Contested Capitalism

This book examines the political origins of financial institutions across 15 developed democracies, with focused case studies on the US, France, Japan, Austria, and Germany.

The institutional arrangements of financial systems are widely seen as a central distinguishing feature of "varieties of capitalism." Through a wide-range of case studies, this book contends that political battles between landed interests, labor, and owners of capital have fundamentally shaped modern financial arrangements. Demonstrating how these conflicts have shaped contemporary financial architecture in a number of different contexts, author Richard W. Carney offers an innovative approach to explaining the distinctive capitalist arrangements of nation-states. By demonstrating the importance of landed interests to nations' institutional configurations, the book has clear implications for developing countries such as India and China.

Providing a detailed account of the development of financial institutions, this book will be of interest to students and scholars of political science, business, finance, law and sociology. It will also offer insights valuable to government policymakers, analysts at international organizations, and the business community.

Richard W. Carney is Assistant Professor of International Political Economy at the S. Rajaratnam School of International Studies in Singapore. He is editor of the book *Lessons from the Asian Financial Crisis* (2008).

Routledge advances in international political economy

Contested Capitalism

The political origins of financial institutions

Richard W. Carney

Routledge
Taylor & Francis Group

LONDON AND NEW YORK

First published 2010
by Routledge
2 Park Square, Milton Park, Abingdon, Oxon OX14 4RN

Simultaneously published in the USA and Canada
by Routledge
270 Madison Ave, New York, NY 10016

Routledge is an imprint of the Taylor & Francis Group, an informa business

Typeset in Times by Wearset Ltd, Boldon, Tyne and Wear
Printed and bound in Great Britain by TJI Digital, Padstow, Cornwall

British Library Cataloguing in Publication Data
A catalogue record for this book is available from the British Library

Library of Congress Cataloging in Publication Data
Carney, Richard W.
Contested capitalism: the political origins of financial institutions/Richard
W. Carney.
p. cm. – (Routledge advances in international political economy)
Includes bibliographical references and index.
1. Capitalism–Case studies. 2. Financial institutions–History–Case studies.
3. International economic relations–Case studies. 4. Economics–Political
aspects–Case studies. 5. Globalization–Economic aspects–Case studies. 6.
Globalization–Political aspects–Case studies. I. Title.
HB501.C249 2009
332.1–dc22
                                                                2009014899

ISBN10: 0-415-54734-2 (hbk)
ISBN10: 0-203-86846-3 (ebk)

ISBN13: 978-0-415-54734-5 (hbk)
ISBN13: 978-0-203-86846-1 (ebk)

Contents

Illustrations

Figures

Tables

Preface

The global financial crisis of 2008 to 2009 started in the United States. It begs the question: what unique features of the modern American financial system enabled such a profound crisis? Many point to the neoliberal policies of the previous 20 years, and the related idea that market participants could, and should, self-regulate. But this is only a proximate cause. A deeper explanation would consider how the financial institutions were initially constructed.

Although it is only by coincidence, the current crisis makes this book timely since it offers an answer to this question. It argues that America's modern financial system is rooted in political bargains struck during the world's last major economic downturn – the Great Depression. Farmers played an important yet overlooked role in the passage of the Glass–Steagall Act, the Securities Exchange Act of 1934, and other important laws commonly regarded as the cornerstones of the modern American financial system. From these laws, protections for minority shareholders were established, enabling capital markets to flourish.

While the present crisis underscores the importance of understanding the historical origins of national financial arrangements and suggests that an over-reliance on capital markets can undermine economic growth in the short term, my interest in this topic was actually motivated by Ross Levine's papers demonstrating a positive long-run relationship between financial development and economic growth. An initial foray into this area gained momentum after I read La Porta *et al.*'s paper "Law and Finance" (1998), as well as an early version of the "Great Reversals" paper by Rajan and Zingales (2003). Since research on this topic had just begun, it appeared to be an area ripe with opportunity; indeed, the legal family argument seemed to offer the perfect foil to a political explanation. And with regard to the advanced democracies that I was focusing on, there were also clear parallels to the ideas in Hall and Soskice's book *Varieties of Capitalism* (2001). Because financial institutions are one of the central distinguishing features of capitalist types, explaining the political origins of financial institutions among wealthy democracies likewise provides insights into the political origins of modern capitalism. A vast literature has been written in both of these areas, yet they rarely speak to one another. This book helps to bridge this gap.

The study was further motivated by the dearth of work offering a political explanation for the structure of national financial systems. Gerschenkron (1962) offered an argument about economic backwardness and financial arrangements in the nineteenth century, but there was a clear gap when it came to modern financial systems. Zysman (1983) seemed to be the closest with his careful and nuanced treatment of several advanced democracies. However, his focus was on how financial systems generated different industrial outcomes, and thus treated financial arrangements as given.

The interdisciplinary component of the topic likewise piqued my interest. I often heard the refrain that the most interesting and innovative work usually occurred at disciplinary intersections, which also made the topic intellectually stimulating. Yet, the very things that made it so attractive also proved to make it more challenging than I anticipated. The research required a multidisciplinary approach, and I wound up presenting papers to academic audiences in a variety of settings, including economic history, finance, political science, business, and sociology. These presentations, and my work, took me from the United States and Canada to Italy, France, the Netherlands, and the UK, and over to Singapore, and China (with regard to extensions of the research). Part of the work on the chapters that cover France is based on my article for the journal *French Politics*, entitled "Varieties of Capitalism in France: Interests, Institutions, and Finance" (Carney, 2006).

Many more people than I can remember offered helpful suggestions along the way. At the project's early stages, I would especially like to thank Miles Kahler, Nathaniel Beck, Takeo Hoshi, and Michael Hiscox. Only after I was well into my project did I find out that Peter Gourevitch was doing work on corporate ownership with James Shinn. This was both a blessing and a curse. It was a blessing in that Peter could offer very helpful advice, but it was a curse to have to work on a similar topic knowing that he was going to produce an incomparably excellent book. As Chapter 1 details, the books are similar in their general approach, yet are clearly different in a variety of important ways, such as the dependent variable (corporate ownership vs. national financial structure), the moment in time examined (contemporary emphasis vs. historical origins), the countries (a wide range of democratic and nondemocratic countries vs. wealthy democracies), and the actors (my emphasis on the role of farmers). In the end, the shortcomings of this book completely rest on my shoulders.

I was also fortunate to receive funding from a variety of sources, including the All-UC Group in Economic History, a Joseph Naiman Fellowship in Japanese Studies at UC San Diego, and a Jean Monnet/Vincent Wright Fellowship at the European University Institute. Helen Wallace, Director of the Robert Schuman Centre at the EUI, provided an excellent environment to think, read, write, and share ideas in a multidisciplinary setting. Martin Rhodes offered helpful and encouraging comments on the France case. And I was very fortunate to have an officemate, Johannes Pollak, who made the time fly by far too quickly with his quick wit.

At the S. Rajaratnam School of International Studies, where I completed the work on the book, I would like to thank Barry Desker for providing research assistance and funding. At the RSIS library, Chong Yee Ming and Jean Lai Foong Yee were both extremely helpful with locating sources. Barkha Shah likewise provided excellent research assistance. John Ravenhill provided wise advice overall as the project neared its completion.

I also taught classes on this topic at RSIS, and interactions with the students in these classes helped me clarify my thoughts, and have generated ideas for further work. In particular, I would like to thank Loh Yi Zheng, Paul Doucet, Luke (Chang Kim Sai), Jet Olfato, Danielle (Loh Wei Lee), Pan Rongfang, and Rifaan Ahmed.

Finally, Sarah shared the final stretch with me and kept the wheels from coming loose despite the numerous bumps, potholes, and unexpected turns. And my parents deserve special mention for their unwavering support and love, no matter how difficult the challenges encountered.

Part I
Questions and explanations

1   Introduction

Why do advanced democracies have such different financial systems? For example, why have the US and UK relied so much on equities markets during the past century, while other countries, such as Germany and Japan, have relied more on bank-based financial arrangements? And why do financial systems change, sometimes dramatically and quickly? For example, the French and Japanese financial systems exhibited many surprising similarities to the contemporary United States before World War II; after the war, they went through radical transformations.

Understanding the structure of national financial systems has attracted attention from across the social sciences in the past decade for two main reasons. First, research has clearly linked economic growth to financial development: the more developed a nation's financial system (i.e., the more sophisticated a nation's capital markets and banking services), the more economic growth it generates (King and Levine, 1993a, 1993b; Levine, 1997, 1998; Levine and Zervos, 1998; Rajan and Zingales, 1998; Levine *et al.*, 2000). Second, the structure of national financial systems is a central distinguishing feature of national varieties of capitalism – coordinated market economies (CMEs) and liberal market economies (LMEs) – which support specific kinds of strategies on the part of firms in international markets. In CMEs, equities markets are less important than in LMEs for firm financing (Hall and Soskice, 2001).

The dominant view to explain differences among financial systems is the legal origins perspective (La Porta *et al.*, 1998, 2008), which argues that contemporary levels of financial development are largely determined by a country's legal tradition; British common law provides better protection to minority shareholders and hence leads to larger financial systems (and equities markets) than civil law. However, alternative political economy explanations have emerged that emphasize the role of political institutions and/or interest groups. The political institutions view suggests that financial development depends on how political institutions mediate conflicts of interest over the security of property rights which then affects the structure of the financial system (e.g., Verdier, 2003; Acemoglu *et al.*, 2004; Lamoreaux and Rosenthal, 2005; Acemoglu and Robinson, 2006; Haber *et al.*, 2007). Interest group explanations take a step back in the causal chain by focusing on the preferences of specific actors and the political coalitions they may form (e.g., Rajan and Zingales, 2003; Roe, 2003; Gourevitch and Shinn, 2005). Both perspectives have merit: allow political institutions to vary while holding actors constant and financial outcomes will vary accordingly; the converse is also true.

This book begins with the premise that institutional inertia has shaped modern financial arrangements in ways that cannot be accounted for by looking solely at contemporary political cleavages or institutions. To understand the causal mechanisms that have produced modern financial arrangements it is necessary to examine the origins, and to consider which actors were most important at that time. But in those moments, not only were new bargains struck over the design of financial institutions, often political institutions were also restructured, as in many countries following World War II (e.g., France, Germany, Austria, and Japan). For this reason, this study places greater emphasis on actors and coalitions.

By looking back to when bargains were struck over the design of modern financial institutions among advanced democracies, it becomes clear that landed interests (farmers) have had a substantial, though frequently overlooked, impact. As a result, this book argues that political battles fought between landed interests, labor, and owners of capital at formative moments in a nation's institutional development have substantially shaped modern financial arrangements. The resultant financial institutions depend upon which actors formed a winning political coalition at that moment. When these battles occur in the wake of a crisis that leads to new political institutions, dramatic changes to the structure of financial institutions are possible; when in the context of pre-existing political institutions, financial outcomes are constrained. The details of the argument are presented in Chapter 2.

This argument differs from the alternatives highlighted above with its focus on the *origins* of contemporary financial institutions, as well as with its focus on *farmers* as a key actor. It shows that farmers have had a substantial impact not only on national banking systems, but also on corporate ownership and equities markets. Further, the study clearly demonstrates that financial arrangements really were different before World War II in many advanced democracies, and offers a parsimonious explanation for the variety of financial arrangements observed across space and time. In contrast to many other studies which emphasize the causal role of political institutions, I see the actors as critical – particularly at those moments when both financial and political institutions change. Once new political institutions are in place, they preserve and bias the evolutionary path of the financial system. This is consistent with Acemoglu and Robinson's (2006) argument that political institutions enable credible commitments to new bargains; but the key causal mechanism is the de facto power that groups wield when the new institutional bargains are struck (as opposed to de jure power, which is granted by the institutions). A final contrast with the aforementioned arguments is with this book's focus on general financial characteristics. That is, financial institutions are seen as complementing one another, and arising from a common political origin.[1] Like varieties of capitalism, financial systems fall along a continuum: at one end, financial institutions complement one another in generating incentives for actors to focus on the short term, as in LMEs; at the other end, financial institutions foster a longer term focus, as in CMEs.[2] The "patient" capital of CMEs allows employment to be more stable and longer term, and enables workers to devote more of their time and energy to cultivating job-specific skills.[3] In this way, financial arrangements complement industrial relations, vocational training, and other dimensions of capitalist systems. Indeed, the varieties of capitalism literature points to the reliance on equities markets and related corporate governance rules as central distinguishing features of capitalist ideal-types. As a result, understanding the origins of financial institutions offers insight into how national varieties of capitalism have emerged and persisted.

Which financial institutions?

To understand how interests impact the structure of the financial system, I focus on four dimensions: the diffusion of corporate ownership, the extent of government intervention via banks, the agricultural bias of the banking system, and the public or private orientation of pension funds. Each of these dimensions has had a substantial impact on the mobility of capital within wealthy economies during the last century. The benefit of looking at this diverse array of financial arrangements is that they each perform different functions, and so taken together they offer a holistic view of a country's financial system as well as a broad assessment of how easy it is to move money from one place to another.

Capital which can easily move between investments generates stronger incentives to focus on short-term results, and ultimately affects how economic actors behave and interact with one another. For example, in the United States, firms frequently turn to the equities market to raise money. This entails selling ownership rights in the firm to a diffuse group of shareholders, which generates a collective action problem in monitoring the firm closely – the Berle–Means (1932) problem of the separation of ownership and control. To compensate for this, managers' compensation packages are closely tied to the firm's share price via stock options, and the firm must provide quarterly earnings updates (among other mechanisms to ensure managers' incentives are aligned with those of shareholders). If the firm fails to meet investors' expectations, investors will sell the company's shares. As a result of these performance updates every three months, firms focus their strategy on meeting, if not exceeding, these expectations. If a firm faces difficulties, cost cutting via layoffs is a common first (and last) line of defense. As a result of these uncertain employment prospects, workers' incentives to acquire firm-specific skills are diminished. But when firm ownership is concentrated among a handful of owners, there is less reliance on using the share price as a quick measure of the company's performance since the owners have the incentive to monitor the firm closely. If necessary, they have the power to intervene. As a result, there tends to be less pressure on meeting quarterly earnings expectations, and a stronger orientation on the long-term competitiveness of the firm. We can then see how diffuse or concentrated ownership generates incentives to focus on the short or long term. One consequence of this tends to be a greater reliance on equities markets in those countries where diffuse ownership is more common, and money quickly moves in and out of the market. The converse of this is that bank lending tends to be more important as a source of external financing in countries with more concentrated ownership (since selling shares would diminish the power of the owners). Money thus tends to be tied up for a longer period of time.

Other dimensions of a nation's financial system likewise affect the speed with which money flows around the economy. For example, the extent of government intervention in the economy via banks can have a substantial impact when the government intervenes in the economy to decide how money gets lent (as part of the economy's regular functioning rather than when the government intervenes on a temporary basis as during a crisis). The greater the level of government intervention in the economy, the more important bank lending becomes, which diminishes pressure to meet short-term expectations as would occur if firms were otherwise selling equity stakes to diffuse shareholders. Because government intervention via banks has played an important role in the structure of national financial arrangements over the past century, this is another key dimension examined in this book.

A third important dimension is the agricultural bias of the banking system. Often there is overlap between this dimension and government intervention since banks that cater to the agricultural sector are often owned by the government. However, banking regulations can arrange for the diversion of financing to the agricultural sector without government ownership of banks, as with interstate bank branching regulations in the United States (Calomiris, 2000; Rajan and Ramcharan, 2008). In either case, banks assume a larger role in handling the nation's stock of capital, and prevent money from flowing to corporations via the equities market. Agricultural banks, such as France's Crédit Agricole or Japan's Norinchukin Bank, became some of the largest financial institutions in the world during the past century, and have had a substantial impact on the structure of national financial arrangements as a result.

The final dimension of financial systems considered in this study is the public/private orientation of pension funds. A heavier reliance on public pensions means that less money will be available for investing in private companies via the equities market. Investing public pension fund money in a nation's equities market is a political minefield (choosing which equities to invest in can lead to charges of corruption, not to mention that equities markets generate volatile returns), so public pension funds avoid this, and instead invest in more politically neutral and less risky assets such as government bonds. But private funds do go into equities markets since they are not constrained by politics. As a result, the more heavily a nation relies on public pension funds, the less money is available for investing in private companies via the equities market.[4]

Together, these four dimensions offer a broad depiction of the way national financial systems have been organized during the past century. Each dimension involves a trade-off that affects how easily money can be moved from one investment to another, with consequences for the long- versus short-term incentives that economic actors face. Concentrated ownership, high levels of government ownership of banks, extensive support for agricultural banking, and public pensions tend to foster investments that are more specific, and thus longer term, which in turn generate longer term incentives in other areas of the economy.

While asset specificity (and its related short- vs. long-term effects) is widely recognized as a defining attribute of different capitalist systems, Peter Hall and David Soskice suggest that government intervention and the size of the agrarian sector could also be important distinguishing attributes of Mediterranean (or mixed) economies, such as France, Italy, Spain, Portugal, Greece, and Turkey (Hall and Soskice, 2001: 21). In this regard, looking at the structure of the financial system is particularly helpful since it can accommodate these additional characteristics while, at the same time, accounting for asset specificity. Government intervention in the economy is straightforwardly reflected in the structure of the financial system by the extent of government ownership of the nation's banks. Indeed, economists point to government ownership of banks as a, if not *the*, critical mechanism by which government intervention in the economy takes place.[5] The importance of the agrarian sector is also reflected in the structure of the banking system. A larger agrarian sector generally requires a greater number of local credit institutions, so the number of these and the size of financing directed to the agricultural sector reflects its importance. Thus, an examination of the financial institutions that correspond to the extent of government intervention and the importance of the agrarian sector, in combination with asset specificity, offers a robust depiction of how the financial system mirrors different varieties of capitalism.

The existing literature

As discussed in the opening section, national financial arrangements are frequently explained with reference to one of three dominant perspectives: the country's legal tradition, interest groups, and political institutions. I begin this section with a brief overview of arguments from each approach. I then turn to a brief summary of the varieties of capitalism literature and how this study contributes to it. Finally, I discuss how my argument fits with respect to the dominant interest group explanations found in political science.

Following the "law and finance" initial emphasis on minority shareholder protections (La Porta *et al.*, 1998), much of the recent literature on financial institutions has focused on corporate governance.[6] Roe (1994), however, offers an excellent illustration of how different facets of the financial system are closely linked, and the wide-ranging impact of interests that wield political influence. He focuses on the political influence of populist interests within the context of a federal political system to explain the development of America's fragmented financial arrangements. His analysis clearly illustrates that an array of financial institutions owe their design to a shared political source. Allen and Gale (2000) further demonstrate that such complementary financial arrangements are not specific to the US, but are common to many countries. And in work since La Porta *et al.*'s 1998 paper, other attributes of financial systems have been examined for their relationship to the country's legal tradition (La Porta *et al.*, 2008). Taken together, these perspectives suggest that there is promise in developing a theory that roots national financial arrangements in a common political origin.

Rajan and Zingales (2003) also emphasize the impact of political interests in a cross-national and historical study of financial development (where more robust securities markets correspond to more financial development). They argue that entrenched businesses lock up access to domestic finance via their political influence, but domestic capital markets do grow, and allow entrants access to finance, as the entrenched firms turn to lower cost financing from international capital markets when trade and capital flows increase. Roe (2003), by contrast, emphasizes political ideology in affecting the diffusion of corporate ownership; where social democracy is weaker, corporate ownership becomes more diffuse and a greater emphasis is placed on meeting shareholders' short-term earnings objectives. Pagano and Volpin (2005) and Perotti and von Thadden (2005) likewise argue that poor shareholder protections correspond to strong employment protections. Gourevitch and Shinn (2005) build on this perspective by considering the outcomes that occur when labor interacts with owners and managers in the political arena, and the manner by which political institutions mediate interactions between these groups.

Interest group arguments have also become increasingly prominent among authors who focus exclusively on the structure of the banking system (and how much it caters to the agrarian sector; e.g., Calomiris, 2000; Rajan and Ramcharan, 2008), government intervention (e.g., Glaeser and Shleifer, 2003), and pension funds (e.g., Baldwin, 1990; Perotti and Schwienbacher, 2007). Given the wide-ranging impact that interests can have on the structure of financial institutions within a single country, as Roe (1994) convincingly demonstrates for the United States, these other studies further suggest that there is promise in developing a general interest group theory to explain financial arrangements across countries.

Other authors emphasize the role of political institutions. For example, Verdier (2003) argues that state centralization facilitates the growth of capital markets by drawing savings out of the interior and channeling them to large industrial enterprises in urban centers. Pagano and Volpin (2005) emphasize the role of electoral systems: owner-managers and workers converge on a political platform featuring low investor protection if the voting system is proportional but not if it is majoritarian. This is mirrored in Gourevitch and Shinn's (2005) analysis which encompasses a broader set of consensus versus majoritarian attributes. The chapters in Haber *et al.* (2007) investigate a wide range of political institutions across countries and time, and convincingly illustrate their important role in shaping financial arrangements.

Among the advanced democratic nations, which this study focuses on, the varieties of capitalism approach has gained wide appeal for its characterization of liberal and coordinated market economies. The financial system is generally recognized as a central, distinguishing feature in which larger equities markets are associated with LMEs (e.g., Dore, 2000; Hall and Soskice, 2001; Amable, 2003; Hall and Gingerich, 2004; Culpepper, 2005). Despite an array of critiques to this approach (e.g., Crouch, 2005; Hancké *et al.*, 2007) it has remained resilient and its influence has spread across the social sciences. A nascent but growing body of research has turned to an examination of the origins of these varieties of capitalism, such as the impact of preindustrial traditions of cooperation and skills development (Thelen, 2004). Others have begun to investigate the impact of electoral and party systems on coordination (Cusack *et al.*, 2007; Martin and Swank, 2008). These studies tend to see modern origins as being rooted in the nineteenth century. However, this study challenges these views about the origins of capitalist arrangements by demonstrating that financial systems changed in the mid-twentieth century in many countries, and that farmers have played an important, yet underappreciated, role.

With regard to the political science literature, this study develops an argument about how actors and the coalitions they form affect economic outcomes in the tradition of Rogowski (1989) and Frieden (1991). By pointing to populist versus corporate interests, Roe (1994) offers an excellent starting point for thinking about the relevant groups with regard to financial outcomes specifically. However, my argument differs from his, and the alternatives mentioned above, in two distinct ways. First, I sharpen the meaning of populist interests by clearly distinguishing between farmers and labor. As will become clear in the rest of the book, it is critical to distinguish between these two groups because they can have very different preferences over financial institutions. I then consider the financial outcomes that result from the political coalitions these actors may form with each other, or with owners of capital (business owners). The second difference is the focus on the timing of when these bargains are struck. Bargains that occur at critical junctures of institutional change matter most, such as the early twentieth century or immediately following World War II.

While my focus on landed interests, labor, and owners of capital superficially resembles that of Rogowski's, it is actually a very different argument. Because of the focus on trade policy, Rogowski's theory explicitly incorporates the idea of factor abundance as articulated in the Stolper-Samuelson theorem. But this does not make sense for explaining the structure of financial institutions, which turns more on identifying those actors that wield political power, independent of factor abundance. For example, both pre-World War II France and Japan relied heavily on securities markets; after World War II they changed to a heavy reliance on banking. Without narrowing in on which political interests wield political influence, and simply applying a generic factor abundance theory, it is impossible to explain these outcomes.

My argument also offers an alternative way of depicting coalitional politics as nations race towards modernity. While Rogowski's theory focuses on urban–rural and class cleavages, I extend the range of coalitional possibilities to also include voice vs. property cleavages, and a social contract outcome, as will be discussed in Chapter 2.

Implications

Several implications arise from the framework offered here. One of the clearest and most pertinent applications of this research regards India and China. These countries are at a point in their development that resembles the process many wealthy countries went through at the beginning of the twentieth century. An immediate question presents itself with respect to India: with its inheritance of British institutions and federal governmental structure, will farmers and business owners dominate the political battles and create an Indian financial system similar to that of the United States? Or, will workers have more of a say, and if so, what will be the consequences? With respect to China, one wonders whether workers and farmers have any influence on policymakers' decisions over reforms made to the country's financial institutions. And what would be the consequences if democratic reforms permit groups representing land, labor, and capital to battle freely in the political arena? The framework developed here enables observers of the global economy to make clearer assessments about the likely institutional trajectories of developing nations in the twenty-first century.

While the argument offers an explanation for the institutional origins of financial systems, it also calls attention to the conditions under which dramatic institutional changes can occur. The theory accomplishes this by deriving seven outcomes based on actors' political interactions; if, at a critical moment of institutional change, the winning coalition differs from that of the prior moment of critical institutional change, then dramatic transformations are possible (e.g., as after World War II for France, Japan, Austria, Germany, and Italy).

This framework also offers a novel perspective on the structure of Japanese capitalism. Specifically, the theory reconciles why Japan has resembled France as an interventionist state, while at the same time resembling Germany with regard to its reliance on relationships for organizing private sector activity.

While few would question the importance of labor and capital to contemporary capitalism, some may view farmers' relevance with skepticism. However, farmers have played a critical role in determining the structure of the contemporary American financial system – the world's largest economy. For example, political power over banking regulations has historically been devolved to state governments that cater to local agricultural interests, which has forced centralized capital markets to arise to offer a coordinating mechanism with which to raise sufficient capital for large corporations in place of commercial or universal banks with nationwide branches (Calomiris, 2000). These conditions have contributed to the emergence of diffuse ownership in American companies (Roe, 1994).

In addition, farmers have played an important role in determining the structure of the world's major institutional investors: pension funds (Baldwin, 1990). Farmers favor public pension systems instead of private pension funds run on behalf of corporations, and where they are public, politicians are reluctant to make investments in seemingly risky assets such as the equities market. This helps to preserve the concentration of corporate ownership and denies an important source of liquidity that would aid the development of equities markets.

But of potentially greater importance is farmers' preference for government intervention which can lead to subsidized lending for farmers and corporations for politically expedient reasons. For example, the funds collected via banks catering to the rural citizenry in Japan (via the Postal Savings Bank) have been commonly lent to industrial firms at subsidized rates through government-operated intermediaries which helps to sustain these firms' reliance on patient capital.

Finally, farmers are an important player in the economies of China and India. In view of their historical importance to OECD economies and their contemporary relevance to these emerging economies and to other developing countries, to ignore farmers would be like ignoring an elephant in the room.

Organization of the book

Chapter 2 details the theory. I discuss the preferences of the key actors with regard to the financial institutions under consideration, the coalitions that may form among them, and the consequent financial system and corresponding capitalist outcomes depending on who wins the political battles.

Chapter 3 looks at broad trends across countries during the twentieth century. It first demonstrates that countries' financial arrangements have changed, and that many of them looked very different before World Wars I and II than after. It then analyzes correlations between the financial variables and actors' political power. Finally it shows the biasing effect of political institutions.

Chapters 4 through 7 examine specific cases based on the coalitions that form among the actors at critical junctures of institutional change. The chapters provide clear evidence for the causal mechanism purported by the theory. The selected cases come primarily from those countries which are the typical nations upon which theories of capitalism have been constructed, including Germany, Japan, the United States, and France. Emphasis is placed on Japan and France since the financial systems of these two countries changed dramatically from their pre- to their post-World War II form as a result of changes in the political power of the key actors – the increase in power of labor and farmers, and the corresponding decline in power of capital owners. It is worth reiterating that the capacity for labor and farmers to accomplish such profound change is of potentially great importance to India and China, where these two groups exert significant influence on leaders' policy decisions (Varshney, 1995; Shirk, 2007).

Chapter 8 concludes with a discussion of the key lessons, including the critical importance of the initial bargains over capitalist institutions, the importance of farmers and the coalitions they form with other actors, the delimiting and biasing effects of political institutions on financial change, and the need to consider how a nation's financial system exhibits complementarities among its constituent parts that constrain and bias change.

2 Theory

Interests – labor, capital, and landed interests – will battle in the political arena over the structure of a nation's capitalist institutions. When these battles occur in the wake of a crisis that leads to new political institutions, dramatic changes to the structure of financial institutions are possible; when in the context of pre-existing political institutions, financial outcomes are constrained. In this chapter, I detail the expected outcomes based on these general mechanisms.

The chapter is broken into two parts: (1) the identification of the relevant actors and their preferences over financial arrangements, the coalitions they may form, and the consequent financial outcomes; and (2) the biasing effects of domestic political institutions over these outcomes.

Actors, coalitions, and outcomes

Important for explaining the structure of a nation's capitalist system, and a financial system more specifically, is identifying those actors with the greatest interest in and power to alter it – this is the topic of the first subsection. Next, I discuss how financial arrangements lead to more or less asset specificity before discussing actors' preferences with regard to those under consideration: corporate ownership, banking, government intervention, and pensions. Finally, I consider the coalitions actors may form and the corresponding outcomes for the financial system and, by extension, the capitalist system.

Identifying the key actors

Which actors should be examined to determine the structure of the financial system? Owing to the transaction costs of lobbying the government (i.e., overcoming collective action problems), only those with special interests (i.e., a lot to gain or lose) will pay the price to express their opinion and influence policymakers. This explains why financial regulation, and bank regulation in particular, seldom maximizes depositors' welfare and why borrowers would be the dominant players in the political regulatory game.[1]

So which interests matter most? Owing to their fundamental importance to the structure of any nation's economy, their political power during industrialized nations' institutional birth and evolution, and because they have strong interests in the structure of the financial system (and the broader capitalist system), landed interests, labor, and owners of capital are examined.

Is it worthwhile considering whether these actors form alternative cleavages over time, or whether subsets of these actors are worthy of investigation? Hiscox (2001) has demonstrated that, with regard to trade issues, actors representing factors of production tend to form sectoral cleavages as factor mobility declines. For example, low-skilled labor working in an auto factory could be easily retrained to work in a shoe factory, creating stronger incentives for labor to form class-based unions. However, more highly skilled labor working in a computer software company would have great difficulty in retraining and finding work in a pharmaceutical firm. By this logic, labor becomes more sector-based as economies rely more heavily on knowledge-intensive production. While this is certainly a valid point, industrialized nations' institutions were primarily created when labor was more class-based. The case studies will clearly demonstrate that it is useful to view labor as a unified actor in the years following World War II, when the most recent examples of institutional change occurred. But does this mean that today's newly democratizing nations are likely to exhibit different cleavages? And, if labor is no longer class-based, are their past institutional victories no longer applicable to the structure of today's economies? I argue no on both points.

Newly democratizing nations are, usually, also newly industrializing nations. As such, their labor force is ascending the development ladder in the same manner that other industrialized nations did during the last century. In this regard, it seems less erroneous to think of labor as class-based than as sector-based in newly democratizing nations.

In addition, past labor victories over the institutional structure of the political economy remain important and valid for today's globalized world because, as Hall and Soskice (2001) explain, complementarities among the numerous institutions of political economies make change difficult. The pre-existing political and economic institutions delimit the choices that actors can make although new cleavages may emerge. And veto points within political institutions, often wielded by minority groups such as farmers, prevent change.

Farmers are viewed as the main landed interest group. One might argue that it would be appropriate to consider large landowners versus small farmers; however, such a breakdown would overly complicate the analysis while adding little value, since their preferences are generally the same for the time periods examined here. Moreover, in the context of democracies, farmers' political power comes from votes, so small farmers (labeled simply as farmers) are viewed as the most appropriate actor representing land. Further discussion on different types of farmers and their preferences will be presented in the subsection below on actors' preferences.

Owners of capital are viewed as owners of firms, which fall along a spectrum from small to large. As will be discussed below, farmers and owners of small firms tend to have similar financing preferences in terms of favoring decentralized bank lending institutions. The critical actor for the development of the financial system (and the structure of capitalism) is the owner of a large firm, since it is this actor more than any other who is likely to favor the development of securities markets. In other words, large firms are a necessary, though insufficient, condition for the growth of equities markets.

Asset specificity and corporate finance

Before thinking about these actors' preferences over the financial institutions of interest, it is necessary to understand whether different financing alternatives lead to corporate strategies that focus more on the short or long term (via impatient or patient financing, which leads to less or more asset specificity, respectively). Companies that focus on achieving short-term performance benchmarks, such as quarterly earnings, are generally driven by the need to meet the expectations of diffuse shareholders who will simply sell the company's shares as a result of underperformance. Longer term corporate strategy does not face such intense short-term pressures since owners are more likely to intervene in the management of the firm to improve its performance, which allows for the development of strategies that require longer term investments with more distant payoffs. By focusing on the long term, corporations in CME countries can develop assets that are highly specific to the manufacture of a particular product (e.g., highly skilled labor and German automobiles). Workers who are more confident of being in their position for a long period of time are more willing to invest in acquiring skills and knowledge specific to their job. In LMEs, corporations often cut costs via layoffs during downturns in the business cycle to keep earnings up, which undermines their workers' incentives to invest in the acquisition of job-specific knowledge and skills.

What are the financing alternatives that corporations generally face, and what kinds of temporal pressures do they create? Corporate finance occurs either through internally generated funds (retained earnings) or with external financing. Internally generated funds tend to preserve the pre-existing incentives for corporate strategy as determined by the ownership structure. Whether firm ownership is concentrated or diffuse, the use of internal financing simply preserves the incentives already in place.[2]

When owners of firms turn to external financing sources, they face two basic choices: taking a loan or issuing securities. Both choices entail substantial costs including information collection and transmittal (that is, costs of creating and enforcing mechanisms that lead to credible monitoring of firms and revelation of the true state of firm finances), and physical transaction costs (costs associated with legal and accounting paperwork, and with physically distributing securities to ultimate holders). Intermediaries offer a useful way to economize on these costs. Commercial banks solve problems of transaction costs and information asymmetry including the physical costs of transacting (clearing payments, liquidating insolvent firms), costs of generating information (monitoring firms' actions and outcomes), and costs of enforcing contractual compliance on the part of firms and bankers (disciplining borrowers and protecting against improper behavior by the banker at the expense of those funding the bank). Investment banks are also seen as providing a low-cost means of generating and disseminating credible information about firms' characteristics, which benefits both securities issuers and purchasers in deciding on the form and price of the security used to finance an investment.

With regard to taking a loan or issuing securities, the recent literature on corporate finance focuses on a continuum of financing instruments defined according to the elasticity of their cost with respect to problems of asymmetric information (Myers, 1984; Myers and Majluf, 1984; Diamond, 1991). As firms mature, they ascend this "pecking order" of finance. Firms just starting out may be forced to rely exclusively on retained earnings and the wealth of insiders. After a successful beginning, the firm may begin to rely on bank loans. The bank spends resources to monitor the firm, and protects itself against adverse selection problems by holding a debt claim on the firm. As the firm matures and develops a track record, its financing will change. Informed intermediaries will be willing to take equity positions in the firm, which will reduce the leverage of the firm and its exposure to financial distress, and provide a positive signal to outside investors. Outside finance through securities may initially take the form of closely held senior instruments (e.g., private placements). Later, firms will graduate to issuing bonds and preferred and common stock on the open market to outsiders, using underwriters as a means for providing credible signals of the firm's value to outsiders.

Alternative corporate ownership arrangements will produce deviations to this simple life-cycle theory of firm financing (e.g., Lamoreaux and Rosenthal, 2005; Pagano and Volpin, 2005). But the important point for the analysis made here is that larger firms are more likely to favor financing via the securities markets than smaller firms, and this is what leads to minority shareholder protections and the growth of equities markets.

Do these various financing options produce different temporal incentives for firm strategy? Bank lending tends to preserve a long-term orientation if corporate ownership is concentrated ex ante. While banks require regular loan payments, if a firm gets into trouble, the bank is likely to work with the firm to determine how it can repay its debt. But bank lending tends to be costly relative to securities markets as firm size increases.

Bond markets, or debt markets, offer a less costly form of financing while at the same time introducing external performance-monitoring deadlines with annual bond ratings. But because these ratings are updated on a yearly basis, they produce weaker incentives to focus on the short term than other financing options, such as issuing equity. Selling shares with voting rights *may* produce stronger short-term incentives since outside shareholders often demand quarterly earnings updates, and other mechanisms to make corporate performance transparent. This, in and of itself, is insufficient, however, since ownership may remain concentrated, with the majority owner denying the requests of minority shareholders, and preferring to intervene in the management of the company rather than selling his ownership stake (or preferring to expropriate company assets and therefore not wanting to make the company's finances available to outsiders). Indeed, selling a large block of shares could be difficult and costly, especially if sold over a short period of time, since it would likely cause the share price to fall; there may also be tax disincentives and regulatory hurdles, especially in the case of mergers and acquisitions, creating further complications.

Short-term incentives tend to arise most strongly when ownership becomes more diffuse. Diffuse shareholding generally arises as majority owners sell their shares to capture the benefits of diversifying their investments, and as firms expand the size and scope of their operations through mergers and acquisitions. In such circumstances, dispersed owners (who face collective action problems to closely monitor the firm) use the share price as an indicator of whether to hold on to their shares or sell them. But in order for a company to attract minority shareholders, the market must offer a credible mechanism for the manager's performance to be tied to the firm's share price (e.g., quarterly earnings reports, transparent accounting, incentivizing options); that is, for the manager to act in the best interests of minority shareholders. Only if the market successfully resolves this agency problem will diffuse shareholding arise. Quarterly earnings reports, and other frequent updates on firm performance, are critical tools by which this is accomplished. Markets that successfully solve this agency problem and allow diffuse ownership to emerge tend to expand in size as a larger pool of investors can be tapped at a lower cost.

Corporate pyramids fall in between concentrated and diffuse ownership structures in terms of generating a long- versus short-term focus. Pyramids attempt to capture the benefits of low-cost financing available through equities markets without sacrificing the benefits of control. To attract investors, there must be sufficiently strong safeguards for minority shareholders – and accompanying mechanisms that resolve the managerial agency problem, such as quarterly earnings reports – since the parent company will retain majority ownership. This leads to some elements of short-term behavior to satisfy minority shareholders' concerns. However, majority ownership by the parent corporation moderates the focus on the short term. This is also true for intercorporate shareholding, as in Japan; there is a bias to the long term though pressures for conforming to shareholders' interests also exist.

Actors' preferences

What are the preferences of these actors – farmers, labor, firm owners – with regard to the four financial dimensions under consideration? Corporate ownership concentration, government intervention via banks, the scope of agricultural banking, and public versus private pensions.

Farmers

While farmers' preferences on other economic dimensions may vary as a result of the different crops they grow (e.g., their preference for tariffs, subsidies, and tax rates), their preferences over the structure of financial institutions remain quite uniform. No matter what is grown, or what kind of livestock raised, all farmers want a reliable, inexpensive source of financing. And while farms could be likened to firms, whose financing preferences vary according to their size, large farms (e.g., plantations) have nowhere near the same financing needs of large industrial corporations. Like their smaller counterparts, owners of large farms want a financing facility that can readily provide capital whenever it is needed. Indeed, both small and large farmers favor banking arrangements that cater to the agricultural sector with numerous local credit facilities, government intervention to divert money away from industrializing sectors of the economy, and diffuse corporate ownership. Divisions over the support for pension funds may occur as a result of income differences; wealthy farmers are unlikely to support a redistributive public pension system. I give a brief discussion of farmers' preferences over these four financial dimensions in turn.

Because farmers, across most countries during the twentieth century, are generally too small to seek financing from capital markets, they must rely on local banks, either in the form of branches of large, networked banks, or in the form of unit banks (i.e., small, local banks without ties to a larger, national banking network). This relationship to the local bank, or agricultural credit bureau, is critical to their survival and success. Keeping capital location-specific with regulations protecting and supporting local banks ensures that lenders will go elsewhere at the expense of local farms. Moreover, keeping banks location-specific ties the bank's fortunes to those of local farmers; local banks will have to continue lending to local farmers despite a long-term negative revision in expectations regarding the profitability of investment (e.g., an expected long-term decline in the terms of trade). This preserves a long-term relationship between the local bank and farmers, and offers a kind of "loan insurance" in the sense that farmers can rest assured that banks will continue to loan to them even in bad times (Calomiris, 2000).

Farmers also tend to favor government intervention in order to divert money away from industrializing sectors, or other areas of the economy where a higher return is likely. With regard to corporate ownership, farmers prefer that it is not highly concentrated (e.g., populist resistance to capitalist oligarchs in the late nineteenth-century US: Chandler, 1977: 498; Roe, 1994). Concentrated economic and financial might would be detrimental to farmers as such oligopolistic power would almost inevitably lead to funds being drained out of the interior, raising their own costs of financing. Further, the concentration of industry would lead to higher transportation and other business services costs, as large firms would take the best and cheapest resources, and charge customers (farmers) higher prices as a result of monopoly. Instead, ownership, corresponding to general wealth (equitable distribution of income) and banking outcomes, will tend to be more dispersed.

Publicly controlled pensions are also likely since they tend to be more inclusive of economic groups not employed in large corporations, where private pension funds tend to be located. Moreover, publicly run pension schemes tend to be redistributive, and generally for the benefit of smaller farmers (e.g., Baldwin, 1990). And when farmers wield political power, they can direct funds collected through a public pension scheme to favored programs (e.g., subsidizing agrarian financing and rural construction projects). It should be noted that pensions tend to emerge only after workers in an industrializing economy press for them. And as mentioned earlier, large wealthy farmers are unlikely to support public pensions since they will be paying more into the system than they will get out of it. But in democratic countries, small farmers tend to dominate politically. As a result of their preference for public pensions (which generally denies funds for investment in equities markets) and government intervention via banks, farmers can foster a bias towards patient capital for corporate finance. For example, in Japan, farmers were important to the success of the postal savings system – the main source of funds for the government's interventionist activities – which enabled subsidized lending to many large corporations. Government ownership of banks in France following World War II likewise led to patient corporate financing, and to the swelling of agricultural assistance.

Together, farmers' preference for local banking, government intervention, and public pensions reduces the availability of funds for investment through securities markets and generates pressure for the emergence of a coordinated market economy. By contrast, farmers' corporate ownership preferences tend to push the capitalist arrangements in an LME direction (e.g., the United States).

Labor

The preferences of workers across the four financial dimensions can have more variability because they turn on whether employees have a low or high income (Perotti and von Thadden, 2006). High-income workers tend to have more of their savings invested in equities markets; above a certain point they will favor a financial system that privileges minority shareholder protections and corresponds with a greater reliance on equities markets. But because this study examines the origins of financial institutions among developed democracies, with the most recent bargains occurring in the wake of World War II, it is appropriate to focus on the preferences of low-income employees. These workers favor more centralized banking arrangements, government intervention, concentrated ownership, and public pensions. I discuss each in turn.

Labor favors a more centralized financial system, via branched banks, which facilitates the financing of urban industries by drawing savings out of the interior. Labor also favors government intervention in the economy, primarily via banks, in order to provide financing to industry during downturns in the economy to avert layoffs (consistent with Keynesian countercyclical monetary and fiscal policy advice). Labor also tends to favor government intervention – when labor controls government – in order to offer specific financing incentives to industries and firms to ensure that they act in the interests of workers. If banks are not a viable option for influencing industry (i.e., securities markets are more dominant), labor still favors government intervention to minimize layoffs, as frequently occurs with mergers and acquisitions. In this regard, they favor "managed markets." Public pension systems are a natural complement to government intervention in the economy since they tend to be redistributive (Baldwin, 1990; Willmore, 1999). Labor also favors concentrated corporate ownership because it reduces pressure to focus on short-term performance benchmarks (i.e., quarterly earnings reports) that often lead to layoffs during a downturn in the business cycle (Roe, 2003). Moreover, the diffusion of corporate ownership facilitates mergers and acquisitions (particularly hostile ones), which likewise lead to layoffs (to cut costs).

Workers' preference for centralized banking arrangements tends to be favorable for the development of equities markets, but these benefits will likely be outweighed by their desire for government intervention (often resulting in state ownership of these banks), concentrated corporate ownership, and public pensions, which tend to stunt the growth of capital markets, and push the economy towards coordinated market arrangements.

Capital

Because the focus here is on developed democracies, two implicit assumptions should be made explicit in the context of capital owners' preferences. First, their preferences depend upon an effective legal system, with strong property rights protection (i.e., investors can lend their money to corporations without fear of not getting it back). Second, private business, not publicly owned corporations, is the focus here. As a result, the preferences of business owners are straightforward with regard to government intervention, pensions, and the structure of the banking system; preferences concerning corporate ownership are more mixed. I discuss each in turn.

Both small and large firms favor minimal government intervention since this reduces inefficiencies in the allocation of capital, and lowers the costs of obtaining financing (e.g., via taxes and regulations). Private pension funds are generally preferable to public funds for large firms since corporations then have control over the allocation of the funds, and they are not redistributive.

Informational characteristics of firms (the availability of a track record, the costs to outsiders of monitoring and controlling activities of the firm) are important determinants of whether firms choose to finance themselves with securities issues or with bank lending. Financing through bank lending tends to be more important in the early stages of the life cycle of the firm; as the firm matures and grows, investment banking services become more heavily relied upon. Financing arrangements that accelerate the process of seasoning a firm, and economize on the costs of information production and corporate governance, can stimulate investment by reducing the costs of external finance. In this light, universal banking (as opposed to separate commercial and investment banking) is favored and encourages a long-term relationship to develop between a firm and its intermediary by allowing the intermediary to vary the form of firm financing as the firm matures.

As firms increase in size and geographical scope, there are advantages for banks to becoming large and operating a branching network. First, if industrial firms find it advantageous to operate large-scale enterprises over a wide geographic area as Chandler (1977) argues, then monitoring the activities of the firm will be easier if a bank has similarly wide geographic scope. Second, large branching banks are better able to take advantage of long-term relationship economies of financing firms through a universal bank owing to their access to both securities purchasers and depositors. Unit banking laws that prohibit the establishment of deposit-taking branches effectively limit banks' access to deposits on a large scale and, therefore, limit large-scale lending to firms.

Furthermore, given the overhead costs of setting up a bank office, restrictions on commercial bank branching limit branching in securities retailing too, and this raises the costs of bringing securities to market. Without access to a large number of securities purchasers, a bank may not be able to internalize all the benefits of collecting information about issuing firms' prospects and about the ultimate demand for firms' securities. The lack of retail branching also creates transactions and signaling costs associated with setting up networks of banks that collect and credibly transmit such information. Finally, branching reduces the physical cost of distributing securities. Consequently, owners of growing or large firms tend to favor regulations permitting universal banking with nationwide branches.

As a result of reaping the benefits of reduced transaction costs via equity sales, business owners thus have incentives to permit the diffusion of their ownership. Yet, some owners of large firms may still prefer to retain dominant ownership as a result of "pride of ownership" or other "ego rents," or even because they can continue to receive more rents than would be possible by diversifying their investments.[3] The simple solution to this is to use a *pyramidal* corporate ownership structure, where the parent firm sells equity stakes to outside investors of a firm it controls, and that firm in turn sells equity stakes of another firm in which it retains majority control. Thus, owners of firms are increasingly likely to favor dispersed ownership as firm size increases, yet they may also seek to retain dominant control over the firm. These dual incentives may give rise to pyramidal ownership structures.

As a result, business owners' preference for centralized banking arrangements, minimal government intervention, and private pensions all foster the development of securities markets. Their preference over corporate ownership likewise favors the growth of securities markets, with pyramidal corporate ownership potentially emerging.

Table 2.1 summarizes actors' preferences over the structure of financial institutions.

Coalitions and outcomes

Financial system outcomes depend primarily upon the coalitions formed between farmers (F), labor (L), and owners of large firms (K_L). It is important to note that

Table 2.1 Actors' financial system preferences

	Corporate ownership	Banking system	Government intervention	Pensions
Farmers	Diffuse	Decentralized	High	Public
Labor (low-income workers)	Concentrated	Centralized	High	Public
Capital owners (owners of big business)	Concentrated/ diffuse (pyramidal)	Centralized	Low	Private

these actors do not necessarily form coalitions to achieve specific financial system outcomes; rather, they form political power-sharing coalitions from which financial and capitalist structures emerge.

The outcomes in Table 2.2 can be arrayed along an LME–CME continuum, as shown in Table 2.3. Recall that the four financial dimensions contribute to an economy's general level of asset specificity, which can be roughly captured by the size of a country's equities market; these expectations will be examined in the next chapter and the case studies.

The outcomes listed in Table 2.2 that occur at critical junctures of institutional change (e.g., the early twentieth century and immediately following World War II) are likely to be the most consequential for contemporary capitalism since the (re)created institutions tend to become mutually self-reinforcing and thereby delimit the extent of subsequent change. Also, these groups are likely to retain the capacity to block radical changes to the capitalist bargains in subsequent decades by retaining veto-power (e.g., farmers in France, Japan, and the United States). I now turn to a brief discussion of the outcomes.

Rural vs. urban politics

FARMERS

Small, rural banks are likely to dominate when farmers wield political power. This is the first stage from which industrialization begins. Government intervention will occur to prevent (or at least slow) capital from being redirected to the growing industrial sectors of the economy, and, as was witnessed in the Scandinavian countries (Baldwin, 1990), public pensions may emerge. For all these reasons (local banks, government intervention, and public pensions), the growth of securities markets is likely to be hampered.

As industrialization proceeds, farmers may form a coalition with capital or labor. Whether democratic political institutions allow farmers to wield vast political power, despite a fall in their economic importance and population size – as in the US – can have considerable ramifications for the structure of the financial system. In such circumstances, political authority over financial regulation is

Table 2.2 Coalitions and financial/capitalist system outcomes

Cleavage	Winner	Financial system outcome	Corresponding capitalist system	Example
Rural vs. urban				
	F	• Diffuse corporate ownership • Increasing government intervention with industrialization • Numerous agricultural banking facilities • Public pensions	Agrarian CME	Early nineteenth century US
F vs. L & KL	L & KL	• Concentrated corporate ownership • Moderate level of government intervention • Few agricultural lending facilities • Public–private pensions	Classic CME	Germany post-World War II
Class conflict				
	KL	• Concentrated and diffuse ownership; Pyramidal ownership likely • Minimal government intervention • Low level of agricultural financing • Private pensions	Owner-Oriented LME	France pre-World War II, Japan pre-World War II
KL vs. F & L	F & L	• Concentrated corporate ownership • High level of government intervention • Moderate level of agricultural financing • Public pensions	Mediterranean	France post-World War II

Voice vs. property				
	L	• Concentrated corporate ownership • High level of government intervention • Few agricultural financing facilities • Public pensions	Statist CME	Austria post-World War II
L vs. F & KL	F & KL	• Diffuse corporate ownership • Minimal government intervention in corporate finance; government intervention for agricultural financing • Moderate level of agricultural financing • Public–private pensions	Managerial LME	Twentieth century US
Social contract	F, L, KL	• Some combination of concentrated and diffuse ownership • Moderate to high government intervention • Moderate level of agricultural financing • Public–private pensions	Inclusive CME	Japan post-World War II

Table 2.3 LME–CME continuum

LME			CME
Owner-oriented LME (France and Japan pre-World War II)	Inclusive CME (Japan post-World War II)	Classic CME (Germany post-World War II)	Agrarian CME (early nineteenth century US)
Managerial LME (Twentieth century US)			Statist CME (Austria post-World War II)
			Mediterranean (France post-World War II)

likely to be administered at the subnational level, especially in large countries. This becomes important to the financial structure that emerges when farmers must forge a coalition with capital or labor, since it is likely to lead to either an LME (in coalition with capital) or Mediterranean (in coalition with labor) style of capitalism.

LABOR AND CAPITAL COALITION

This coalition is the classic one that leads to a coordinated market economy, as found in Germany. Corporate finance will have a bias towards the long term, via internal financing, bond sales, and/or equity sales while retaining concentrated ownership (via individuals, banks and other financial institutions, and nonfinancial corporations). These financing structures allow greater employment stability for labor. Government intervention is also likely, albeit in a more indirect (or muted) manner than that found when labor, or labor and farmers, exercises political control. A mix of public and private pension funds is likely to emerge, and financing to the agricultural sector will be relatively low as money flows to urban industries via branched banks.

Class conflict

CAPITAL

When owners of large firms control politics, they are likely to press for the development of securities markets to reduce the transaction costs of external financing, while also seeking to retain controlling blocks in corporations. Pyramidal ownership structures offer a useful solution, and are likely to arise in this circumstance. Government intervention will be minimal, and agrarian financing will be low. Banks will be universal with branches in rural areas to draw deposits out of the interior. Pensions, to the extent that they exist, will be private.

FARMERS AND LABOR

This populist coalition leads to a combination of centralized commercial banking to finance industrial development and local agricultural banking, complemented by economy-wide government intervention. Public pensions stymie the growth of equities markets. What is particularly interesting about this case is the difficult transition that occurs as capital owners become more influential (e.g., since the 1980s). Because institutions were originally designed according to the preferences of labor and farmers, they do not easily accommodate capital owners' growing influence. Consequently, growing pains occur for the political economy as actors must use institutions ill-suited to accommodate capital owners' needs, as in France.

Voice vs. property

LABOR

When labor wields dominant political power, a centralized, government-controlled banking system emerges, as in Austria after World War II. Labor seeks to control the financial system through nationalized, government-run banks in order to direct lending to specific firms and industries in exchange for high and stable employment. Pyramids may likewise arise to allow the state to influence multiple firms easily. At the same time, public pension funds prevent the diversion of funds to equity markets. As capital owners become influential (with globalization), managed markets that favor a long-term corporate strategy (e.g., via concentrated ownership) are likely to emerge in place of directed bank lending.

FARMERS AND CAPITAL COALITION

When farmers exercise political power in democratic governments they implement a decentralized banking structure, which may precede the advent of capital's political power and economic importance. Once capital forms a coalition with farmers, capital requires the creation of centralized capital markets to finance industry since the banking system is decentralized. As part of farmers' general antipathy towards oligarchic capital, they seek to prevent the emergence of concentrated banking and large corporations, which creates political pressure for diffuse ownership. The US offers a clear example of the financial structure resulting from this power-sharing coalition (e.g., Roe, 1994; Calomiris, 2000). Private pension funds emerge eventually, which allow funds to flow to equity markets, and bolster the diffusion of corporate ownership. Government intervention for agriculture persists, but not for the corporate sector.

Social contract

This occurs when labor, capital, and farmers come to a three-way compromise on the structure of the financial system. This is more likely to occur when an exogenous force, such as a foreign power or a small state coping with a global economy, causes these actors to find a socially inclusive compromise. A clear example of this is American influence on post-World War II Japan. If it were not for American involvement, a labor–farmer outcome would have been likely, but US pressure forced a capital–labor–farmer compromise. Globalization like-wise places pressure on small states to form a corporatist compromise such as found among many small European countries (Katzenstein, 1985). As capital gains increasing leverage via globalization, a transition may occur from a reli-ance on banking to managed markets so as not to alienate labor and farmers (i.e., limited government intervention). A public–private mix of pension systems is likely to emerge, along with some degree of agriculture-oriented banking. A substantial level of government intervention is expected since both labor and farmers favor it.

Biasing effects of domestic political institutions

The bargaining strength of these actors, within the context of stable democracies, can be substantially altered by the structure of the political institutions. Thus, to understand the distribution of political power among interests representing land, labor and capital, it is necessary to consider the biasing effects of domestic polit-ical institutions.

Specialists in the comparative political institutions of democracies (e.g., Shugart and Carey, 1992; Cox, 1997; Lijphart, 1999) find it useful to stylize them as exhibiting the traits of one of two ideal-types: consensus or majoritarian democracy. Three key institutional attributes distinguish these democratic models from one another: electoral systems (and the consequent party divisions), legislative–executive relations, and veto-points. Electoral systems offer the clearest illustration of the differences between consensus and majoritarian systems: proportional representation electoral rules – common to consensus systems – allow many interests to gain representation to the legislature and thereby lead to coalitions after elections are held in the form of coalition govern-ments. Proportional representation is prominently found in continental Europe, including Austria, Belgium, Denmark, Finland, Germany, Ireland, Italy, the Netherlands, Norway, Spain, Sweden, Switzerland, and New Zealand since 1996. Plurality electoral rules, which lead to single-member districts – common to majoritarian systems – reward interest aggregation before elections are held so that they can achieve the plurality needed for victory. Plurality electoral rules are common to the UK and its former colonies, including the US, Canada, Aus-tralia, and New Zealand (before 1996), and France. Japan is considered semi-proportional owing to its unique single non-transferable vote system. This will be discussed in more detail in Chapters 4 and 5.

Of additional importance is the number of veto-points; they are generally greater in consensus systems than in majoritarian ones, and make change diffi-cult (Tsebelis, 1995). This is consistent with Lijphart's (1999) main theme that majoritarian systems concentrate power in the hands of the majority and allow for more dramatic policy changes to occur while consensus systems diffuse power and thereby make change more difficult. But countries frequently combine attributes of each category (e.g., the US, with a majoritarian electoral system, has many veto-points owing to its federal system of government and division of powers). Consequently, it is important to remain sensitive to the institutional arrangements of individual nations.

Although majoritarian systems tend to permit more policy change because they have fewer veto-points and because small shifts of votes can lead to larger policy swings, such change is often slow in coming, or occurs more moderately than one might expect, because the electoral system encourages the two political parties to cater to the median voter. So, political change often occurs only as the median voter shifts to the left or right.

With regard to executive–legislative relations, in majoritarian systems the executive usually dominates, while the consensus model is characterized by a more balanced executive–legislative relationship. According to Lijphart's classification, the United States is the major exception, where the legislature dominates the executive (Lijphart, 1999). Otherwise, countries generally cluster into the consensus-majoritarian categories as expected.

An additional feature of political institutions that is of importance is the centralization or decentralization of government policymaking powers. With high decentralization, as with federalism in the United States, local governments have greater authority over economic policy, including legislative and enforcement powers. Greater decentralization stymies financial development, including the growth of securities markets, since it keeps finance local and prevents economies of scope and scale from developing to finance large-scale industry (Verdier, 2003). The US market succeeded in spite of these constraints.

In addition to a federal structure of government, policy outcomes may be skewed towards local interests as a result of electoral rules that favor the election of representatives based on personal reputation rather than their political party (which causes representatives to build a narrow and local group of loyal voters, as in Japan), and malapportionment.

Malapportionment, or unequal representation, is broad and systematic variance in the size of electoral constituencies resulting in disproportionate representation for a given voter (e.g., more seats assigned to a district than its share of the population deserves). Malapportionment is only possible with electoral systems that have districted constituencies – an electoral system with only one national constituency, such as those in Israel and the Netherlands, cannot be malapportioned. For example, the United States Senate is deliberately malapportioned, granting two senators to every state regardless of population size, and resulting in two senators representing over 36 million Californians and two senators representing half a million citizens of Wyoming. An individual voter in Wyoming therefore has 72 times the Senate voting power of a Californian. At the time the US constitution was written, the Senate was intended to represent the interests of the states themselves rather than the residents of those states, and thus apportionment was divided equally among the states rather than among the population at large. In fact, the Constitution specifies that the equal representation of states in the Senate cannot be changed by amendment except with the consent of all affected states (Article V). This effectively entrenched that system.

The United States Senate has become steadily more malapportioned since its creation. In 1787, half of the Senate could theoretically have been elected by 30 percent of the nation, while in 2005 it would take only 17 percent of the nation to elect half the Senate. Extremes of representation have also increased. Virginia's population in 1787 was only 12 times that of Delaware. Today, California's population is 72 times greater than Wyoming's. Owing to the concentration of the population along the coasts, urban areas have become under-represented in the Senate while rural areas have become over-represented. As a result, farmers have retained their political power despite their shrinking importance to the national economy, and their declining size of the nation's population. The phenomenon of malapportionment preserving farmers' political power is common across developed democracies, but its effects are particularly noticeable in France, Japan, and the United States.

Financial system consequences

An electoral system that permits the representation of numerous political parties (i.e., proportional representation), and a political system with more veto-points, tend to preserve the status quo.[4] Moreover, where the legislature is more important, more political interests (and parties) have formal policymaking power. Consensus systems (more political parties, more veto-points, and greater power in the legislature) tend to produce more public pension systems since universalistic welfare outcomes are more likely with many interests requiring accommodation. Less change in the structure of the financial system will occur as groups seek to prevent changes to the status quo financial–industrial relationships (e.g., via banks or concentrated corporate ownership). Whatever the pre-existing financial structure – CME or LME – it will change less. Depending on which groups successfully bargained for the structure of the financial system, consensus systems will help preserve that bargain. So, if labor and farmers were highly influential, a CME system would likely emerge and persist.

Arguments that put the primary emphasis on electoral systems, or related political institutions, have difficulty accounting for major institutional changes in the mid-twentieth century. In many countries (e.g., France, Germany, Austria, Italy, and Japan), bargains struck in the late nineteenth and early twentieth century were renegotiated in the wake of World War II, leading to new constitutions and institutional arrangements. Another difficulty for the electoral system argument is that many countries were not truly democratic in the pre-World War II period; as a consequence, bargains over the electoral system may not translate into meaningful political influence. Instead of using the electoral system as a mechanism for containing the Left, the division of power between the Upper and Lower Houses, or between the executive and the legislature, may have achieved the same objective. As a result, bargains over the electoral system may occur without business interests relinquishing power, and thus offer false evidence. Among the countries examined here in which such arrangements existed include Japan (with its Meiji Constitution), pre-World War I (Imperial) Germany (Japan used Imperial Germany's constitution as a model for its own Meiji Constitution), France (with its Third Republic), pre-World War II Italy, and pre-World War I Austria (the Austro-Hungarian Empire). And although Germany and Austria adopted democratic governments in the interwar period, these were so short-lived that bargains re-struck after World War II are more likely to have had meaningful long-term effects. The key point is that we must be sensitive to the timing of when institutional bargains were struck in seeking to account for modern capitalist arrangements.

Of course, most countries do not have purely consensus or majoritarian institutions; frequently, countries combine elements of each. So, where did these institutions come from? Political institutions are political decisions. They emerge from bargains struck among interest groups, with actors representing land, labor, and capital playing important and often leading roles. Certainly, many aspects of political institutions cannot be clearly determined by looking at the bargaining that takes place among these groups; however, some important attributes can, and others are at least consonant with preserving or enhancing the power of these actors. But answering this question is beyond the scope of this book. I take political institutions as given, and proceed from there.

Part II
Broad patterns

3   Patterns during the twentieth century

Before delving into an analysis of whether the theory accurately describes the causal mechanisms that lead to different capitalist styles, it is useful to observe some of the broad patterns that countries have displayed over time. In this chapter, I begin by illustrating patterns across time and space for the financial system variables of interest, where data are available: countries' general reliance on equities markets, to which corporate ownership outcomes closely correspond; government ownership of banks; and the size of public pension funds. It is difficult to get a consistent cross-national measure of the degree to which banking institutions cater to the agricultural sector, so this is saved for the case studies. I then look at how financial systems changed following a change in the country's constitution. As the theory articulates, dramatic changes to political institutions will likely correspond to changes in financial institutions. But more fundamental to the subsequent financial structure are the new political bargains struck among actors since the political institutions are seen as preserving and biasing the evolutionary path of the bargains. So, in the third section, I test for correlations between the financial variables and government partisanship, which proxies for labor's power versus capital owner's power, *at the time new bargains were struck*. Because it is difficult to get a consistent and accurate measure of farmers' power across countries, in the fourth section I look within the United States to see whether legislators' votes on key laws correlate with the value of agricultural production in their home constituency. Fifth, I test whether countries with more consensus forms of political institutions exhibit less financial change over time. Finally, I conclude with an overview of the results.

Financial systems across time and space

Table 3.1 presents a series of variables to measure countries' general reliance on equities markets, government ownership of banks, and the size of public pension funds. I discuss each in turn.

The size of a country's stock market relative to GDP is a common indicator for financial development. Hall and Soskice (2001) also use stock market capitalization relative to GDP as a general indicator for a nation's reliance on arm's length interactions relative to relationship-based interactions. With respect to the varieties of capitalism (VoC) debate, this is a good measure of asset specificity, but it needs to be treated with caution. Stock markets are known for occasional bubbles and busts, making it a potentially unreliable measure if examining only one point in time.[1] In the long term (over decades), stock markets tend to settle around an equilibrium price level (e.g., 10 percent increase per annum for the NYSE), making it preferable to measure a country's reliance on stock markets across long periods of time to gauge a country's overall reliance on markets.

At the same time, looking exclusively at stock markets only captures one half of the asset specificity variable. It would be preferable to have a measure for a nation's reliance on banks as well, such as bank loans relative to GDP, or bank deposits relative to GDP (from which bank loans are derived). This measure, on its own, is also subject to problems. Specifically, a nation with a low level of savings will likely have a low level of bank deposits (and thus bank lending) and a low stock market capitalization (conversely, high levels of savings could lead to high levels of bank deposits and a high stock market capitalization), holding foreign portfolio investment constant. To avoid this problem, we can take the ratio of the two – bank deposits/stock market capitalization – to achieve a more balanced assessment of a country's overall reliance on arm's length vs. relationship-based forms of economic activity.[2]

From Panel a in Table 3.1, we can see that there have been considerable changes between the pre- and post-World War II periods with regard to countries' reliance on equities markets. The ordering of countries in the postwar period, however, raises some questions with regard to the utility of the stock market capitalization measure as an indicator for the LME–CME orientation of a country since some countries seem out of place, such as Switzerland (being too LME), and the USA (being too CME) relative to conventional assessments of their financial, and capitalist, systems. This is consistent with the point made above that it is preferable to also account for the dependence on banks. Panel b illustrates the ratio of stock market capitalization to bank deposits.[3] Compared to the stock market capitalization table, the country orderings seem more in line with LME–CME expectations: the USA is appropriately LME for the postwar period; Switzerland remains on the LME side, but less so than before. And, as in Panel a, we see movement of countries along the LME–CME continuum – notably Japan and France. Some may prefer a corporate governance measure, but data are not available across time; however, analysis will be conducted across countries for the contemporary period (see below).

To assess the extent of government intervention, Panel c illustrates government ownership of banks in 1970 before privatization waves began, and in 1995. What is notable about these data is the stability of countries relative to one another in 1970 and 1995, suggesting that underlying institutional rigidities constrain the extent of change along the LME–CME continuum. Data are not available for the prewar period. Panel d offers an additional measure of state intervention in the broad economy, which shows a fairly similar country ordering. Panel e provides cross-sectional data on public pension assets and illustrates that countries again group together into the general LME–CME patterns observed in the other panels.

Table 3.2 illustrates pairwise correlations among the financial variables, which exhibit fairly high levels of correlation; they are all greater than 0.5. Given the general similarity of country groupings for the financial system variables in Table 3.1, this high level of correlation should not be too surprising, and mirrors the comparison of national financial systems made by Allen and Gale (2000). The high level of correlation among these variables suggests that it is important not only to consider how financial variables are constrained by the broader institutions of capitalism (as Gourevitch and Shinn (2005) note with respect to corporate governance), but also to consider how the financial variables themselves constrain change among each other. Moreover, the high levels of correlation again point to the importance of the initial bargains over the structure of financial institutions since they seem to group together once the rules are established. Summary statistics of the variables are provided in the Appendix to this chapter.

Constitutional and financial change

Among wealthy democracies, industrialization during the nineteenth and early twentieth centuries altered the existing agrarian-based economy and created a new, "modern" form of capitalism. Following World War I, labor's political influence surged across many European countries, leading to new bargains being struck with regard to the structure of the new institutions of capitalism. But for some countries, the depression and World War II disrupted the structure of these new institutional arrangements, and led to a new set of institutional bargains after the war ended. Table 3.3 lists the dates of the last major constitutional change for the 15 countries examined here, which corresponds to major changes in their financial (and capitalist) institutions, illustrating that five countries in the sample significantly altered their institutions following World War II: France, Germany, Japan, Austria, and Italy.[4]

Table 3.4 shows changes to the financial system for the pre- and post-World War II periods. The table also shows the magnitude of the change in these variables, and the expectation of the size of the change – a small change is expected for those countries that kept their pre-existing constitution, and a big change for those that changed their constitution. Using the stock market capitalization measure, there is, on average, a small decrease among those countries with no change in their constitution; the size of the stock market increased for some of these countries in the postwar period while for others it decreased. But for countries in which the constitution changed, there is, on average, a large decrease in the size of the stock market capitalization.

The preferred measure for the LME–CME orientation of the capitalist economy – stock market capitalization over bank deposits – likewise demonstrates a more major change for those countries that changed their constitutions. Countries without a constitutional change tended to change towards banks or markets nearly evenly, while those with constitutional changes all moved towards a greater reliance on banks in truly dramatic fashion.

The box plots in Figures 3.1a and 3.1b likewise demonstrate that the post-

Table 3.1 Financial system variables

	LME										CME				
Panel a: Stock market capitalization to GDP															
Pre-World War II[a]	UK 1.24	BEL 1.15	FRA 1.04	JAP 0.85	AUT 0.76	CAN 0.74	SWI 0.58	USA 0.57	NET 0.56	AUS 0.445	SWE 0.44	GER 0.44	DEN 0.27	NOR 0.19	ITA 0.17
Post-World War II[b]	CAN 1.12	SWI 0.96	UK 0.93	AUS 0.64	JAP 0.52	USA 0.52	NET 0.42	NOR 0.29	BEL 0.23	DEN 0.23	SWE 0.21	GER 0.19	ITA 0.17	FRA 0.17	AUT 0.1
Panel b: Ratio of stock market capitalization to bank deposits															
Pre-World War II[a]	JAP 4.8	CAN 4.23	UK 3.09	FRA 2.42	NET 2.07	BEL 1.98	USA 1.73	AUS 1.1	GER 1.1	AUT 1.02	ITA 0.77	SWE 0.64	SWI 0.58	DEN 0.43	NOR 0.25
Post-World War II[b]	CAN 2.89	UK 2.77	USA 1.97	JAP 1.56	AUS 1.4	SWI 1.37	NET 1.18	GER 0.74	DEN 0.7	NOR 0.66	BEL 0.61	FRA 0.49	SWE 0.42	ITA 0.32	AUT 0.2
Panel c: Government intervention: government ownership of banks (% of total ownership)[c]															
1970	UK 0	USA 0	JAP 0.07	NET 0.08	DEN 0.098	CAN 0.11	SWE 0.21	AUS 0.21	SWI 0.25	BEL 0.4	GER 0.52	NOR 0.55	AUT 0.71	FRA 0.74	ITA 0.76
1995	UK 0	USA 0	JAP 0	CAN 0	DEN 0.09	NET 0.09	AUS 0.12	SWI 0.13	FRA 0.17	SWE 0.23	BEL 0.28	ITA 0.36	GER 0.36	NOR 0.44	AUT 0.5

Panel d: Government intervention: state control[d]

	UK	USA	AUS	CAN	JAP	SWE	GER	SWI	AUT	NET	DEN	FRA	BEL	NOR	ITA
Mid-1990s	0.55	0.85	1.26	1.29	1.29	1.51	1.76	2.08	2.11	2.28	2.46	2.63	2.78	3.19	3.95

Panel e: State public pensions (% of GDP)[e]

	AUS	JAP	USA	CAN	DEN	BEL	UK	SWI	AUT	NOR	NET	FRA	GER	SWE	ITA
1980–1996	2.55	2.9	3.33	4.17	4.69	4.77	4.91	5.4	5.56	5.89	6.02	6.95	6.98	7.75	8.34

Notes

a avg. 1913–1929 (unless change of government after World War I, then 1913 only; includes Austria, Germany, and Italy since the stability of the interwar period was too short to allow new institutions to take root). 1938 is excluded because it is a clear outlier from countries' normal reliance on markets versus bank financing.

b avg. 1950–1990.

c Source: La Porta *et al.* (2000).

d Source: Nicoletti *et al.* (1999: 74). Ranking described as capturing "public ownership" (in turn taking into account the "size" and "scope" of the public sector, "control of public enterprises by legislative bodies," and "special voting rights") and "(state) involvement in business operation" (in turn including "price controls" and "use of command and control regulations").

e *Source*: State Public Pensions, category 1.1 of the Social Expenditure Database 1980–1996.

Table 3.2 Pairwise correlations between financial variables (significance in parentheses)

	Market cap. postwar avg.	Market cap/bank deposits postwar avg.	Gov. owned banks	State control	Public pension assets	Widely held corporate ownership	Family and state corporate ownership	Diffuse ownership aggregated
Market cap/bank deposits postwar avg.	0.902 (0.00)							
Gov. owned banks	-0.682 (0.01)	-0.772 (0.00)						
State control	-0.58 (0.02)	-0.726 (0.00)	0.644 (0.01)					
Public pension assets	-0.512 (0.05)	0.593 (0.02)	0.58 (0.02)	0.59 (0.02)				
Widely held corporate ownership	0.764 (0.00)	0.848 (0.00)	-0.778 (0.00)	-0.683 (0.01)	-0.591 (0.02)			
Family and state corporate ownership	-0.64 (0.01)	-0.77 (0.00)	0.82 (0.00)	0.701 (0.00)	0.601 (0.02)	-0.804 (0.00)		
Diffuse ownership aggregated	0.53 (0.04)	0.65 (0.01)	-0.694 (0.00)	-0.7 (0.00)	-0.601 (0.02)	0.715 (0.00)	-0.89 (0.00)	
Coordination index	-0.78 (0.00)	-0.87 (0.00)	0.76 (0.00)	0.67 (0.00)	0.54 (0.03)	-0.8 (0.00)	0.7 (0.00)	-0.77 (0.00)

Table 3.3 Most recent year of major constitutional change

	AUS	AUT	BEL	CAN	DEN	FRA	GER	ITA	JAP	NET	NOR	SWE	SWI	UK	USA
Year of last key change of constitution	1901	1945	1831	1867	1901	1946	1949	1948	1946	1848	1814	1866	1874	NA	1787

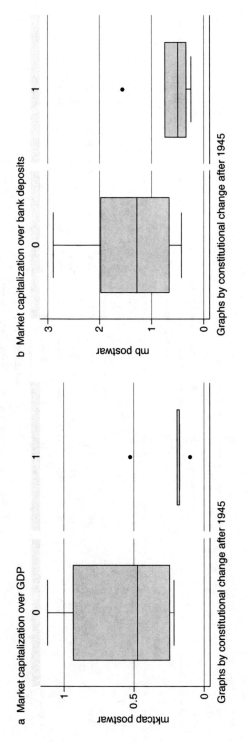

Figure 3.1 Box plots of market reliance during the post-World War II period for countries without and with constitutional change after World War II.

Note
The box plot on the left is for the ten countries without constitutional change after World War II; the box plot on the right is for the five countries that did change their constitutions after World War II (France, Italy, Germany, Austria, and Japan).

Table 3.4 Market reliance across time

Panel A: Stock market capitalization over GDP

High (LME) → Low (CME)

Row	Values (country value)
Pre-World War II	UK 1.24, BEL 1.15, FRA 1.04, JAP 0.85, AUT 0.76, CAN 0.74, SWI 0.58, USA 0.57, NET 0.56, AUS 0.445, SWE 0.44, GER 0.44, DEN 0.27, NOR 0.19, ITA 0.17
Post-World War II	CAN 1.12, SWI 0.96, UK 0.93, AUS 0.64, JAP 0.52, USA 0.52, NET 0.42, NOR 0.29, DEN 0.23, BEL 0.23, SWE 0.21, GER 0.19, ITA 0.17, FRA 0.17, AUT 0.1
Difference	AUS 0.195, AUT -0.66, BEL -0.91, CAN 0.38, FRA -0.87, GER -0.25, DEN -0.03, ITA -0.004, JAP -0.32, NET -0.13, NOR 0.104, SWE -0.23, SWI 0.38, USA -0.31, UK -0.05
Expectation[a]	s, b, b, s, s, b, s, s, s, s, s, s, s, s, s

Average change
Small change expected: -0.06   Big change expected: -0.42

Panel B: Ratio of stock market capitalization to bank deposits

High (LME) → Low (CME)

Row	Values (country value)
Pre-World War II	JAP 4.8, CAN 4.23, UK 3.09, FRA 2.42, NET 2.07, BEL 1.98, USA 1.73, GER 1.1, AUS 1.1, AUT 1.02, ITA 0.77, SWE 0.64, SWI 0.58, DEN 0.43, NOR 0.25
Post-World War II	CAN 2.89, UK 2.77, USA 1.97, JAP 1.56, AUS 1.4, SWI 1.37, NET 1.18, GER 0.74, DEN 0.7, NOR 0.66, BEL 0.61, SWE 0.49, FRA 0.49, ITA 0.42, AUT 0.2
Difference	AUS 0.36, AUT -0.78, BEL -1.38, CAN -1.3, DEN 0.26, FRA -1.93, GER -0.36, ITA -0.45, JAP -3.26, NET -0.89, NOR 0.41, SWE -0.22, SWI 0.79, UK -0.32, USA 0.24
Expectation[a]	s, b, s, s, s, b, s, s, b, s, s, s, s, s, s

Average change
Small change expected: -0.2   Big change expected: -1.36

Source: Rajan and Zingales (2003).

Notes

a s = small change; b = big change.

World War II financial systems differed markedly depending on whether a country's constitution changed after the war. For both measures, the reliance on markets is less than half that of those countries whose constitutions did not change.

What caused such dramatic and long-lasting changes? I argue that a new institutional bargain was reached among interests representing the economy's factors of production and the constitution preserved that bargain.

Labor versus capital owners

According to the argument, we must look at the power of actors during the period of time when they struck new bargains over financial institutions. For some countries this occurred at the end of the nineteenth and beginning of the twentieth century, when the institutions of modern capitalism were initially constructed. For these countries, the pre-existing constitution remained intact throughout the twentieth century, thus preserving the initial bargains. For other countries, however, political battles were fought after World War II, and political and capitalist institutions changed (as in France, Germany, Austria, Italy, and Japan). It is important that we are sensitive to the period of time when actors fought their most recent political battles over a nation's capitalist institutions since it is the outcome of that particular battle which has the most influence on the contemporary situation.

To assess the political power of labor versus capital owners, I measure the level of partisanship. Specifically, I use a measure constructed by Franzese (2002), which takes the average ideological value assigned to political parties by multiple expert studies, and is then weighted according to the number of cabinet posts held by each party.[5] I extend this measure to the pre-World War II period (see the Appendix for details). This variable allows for the placement of countries on a Left–Right political spectrum – the higher the value, the more left-wing the government, and thus the more sympathetic to labor. It measures government partisanship for ten countries in the interwar period, and is updated to 1950 for the five countries whose constitutions, and broader economic institutions, changed after World War II. I use the acronym POMCI in place of the more cumbersome, "Partisanship at the Origins of Contemporary Capitalist Institutions."[6] To illustrate the robustness of the POMCI measure, I compare regression results for it relative to two alternative partisanship measures: one which measures partisanship in 1950 to account for the possibility of new bargains being struck after the war (viewed by many authors as a key turning point for most OECD countries and their capitalist economies), and a second partisanship measure which is determined by taking countries' average level of partisanship during the post-World War II period.

According to the VoC literature, those economic institutions that exhibit strong complementarities to other institutions offer the broadest implications for understanding the influence of initial bargains on contemporary outcomes. Hall and Gingerich (2004) constructed an index that measures the degree of coordination among institutions. The institutions used to calculate the coordination index include shareholder power, dispersion of control, size of stock market, level of wage coordination, degree of wage coordination, and labor turnover. High levels of coordination are associated with a more coordinated market economy. I also examine correlations with the key dependent variables – stock market capitalization over GDP, bank–market orientation, government intervention, and public pensions – and with corporate governance variables that are commonly associated with LME and CME systems. While plenty of work has been done to demonstrate the correlation between partisanship and several of these variables at the same moment in time, to my knowledge none has tested for the political power of actors when bargains over capitalist institutions were initially struck and the structure of the institutions several decades later; in other words, whether partnership at time 0 correlates with institutional arrangements at time 10.

I test first for correlations with respect to the coordination index. The main drawback of this measure is that it is a static measure for the post-World War II period alone, and is calculated with data for the 1990s only. Although Hall and Soskice (2001) argue that complementary institutions would constrain change across the post-World War II period, it would be useful to have a measure that averaged the variables that comprise this index across the entire period. Nevertheless, the tests illustrate that the POMCI variable is the only partisanship variable to display statistically significant results, as shown in Table 3.5. The results illustrate the importance of being sensitive to the timing of when initial bargains over institutional design are struck.

The scatterplot in Figure 3.2 shows that Japan is a clear outlier. However, its placement at such a right-wing extreme is problematic since the left exercised considerable bargaining power in the years immediately following the war, when bargains over capitalist institutions were struck, as discussed in Chapter 5. That Japan is too far to the Left is a result of the partisanship variable being measured in 1950, immediately after the bargains were largely concluded, and the LDP had begun consolidating its political power.

Table 3.5 Partisanship measures and institutional coordination

	DV: coordination index			
	All countries			Japan excluded
POMCI	0.09** (2.13)			0.15*** (3.16)
Post-World War II average partisanship[a]		0.09 (1.38)		
Partisanship 1950			−0.002 (−0.04)	
Adjusted R^2	0.2	0.06	−0.07	0.41
N	15	15	15	14

Notes
a calculated from the partisanship levels at decade intervals from 1950 to 1990.
*** statistical significance at the 1% level; ** statistical significance at the 5% level.
t-statistics in parentheses.

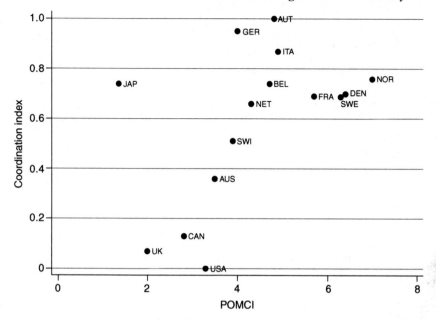

Figure 3.2 POMCI and institutional coordination.

Next, I consider measures for the reliance on stock markets: the post-World War II average stock market capitalization relative to GDP and the post-World War II stock market capitalization relative to bank deposits.[7] Table 3.6 presents both pre- and post-World War II correlations. While it is useful to observe the pre-World War II correlation, as it shows the robustness of the argument across time, more important to contemporary outcomes is the strength of the POMCI measure relative to the other partisanship measures for the post-World War II period.

Table 3.6 illustrates the robustness of the POMCI variable when controlling for legal family: common or civil law (La Porta *et al.*, 1998). The pre-World War II tests are particularly illuminating since they demonstrate no statistically significant correlation to the legal family variable, while the partisan variable remains statistically significant across both periods. This evidence offers support for critiques of the legal family argument, which charge that it fails to account for the underlying political mechanisms from which legal structures arise, and are conditioned by. The post-World War II results are generally consistent with those of the pre-World War II results. The POMCI variable returns stronger results than the alternative measures for partisanship, and it is robust to the inclusion of the legal family and proportional representation variables with respect to the stock market capitalization over bank deposits measures. Weaker results are observed for the average stock market capitalization over GDP in the post-World War II period, but the results do not suggest that legal family or PR are any better. In summary, the results are strongly supportive of the POMCI measure relative to other partisanship measures, and with respect to the legal family or the electoral system.

Table 3.6 Partisanship and market reliance

Dependent variables	Pre-World War II partisanship	POMCI	1950 partisanship	Post-World War II partisanship avgerage	Common law	PR	Constant	N [Adj. R²]
Panel A: Pre-World War II market reliance								
Pre-World War II market cap/bank deposits	-0.67*** (-4.41)						4.54*** (6.82)	13 [0.61]
	-0.68*** (-3.57)				-0.37 (-0.32)	-0.31 (-0.29)	4.86*** (3.96)	13 [0.52]
Pre-World War II market cap.	-0.12** (-2.83)						1.15*** (6.29)	13 [0.37]
	-0.12** (-2.56)				-0.37 (-1.29)	-0.31 (-1.13)	1.48*** (4.74)	13 [0.35]
Panel B: Post-World War II market reliance								
Post-World War II market cap/bank deposits		-0.39*** (-4.11)					2.86*** (6.48)	15 [0.53]
			-0.1 (-0.73)				1.6** (2.41)	15 [-0.03]
				-0.43** (-2.8)			3.01*** (4.39)	15 [0.33]
		-0.22*** (-2.59)			1.15*** (2.17)	0.08 (0.18)	1.75*** (2.71)	15 [0.74]
Post-World War II market cap.		-0.13*** (-3.1)					1.02*** (5.2)	15 [0.38]
			-0.04 (-0.83)				0.65** (2.5)	15 [-0.02]
				-0.14** (-2.14)			1.04*** (3.61)	15 [0.2]
		-0.07 (-1.61)			0.41 (1.36)	0.09 (0.35)	0.61 (1.68)	15 [0.45]

Notes
*** statistical significance at the 1% level; ** statistical significance at the 5% level; * statistical significance at the 10% level.
t-statistics in parentheses.

The concentration of corporate ownership is widely considered to be another important indicator corresponding to the general structure of capitalist systems, with coordinated market economies exhibiting more concentrated ownership than liberal market economies. Indeed, it is one of the components of Hall and Gingerich's index. I look at three measures for ownership concentration: (1) the commonly used measure of widely held ownership; (2) a concentrated ownership measure that combines the extent of family and state ownership; and (3) an aggregate diffuse ownership measure which combines the widely held measure with ownership by widely held financial corporations and widely held nonfinancial corporations. Together, these measures offer a robust series of tests for whether POMCI exhibits correlations to general corporate ownership outcomes. Data on these indicators come from La Porta *et al.* (1998). I expect a negative relationship for the first corporate ownership measure (widely held top 10), a positive correlation for the second (family and state ownership top 10), and a negative correlation for the third (diffuse ownership aggregated top 10). Table 3.7 illustrates that the POMCI variable exhibits stronger correlations compared to the alternative partisanship measures, and remains robust to the inclusion of the proportional representation and legal family variables across all three corporate ownership measures.

Indeed, government partisanship at the time when capitalist institutions were created explains a greater amount of variation in the widely held measure (60 percent) than other widely cited contemporary partisanship measures (e.g., Roe (2003), with an adjusted R-squared value equal to 45 percent). Weaker results are observed with respect to medium-sized firms, as shown in Table 3.8. This may be due to actors' greater attention to rules affecting the largest firms, which are more likely to have been important to, and present during, the initial bargains.

The extent of government intervention is examined next; the results are presented in Table 3.9. An economy with higher levels of intervention is generally equated with exhibiting stronger features of a coordinated market economy. Government ownership of banks before the privatization wave is tested to illustrate that countries retain their spatial ordering with regard to the POMCI measure despite the liberalization of their financial sectors. The evidence is consistent with the argument that initial institutional bargains constrain changes to the capitalist system once the institutions are in place, though the results for the POMCI measure become statistically insignificant in the presence of the control variables. A measure for overall state intervention is also tested with a measure constructed by Nicoletti *et al.* (1999: 74) and is described as capturing "public ownership" (in turn taking into account the "size" and "scope" of the public sector, "control of public enterprises by legislative bodies," and "special voting rights") and "(state) involvement in business operations" (in turn including "price controls" and "use of command and control regulations"). The higher adjusted R-squared for the correlation to this variable (42 percent) in comparison to the government ownership of banks suggests a stronger relationship between the initial institutional bargains struck between labor and capital and government's involvement in the broader structure of the economy.

Finally, the size of public pension assets (as a percentage of GDP) also displays a statistically significant correlation to government partisanship at the time

Table 3.7 Partisanship and corporate ownership concentration

Dependent variables	POMCI	1950 partisanship	Post-World War II partisanship avg.	Common law	PR	Constant	N [Adj. R^2]
Widely held top 10	-0.14*** (-4.66)					0.94*** (6.82)	15 [0.6]
		-0.03 (-0.74)				0.49** (2.18)	15 [-0.03]
			-0.14*** (-2.74)			0.95*** (4.09)	15 [0.31]
	-0.1*** (-3.54)			0.1 (0.61)	-0.19 (-1.3)	0.87*** (4.08)	15 [0.81]
Family and state owned. top 10	0.11*** (4.18)					-0.06 (-0.51)	15 [0.54]
		0.04 (1.22)				0.2 (1.15)	15 [0.03]
			0.14*** (3.9)			-0.2 (-1.23)	15 [0.5]
	0.09*** (3.07)			0.03 (0.17)	0.2 (1.27)	-0.12 (-0.54)	15 [0.6]
Diffuse owned. agg. top 10	-0.12*** (-3.38)					0.98*** (6.1)	15 [0.43]
		-0.03 (-0.81)				0.64*** (2.9)	15 [-0.02]
			-0.12** (-2.23)			0.99*** (4.09)	15 [0.22]
	-0.07** (-2.59)			-0.001 (-0.01)	-0.35** (-2.26)	1.03*** (4.65)	15 [0.73]

Notes

a Top 10 refers to a sample of the 20 largest firms with 10% as the cut-off for control, as measured by La Porta *et al.* (1999).

b Family and state ownership = family ownership + state ownership.

c Diffuse ownership aggregated= widely held + widely held financial corporations + widely held nonfinancial corporations.

*** statistical significance at the 1% level; ** statistical significance at the 5% level.

t-statistics in parentheses.

Table 3.8 POMCI and corporate ownership II

	Widely held top 20[a]	Family and state owned top 20[a]	Diffuse owned agg. top 20[a]	Widely held med 10[b]	Family and state owned med 10[b]	Diffuse owed agg. med 10[b]	Widely held med 20[c]	Family and state owned med 20[c]	Diffuse owned agg. med 20[c]
POMCI	-0.1***	0.08***	-0.09***	-0.02	0.08*	-0.02	-0.02	0.08**	-0.01
	(-2.88)	(2.95)	(-2.9)	(-0.89)	(1.94)	(-0.64)	(-0.61)	(2.18)	(-0.61)
Common law	-0.14	0.03	-0.05	0.2	0.03	0.12	0.53**	-0.1	0.39*
	(-0.62)	(0.2)	(-0.27)	(1.09)	(0.15)	(0.64)	(2.29)	(-0.4)	(1.96)
PR	-0.35	0.19	-0.29	0.08	-0.009	-0.02	0.15	-0.03	0.03
	(-1.73)	(1.2)	(-1.67)	(0.54)	(-0.04)	(-0.18)	(0.8)	(-0.17)	(0.18)
Adjusted R^2	0.57	0.57	0.63	0.14	0.11	0.11	0.5	0.3	0.53
N	15	15	15	15	15	15	15	15	15

Notes

a corporate ownership for a sample of the 20 largest companies with 20% share ownership as the cut-off for blockholding.
b corporate ownership for a sample of companies worth more than $500 million with 10% share ownership as the cut-off for blockholding.
c corporate ownership for a sample of companies worth more than $500 million with 20% share ownership as the cut-off for blockholding.
*** statistical significance at the 1% level; ** statistical significance at the 5% level; * statistical significance at the 10% level.
t-statistics in parentheses.

Table 3.9 POMCI and government intervention

Dependent variables	POMCI	1950 partisanship	Post-World War II partisanship avg.	Common law	PR	Constant	N [Adj. R²]
Government ownership of banks 1970	0.08** (2.13)					-0.06 (-0.34)	15 [0.2]
		0.02 (0.52)				0.2 (0.92)	15 [-0.05]
			0.11* (2)			-0.16 (-0.67)	15 [0.17]
	0.04 (0.9)			-0.54* (-1.86)	-0.33 (-1.35)	0.49 (1.41)	15 [0.28]
Government ownership of banks 1995	0.06** (2.75)					-0.08 (-0.84)	15 [0.32]
		0.02 (0.94)				0.06 (0.51)	15 [0]
			0.09*** (3.35)			-0.22* (-1.78)	15 [0.42]
	0.04 (1.73)			-0.006 (-0.04)	0.12 (0.84)	-0.1 (-0.49)	15 [0.33]
State control	0.38*** (4.76)					0.35 (0.96)	15 [0.42]
		0.1 (0.99)				1.5 (3.08)	15 [-0.0009]
			0.37*** (2.88)			0.43 (0.76)	15 [0.2]
	0.23* (1.76)			-0.98 (-1.19)	-0.07 (-0.1)	1.29 (1.29)	15 [0.48]

Notes
*** statistical significance at the 1% level; ** statistical significance at the 5% level; * statistical significance at the 10% level.
t-statistics in parentheses.

modern capitalist institutions were created (Table 3.10). While partisanship during the post-World War II period correlated more strongly with government ownership of banks in 1995, this was an exception to the general result that government intervention correlates with the POMCI variable. In the case of public pensions, this is the first instance that the postwar partisanship variable clearly exhibits a stronger correlation than the POMCI variable. However, the POMCI variable remains statistically significant at the 5 percent level, thus suggesting that the political origins of capitalist institutions remain valid for the contemporary public–private orientation of pension systems.

Farmers

Farmers' power is difficult to measure accurately across countries, although evidence from agricultural tariffs and the failure to reduce them in GATT and WTO rounds demonstrates that they wield substantial political influence. Indeed, American, French, and Japanese farmers are especially well known for their outsized political influence (e.g., Sheingate, 2001). Part of this is due to institutional rules that grant them a minimum number of representatives which are often sufficient to veto changes to the status quo (this institutional bias usually occurs with an increasing level of malapportionment over time). Unfortunately, it is difficult to measure accurately their political power across countries, so their influence on countries' specific financial systems will be examined in the case studies. However, statistical tests assessing the correlation between their importance to votes on financial legislation in the US during the 1920s and 1930s is examined here.

Because it is difficult to measure farmers' power across countries, I look within a single country to ascertain their importance to financial outcomes. This section may be more appropriately placed in the chapter on the twentieth-century US (Chapter 7); I put it here since it complements the statistical tests for partisanship. However, it is useful to refer to the US case for a more comprehensive view of the political dynamics at work.

Table 3.10 Partisanship measures and pensions

	DV: public pensions assets (% of GDP)		
POMCI	0.61** (2.58)		
Post-World War II average partisanship		1*** (3.55)	
Partisanship 1950			0.56** (2.36)
Adjusted R^2	0.29	0.45	0.24
N	15	15	15

Notes
*** statistical significance at the 1% level; ** statistical significance at the 5% level.
t-statistics in parentheses.

Five laws of great importance to the structure of the American financial system in the twentieth century are examined: the McFadden Act of 1927, the Glass–Steagall Banking Act of 1933, the Securities Exchange Act of 1934, the Public Utility Holding Company Act of 1935, and the Revenue Act of 1935. Together, they have had considerable influence on the structure of the American financial system in the twentieth century. I begin with tests for the first three laws which were of primary importance to the banking system and equities markets. The latter two focus on corporate ownership, and are examined next.

The intent of the McFadden Act was to make national banks equally competitive with state-chartered banks by allowing national banks to branch within the state to the extent permitted by state law.[8] This would be a precedent-setting law of potentially great importance since it would be the first legislation to allow national banks to open branches within a state. Owners of large enterprises and their employees, as well as large city banks would be the main supporters of the Act. Those who depended on the security of local banking facilities (i.e., unit banks and state chartered banks), particularly farmers, would comprise main opponents to the Act as it would likely lead to the draining away of money from the interior to urban, industrial centers.

The Glass–Steagall Banking Act of 1933 sought to separate the activities of commercial banks and securities firms as well as introduce federal deposit insurance.[9] Farmers, who depended on the services of local banks (via the insurance argument discussed in Chapter 2), would benefit most from the Act while wealthy industrialists (firm owners) and those who worked in them would be the losers as a result of inefficiencies in the banking system leading to a lower supply of lending and higher costs (both explicit via the lower supply, and implicit via the moral hazard cost of providing deposit insurance).

Another critical piece of legislation that would have decades-long consequences for the structure of the American financial system was the Securities Exchange Act of 1934. One of its key features was the protection of minority shareholders in the secondary market. While the 1933 Securities Exchange Act, which dealt with the issuing of securities in the primary market, contained an antifraud provision, questions remained about its reach. The 1934 Act broadened the scope, and thereafter it was commonly invoked for insider trading cases; it has also been used against companies for price fixing (artificially inflating or depressing stock prices through stock manipulation), bogus company sales to increase stock price, and even a company's failure to communicate relevant information to investors. The main losers from this legislation were those with access to private information – wealthy owners and investors – while those who supported it were those who sought to limit the scope and power of large financial institutions and corporations, notably farmers.

For the tests conducted here, the dependent variable is the legislator's "yea" vote for a bill (coded as 1 or 0 otherwise), obtained from the *Congressional Record*. As a basic measure of the importance of farmers in each state, I use the total value of agricultural production as a fraction of state income.[10] Workers' influence is measured by the proportion of a state's total population that works in the manufacturing sector.[11] Capital's influence is measured by the level of manufacturing value added minus total wages as a fraction of the state's total income.[12] I also identify members as Democrat or Republican, which is consistent with the partisanship measures used in the cross-country tests. Table 3.11 presents the results from probit estimations for House and Senate votes on these three pieces of legislation.

Models 1 through 3 illustrate that representatives from farming states voted differently from their counterparts in worker- and capital-dominant states for each Act. An analysis of the voting patterns demonstrates that workers and capital tended to vote with, and be represented by, Republicans (known for representing industry at this time); agriculture tended to ally with Democrats. As a result, this can create some difficulties for clearly discerning the impact of farmers when Democrats vote along party lines and in a way that is consistent with farmers' preferences. It is unclear whether party identification, or interest groups from the home constituency, are the main reason. As a result, the impact of farmers is clearest when Republicans from states with a high level of agricultural output break ranks with their party. This is evidenced by statistically significant results for agriculture after controlling for party identification. Model 4 illustrates that this, in fact, occurred. Indeed, farmers exerted more influence in this regard than workers or capital (i.e., Democratic representatives did not break from their party and vote with Republicans). In other words, the agricultural sector wielded a critical swing vote.

With regard to the McFadden Act in the House and the Senate, agriculture proved to have a critical influence in getting Republicans to vote with Democrats since Democrats would not have otherwise had enough Yes votes to pass the Act. With respect to the passage of the Glass–Steagall Act, Democrats had a sufficiently large majority in the House to pass the legislation without Republican support; so we cannot be sure if agriculture played a critical role, or if party identification was the primary influence. The passage of the Securities Exchange Act of 1934 in the House was similar to the Glass–Steagall Act in that Democrats had enough votes without Republican support, though 24 Republicans did vote in favor, and the results suggest that agriculture played a role. In the Senate, however, Democrats lacked a majority (45 Yes votes for the Securities Exchange Act), and 15 Republicans appear to have sided with the Democrats as a result of the importance of agriculture to their home state.

The next two pieces of legislation, the Public Utility Holding Company (PUHC) Act and the Revenue Act (both in 1935), sought to end pyramidal corporate ownership structures. In the utilities industry, holding companies became massive, and highly concentrated. For example, in 1930, 90 percent of all operating companies were controlled by 19 holding companies. The strength of the holding companies was intensified by the existence of interlocking directorates. The Federal Power Commission commented that:

> 48 major projects fall under the control of 10 groups which service 12,487 communities with a population of more than 42 million. The community of interest between the 10 groups is evidenced by the fact that 19 directors or officers were directors in at least 2 groups.[13]

Table 3.11 Interests and US financial legislation

	DV: Yes vote for the McFadden Act, 1927		DV: Yes vote for the Glass-Steagall Banking Act, 1933		DV: Yes vote for the Securities Exchange Act, 1934		DV: Yes vote for the PUHC Act, 1935		DV: Yes vote for the Revenue Act, 1935	
	House	Senate	House	Senate	House	Senate	House	Senate	House	Senate
1 Value of farm production	-0.02***	-0.03***	0.02***	-0.01*	0.03***	0.02***	0.03***	0.02***	0.02***	0.024***
	(-4.03)	(-4.05)	(4.82)	(-1.8)	(6.77)	(2.72)	(5.44)	(2.83)	(4.74)	(2.81)
Pseudo-R^2	0.04	0.2	0.04	0.02	0.09	0.07	0.07	0.075	0.04	0.072
N	365	93	428	86	428	94	425	92	426	94
2 Manufacturing population	0.04***	0.07**	-0.07***	0.02	-0.12***	-0.08***	-0.098***	-0.09***	-0.08***	-0.1***
	(3.28)	(2.24)	(-5.52)	(0.92)	(-7.64)	(-2.88)	(-5.83)	(-3.31)	(-5.61)	(-3.35)
Pseudo-R^2	0.025	0.05	0.05	0	0.11	0.07	0.07	0.094	0.06	0.095
N	365	93	427	86	428	94	425	92	426	94
3 Capital value added	0.003	0.05***	-0.01**	0.009	-0.03***	-0.01	-0.028***	-0.039***	-0.02***	-0.02
	(0.51)	(2.82)	(-2)	(0.68)	(-4.63)	(-1.04)	(-3.83)	(-2.74)	(-3.51)	(-1.46)
Pseudo-R^2	0	0.09	0.006	0	0.039	0	0.03	0.06	0.02	0.01
N	365	93	428	86	428	94	425	92	426	94
4 Value of farm production	-0.02***	-0.06***	0.01*	-0.02*	0.01**	0.03**	0.028***	0.02	0.01	0.02**
	(-3.3)	(-3.69)	(1.82)	(-1.72)	(1.88)	(2.19)	(2.61)	(1.43)	(1.25)	(2.0)
Manufacturing population	-0.01	-0.17**	0.003	-0.03	-0.02	-0.1	0.05	-0.012	-0.008	-0.04
	(-0.58)	(-2.44)	(0.12)	(-0.63)	(-0.61)	(-0.27)	(1.5)	(-0.24)	(-0.27)	(-0.8)
Capital value added	-0.02**	0.02	0.005	-0.004	-0.009	0.03	-0.02**	-0.02	-0.008	0.02
	(-2.02)	(1.16)	(0.56)	(-0.22)	(-0.89)	(1.46)	(-2.01)	(-0.89)	(-0.88)	(1.06)
Democrat	-0.51***	-0.62*	2.08***	-0.1	1.6***	0.97***	1.8***	0.86**	1.4***	1.1***
	(-2.97)	(-1.7)	(9.88)	(-0.34)	(9.44)	(2.92)	(10.47)	(2.44)	(9.01)	(3.0)
Pseudo-R^2	0.07	0.28	0.3	0.03	0.29	0.16	0.34	0.15	0.22	0.18
N	363	93	418	86	427	94	424	92	425	94
Log-likelihood	-200.84	-36.67	-200.6	-57	-194.43	-51.13	-157.12	-52.84	-213.55	-51.75

Notes
*** statistically significant at the 1% level; ** statistically significant at the 5% level; * statistically significant at the 10% level.
z-statistics are shown in parentheses.

This high level of concentration and control led to the PUHC Act in 1935. The Revenue Act complemented and extended the PUHC Act beyond the utilities sector by imposing extra taxation on corporations on the basis of size, and thereby sought to eliminate unnecessary holding companies.[14] Farmers would be expected to support these acts, while labor is expected to oppose them (as concentration of ownership tends to enhance employment stability), and owners of capital are also expected to oppose them since the pyramid structure enhances profitability.

The results are consistent with expectations: farmers supported these Acts, while labor and capital opposed them. With regard to the passage of the PUHC Act of 1935, Democrats had enough votes to pass the legislation in the House without Republican support, though some Republicans did vote in favor and appear to have done so in line with the importance of agriculture to their home state. Senate voting occurred primarily along party lines so it is not clear how important agriculture was. The same may be said for the passage of the Revenue Act in the House. In the Senate, however, the Democrats relied on Republican support (Democrats had only 46 Yes votes), which appears to be influenced by the importance of agriculture to the Senator's state (eight Republicans voted Yes).

The analysis here of federal legislation complements that of Rajan and Ramcharan (2008) who focus on the state level. The findings in this chapter are consistent with their findings that agriculture has had a substantial impact on the structure of the American financial system. The evidence demonstrates that farmers played an important role in weakening the big bankers and financiers and their control over corporations, and cemented the emerging trend of fragmentation that would come to characterize the structure of the American financial system.

Political institutions and financial change

Political institutions cement the bargain struck among the interest groups, making substantial change difficult to implement later. In contrast to Pagano and Volpin (2005), who see the political institutions (proportional representation) as encouraging blockholding, I see the initial bargains as critical. These bargains are preserved more strongly in consensus systems, and insofar as blockholding is more prevalent among these countries, it is likely that interests are compromised on this solution either within pre-existing consensus political institutions, or interests are compromised on both the political institutions and capitalist institutions simultaneously, with the political institutions preserving the blockholding bargain.

In Table 3.12, regressions among political institutions and financial system measures exhibit weaker correlations overall relative to the partisanship variable (see above), suggesting that political interests have a stronger influence; political institutions have a secondary effect.

In my view, proportional representation and political cohesion correlate with financial outcomes by preserving the initial bargains that are struck. Table 3.13

Table 3.12 Political institutions and financial variables

	Market–bank ratio postwar	Government ownership of banks, 1970	Government ownership of banks, 1995	State control	Public pension assets
Proportional representation	–1.1*** (–3.12)	0.15 (1.01)	0.19** (2.37)	1.02** (2.34)	1.4 (1.6)
Adjusted R^2	0.38	0.00	0.25	0.24	0.1
N	15	15	15	15	15
Political cohesion	–1*** (–3.24)	0.21* (1.74)	0.12 (1.65)	1.01*** (2.92)	1.63** (2.3)
Adjusted R^2	0.4	0.12	0.1	0.35	0.24
N	15	15	15	15	15

Notes
Executive-legislative dominance was also tested for the postwar period; however, the results were not significant. Measures for the pre-World War II period would be useful to test since clear differences seem to arise, as the case studies illustrate.
*** statistical significance at the 1% level; ** statistical significance at the 5% level.
t-statistics in parentheses.

illustrates that the political institution variables offer weaker correlations than the POMCI (and legal code) variable for the market–bank ratio – the dependent variable with which the political institution variables exhibit the strongest correlation in Table 3.12. These correlations point to the importance of the initial bargains; political institutions tend to preserve the status quo to varying degrees, and bias the evolutionary path of the financial system. The biasing effect of political institutions is observed when considering the extent of change of the financial system over time, as in Table 3.14 and Figure 3.3.

Table 3.13 Interests, institutions, law, and finance

	DV: Market–bank ratio post-World War II					
POMCI	–0.29*** (–3.12)		–0.22** (–2.63)	–0.3*** (–3.5)		–0.22** (–2.59)
Political cohesion	–0.6** (–2.26)	–0.19 (–0.54)	–0.11 (–0.4)			
Proportional representation				–0.7** (–2.5)	0.29 (0.53)	0.08 (0.18)
common law		1.3*** (2.96)	0.98** (2.48)		1.78*** (3.08)	1.16** (2.17)
Adjusted R2	0.64	0.63	0.75	0.67	0.62	0.75
N	15	15	15	15	15	15

Notes
*** statistical significance at the 1% level; ** statistical significance at the 5% level.
t-statistics in parentheses.

Table 3.14 Changing financial systems and political cohesion

	DV: change in the market–bank ratio 1950–1970 avg. and 1980–1990 avg.			
	All countries		*Excluding Switzerland*	
Political cohesion	−0.5* (2.06)	−0.25 (−1.04)	−0.8*** (4.2)	−0.63** (−2.76)
POMCI		−0.19** (−2.28)		−0.11 (−1.6)
Adjusted R²	0.19	0.39	0.56	0.61
N	15	15	14	14

Notes
*** statistical significance at the 1% level; ** statistical significance at the 5% level.
t-statistics in parentheses.

I control for partisanship to assess whether it could be driving the results. When Switzerland – a clear outlier in Figure 3.3 – is excluded, the results illustrate the expected relationship; more cohesion correlates with less financial change. Why and how Switzerland changed so substantially despite being a highly consensual political system would be an interesting case for future research.

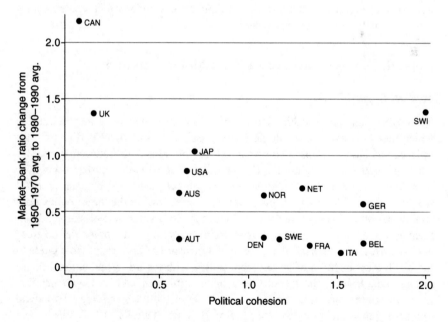

Figure 3.3 Scatter plot of changing market–bank orientation and political cohesion.

Conclusions

The high correlation among the financial variables, as well as the grouping of countries along the LME–CME spectrum, suggests the possibility of a common political origin, and the wide-ranging impact of political interests when institutional bargains are initially struck. But one of the most interesting findings is the big change in the market–bank orientation from the pre- to the post-World War II period for those countries that changed their constitution. Those countries that changed exhibited far less reliance on markets in the post-World War II period relative to those that did not change, suggesting that either the constitution or the new bargains struck by newly empowered political interests led to the change. The robustness of the correlations between the POMCI measure and various financial system variables suggests that political interests – workers and capital owners – likely play a key causal role. The regressions for farmers and financial regulations in the United States offer strong evidence for their relevance to financial outcomes as well. The lack of robust correlations between political institutions and the financial variables lends further support to the potential importance of political interests as the common root cause. Political institutions seem to matter most when affecting the extent of change after bargains are struck – where more veto-points exist, less change occurs. Taken together, these results are consistent with the theory: initial bargains among key political interests have considerable and long-lasting influence on the structure of the country's financial system, and, by extension, its capitalist system. Of course, these correlations do not allow for conclusions to be made regarding a causal relationship; thus it is necessary to investigate the historical circumstances under which contemporary capitalist institutions were (re)created.

Appendix: measurement issues and additional matters

Measuring partisanship

For government partisanship, I use a measure compiled by Franzese (2002), which takes the average ideological value assigned to political parties by multiple expert studies. This ideological value, normalized to between 0 and 10, where 10 is the most right-wing (I invert it so that 10 is the most left-wing), is then weighted according to the number of cabinet posts held by each party. It would be preferable to adjust this government measure for the larger policy constraints set by Parliament, but it is difficult to justify some sort of single adjustment across countries since policy constraints vary so greatly among issue areas and countries. Nonetheless, the government measure offers a reasonable guide to the ideological position of government policy with regard to the national financial system. Indeed, the treasury and other ministries involved with national financial matters are almost always under the executive's purview. To extend Franzese's measure prior to World War II, I use Dodd's (1976) ideological placement of political parties during the interwar period. I normalize his score so

Table 3.A1 Summary statistics

	Mean	Standard deviation	Minimum	Maximum	Observations
Stock market capitalization over GDP post-World War II	0.447	0.328	0.09	1.11	15
Market–bank ratio pre-World War II	1.71	1.4	0.25	4.8	15
Market–bank ratio post-World War II	1.15	0.84	0.24	2.9	15
Government ownership of banks, 1970	0.31	0.27	0	0.76	15
Government ownership of banks, 1995	0.18	0.16	0	0.5	15
State control	2	0.91	0.55	3.95	15
Public pension assets	5.34	1.71	2.55	8.34	15
Widely held corporate ownership top 10	0.34	0.28	0	0.9	15
Family and state corporate ownership top 10	0.42	0.23	0.05	0.85	15
Diffuse ownership aggregated top 10	0.47	0.27	0.05	0.95	15
Partisanship at origins of capitalist institutions (pre-World War II)	3.98	1.68	1	7	15
POMCI	4.33	1.57	1.35	7	15
Political cohesion	1.04	0.55	0.04	2	15
Proportional representation	0.67	0.47	0	1	15

that it corresponds to the 0–10 scale. Data on the partisan composition of government are obtained with Mackie and Rose's (1990) and Flora's (1987) data which, respectively, provide the proportion of seats in Parliament held by each political party as well as the coalition parties forming a government, if a coalition occurred. Based on observation of such coalitions in the postwar period and coalitions in the interwar period where data are available (e.g., Australia), cabinet seats are generally assigned to parties according to the proportion of seats the coalition partner holds as a percentage of total coalition seats. Thus, based on the proportion of parliamentary seats each coalition party holds, we can determine the percentage of cabinet seats the party held, and then calculate the average partisan score for each government. These data are available for 1929. Left-wing power in 1913 can be determined only approximately by using the proportion of parliamentary seats held by left-wing political parties. This lacks a measure for ideological position, but it is clear that left-wing parties were far weaker at this time than in 1929, which supports the findings.

Partisanship at the Origins of Capitalist Institutions (POMCI)

This variable measures government partisanship for ten countries in 1929, and is updated to 1950 for the five countries whose constitutions, and broader economic institutions, changed following World War II.

Table 3.A2 Pairwise correlations between country-level variables (significance in parentheses)

	POMCI	Proportional representation	Political cohesion
Proportional representation	0.39 (0.00)		
Political cohesion	0.46 (0.00)	0.62 (0.00)	
Common law	−0.55 (0.00)	−0.85 (0.00)	−0.74 (0.00)

Table 3.A3 Partisanship at the Origins of Capitalist Institutions (POMCI)

	POMCI
AUS	3.5
AUT	4.8
BEL	4.7
CAN	2.8
DEN	6.4
FRA	5.7
GER	4
ITA	4.9
JAP	1.35
NET	4.3
NOR	7
SWE	6.3
SWI	3.9
UK	2
USA	3.3

Part III

Cases

4　Class conflict

Political battles that occur with owners of capital on one side, and labor and landed interests on the other, are labeled class conflict. When capital owners win, an owner-oriented liberal market economy arises, as in pre-World War II Japan and France. A low level of government intervention is expected, along with private pensions, centralized banking arrangements, pyramidal corporate ownership, and a heavier reliance on equities markets than when labor and farmers dominate. When landed interests and labor win, economy-wide banking prevails, which corresponds to Mediterranean capitalism, as exemplified by post-World War II France. A high level of government intervention is likely, as well as public pensions, a combination of centralized and decentralized banking arrangements, concentrated corporate ownership and a lighter reliance on equities markets. In this chapter I discuss these two outcomes, with the three cases just mentioned.

Capital wins: owner-oriented LME

Japan, pre-World War II

Japan's financial system in the prewar era corresponds neatly to expectations; it is characterized by a high reliance on securities markets, pyramidal corporate ownership, low levels of government intervention, weak agricultural financing, and private pension funding (where it existed). Its politics likewise reflect strong links between the rapidly growing business sector and government officials, with a select group of rural elites also wielding political influence. Political institutions placed power in the hands of the oligarchs who surrounded the emperor (the Genrō and the Privy Council) with some political power accorded to the Upper House of the Diet (the House of Peers). These institutions kept policymaking out of the hands of popular influence (labor and small farmers), and thereby cemented the power of the elite – particularly the business elite. Consequently they determined domestic economic policy, and enabled business owners to capture the benefits of low transaction costs via securities markets without sacrificing ownership of the firm via pyramidal ownership structures. Government intervention was low, and because such a small proportion of agrarian interests wielded meaningful political influence, agricultural financing remained low.

In this section on prewar Japan, I first discuss the structure of the financial system, followed by the structure of the political institutions, and then examine how the dominant political power of capital owners correspond to and entrenched the owner-oriented LME financial system.

Structure of the financial system

Japan's dependence on equity finance began in 1880. After a decade of direct government investment in mines, railroads, and factories, the government privatized them, with the big merchant houses of Mitsui, Mitsubishi, Sumitomo, Yasuda, Furukawa, Okura, and Asano (later becoming known as the zaibatsu) as the largest beneficiaries (Johnson, 1982: 84). Deep personal and unofficial relations developed between the Meiji government and the owners of these enterprises. This privatization of the economy facilitated the development of securities markets, which flourished (Hoshi and Kashyap, 2001). Japan remained staunchly reliant on markets during the prewar era despite momentous political and economic events, including the Sino-Japanese War (1894–1895), the adoption of the Gold Standard in 1897 which stopped a fall in the exchange rate but adversely affected the balance of payment, thereby causing several financial crises, the Russo-Japanese War (1904–1905), the postwar financial crisis in 1920 and a concomitant surge in tariffs, the Great Kantō Earthquake of 1923, a run on banks and a severe financial crisis in 1927, and the Great Depression which spread to Japan in 1930 to 1931. Despite all of this, securities markets remained the dominant source of external finance for large firms up until the 1930s, when the military took power. This long reliance on markets despite numerous crises is notable because banks are commonly turned to for their insurance services (Allen and Gale, 2000). Instead, banking services were largely used to bolster firms' securities markets financing activities, making bank financing "the least important source of funds" for the Japanese economy during the 1889 to 1937 era (Hoshi and Kashyap, 2001). Not until the balance of political power among competing interest groups tilted towards the military in the 1930s (and especially with the Sino-Japanese War in 1937) did bank lending increase substantially, as may be seen in Table 4.1.

But tapping additional funding from outsiders – via equities markets – could allow new investors to seize control, reducing the family to a limited partner. For example, both the Shimomura and Ohmura zaibatsu brought in outside investors who took control, only to see these new shareholders shift the business out of their (money-losing) traditional Japanese clothing businesses and into department store-based retailing. To tap additional low-cost funding via equities markets without sacrificing control of the firm, owners began using pyramidal groups as an elegant solution to this problem. As Yoshisuke Aikawa, founder of the Nassan zaibatsu, wrote in his 1934 memoirs, pyramids preserve total control by insiders while permitting access to limitless capital (Morck and Nakamura, 2005: 381).

The founding of the Tokyo and Osaka Stock Exchanges in 1877 allowed Japanese companies to tap capital from individual investors. This enabled the four

Table 4.1 Sources of external funds for industries, 1931–1955 (percentage distribution of total)

Year	New share issues	New bond issues	Net new bank loans
1931	56.5	29.92	13.57
1935	68.06	2.17	29.77
1940	38.42	7.96	53.63
1945	6.11	0.64	93.24
1950	6.22	8.48	85.3
1955	14.12	3.92	81.95

Source: Bank of Japan, *Statistical Annual* (1960).

largest zaibatsu – Mitsui, Sumitomo, Mitsubishi, and Yasuda – to expand by constructing pyramids in the late nineteenth century (Morck and Nakamura, 2005: 383).

With regard to the banking system, most of the financing went to industry, rather than agriculture or small firms in the prewar period, as Table 4.2 illustrates with the row on mutual banks, and so on. But it is noteworthy that a secular increase occurred in the postwar period. That this corresponds to an increase in small firms' political power, via the electoral system and more power concentrated in the legislature, will be discussed in the next chapter.

In summary, the prewar financial system was heavily reliant on securities markets with corporate pyramids emerging in the late nineteenth century (assisted by the founding of the Tokyo Stock Exchange), with little government intervention after 1880, and a small fraction of bank lending directed towards agriculture. Pension programs were of relatively minor importance, but where they existed, they were primarily managed by employers and for narrow groups of employees – the highly skilled workers that employers were afraid to lose (Manow, 2001a).

Politics

During the prewar period 1889 to 1937, the Meiji constitution structured the balance of power among Japan's political institutions (House of Representatives, House of Peers, Premier, Cabinet, Bureaucracy, Army and Navy, Privy Council, and Emperor). It was modeled after the Constitution of the German Empire (1871–1919) and in both cases, capitalist oligarchs retained dominant political control. In Japan, factions developed among the oligarchs that were more or less sympathetic to the interests of other political actors, such as the popular political parties, the military, and big business. During the 1920s political parties gained more influence, and in the 1930s the power of the military increased until it dominated government. But to understand why particular policy outcomes resulted and how these affected the financial system, we must examine how political institutions coordinated the bargaining arrangements among actors, and privileged particular interests over others.

64   *Cases*

Table 4.2 Proportion of deposits and financial bonds of various financial institutions in aggregate deposits and bank debentures (percent)

	1910	1920	1930	1940	1950	1960	1970	1979	1987
Commercial banks and savings banks[1]	72.8	70.3	47.4	46.4	57.4	49.9	41.9	35	35.7
Long-term credit banks[2]	14.4	14.9	13	10.4	8.9	5.7	6	5.7	5.4
Trust institutions	–	–	7.6	8.1	2.7	10.1	9.6	11.7	11.9
Mutual banks, shinkin banks, credit associations, including cooperatives[3]	0.3	2.2	7.1	13.5	17.4	19.5	25.5	25.1	22.7
Life insurance companies	3.8	4.4	6.6	5.6	2	4.1	6	5.7	9.3
Post office	8.6	8.2	16.3	16	11.5	10.7	11	16.8	15
Total	99.9	100	98	100	99.9	100	100	100	100

Source: Sakakibara (1993: 18).

Notes
1 Figures are the totals of the commercial and savings banks. There were no savings banks after the war.
2 The prewar figures are for specialty banks (tokushu ginkō).
3 Including the Shoko Chukin Bank (Commerce-Industry Cooperative Central Fund) and the Norinchukin Bank (Agriculture-Forestry Central Fund).
See Table 5.10b for data from 1985 to 2005.

In theory, the emperor exercised absolute political power. The Constitution was subordinate to the throne, and thereby to the Sat-Cho[1] oligarchs who controlled the throne.[2] The Constitution placed the Privy Council, the Cabinet, and the House of Peers effectively out of any popular control. Moreover, the powers of the House of Representatives were sufficiently limited to give popular government little positive power and weak veto-power. It was weak because the oligarchs retained the ability to circumvent uncooperative legislatures; they could often avoid statutes through Imperial Orders, they could keep the budget beyond real legislative control (e.g., by implementing the previous year's budget and deflating the currency to increase its relative size), and the oligarchs could even dissolve the legislature if necessary.

One of the most powerful mechanisms for undermining popular rule was the Genrō (Elder Statesmen). They made important political decisions in the Emperor's name, such as recommending the prime minister to the legislature, and served as the real centralized power of the state up until the 1920s.[3] No political institution was as powerful as the Genrō in the early constitutional period. Although they lost their influence as fewer members survived to advise the emperor in the 1920s, the Privy Council also acted as an advisory council. These members were appointed by the emperor for life, but the Council was a constitutionally recognized body and could more easily be reined in, unlike the Genrō.

Members of the House of Peers were either appointed by the emperor or were aristocrats who inherited their membership. The Peers often sought to protect the bureaucracy by vetoing the Lower House's anti-bureaucracy legislation since all policies required concurrent Peer-House approval.

For most of the period, the House of Representatives was not popularly elected since only wealthy taxpayers were permitted to vote – usually business-men and wealthy landowners. The Elections Act of 1889 enfranchised only 453,000 voters out of a total population of 42 million. Subsequent election laws in 1900, 1919, and 1925 raised the voting population, ultimately to the entire male population aged 25 or more, totaling 12.5 million voters, or 21 percent of the population. During the 1920s, political parties' influence increased and policy outcomes reflected more of the parties' objectives via the Diet's power to approve the premier, who was recommended by the emperor. Because the premier selected Cabinet members, this was the Diet's one way to influence the administration. Frequently, the premier would bargain with party leaders to ensure his election, and in doing so would offer Cabinet positions to them.[4]

Although the 1920s witnessed increasing party influence, it was insufficient to substantially alter government policies. The levers of power were controlled by the oligarchy (the Genrō, Privy Council, and House of Peers) until the military began exercising greater control over government policy in the 1930s.[5] Thus, to understand Japan's economic policies during this period, we must deter-mine which interest groups were most closely tied to the oligarchs.

CAPITAL OWNERS

Strong informal ties existed between the leaders of the zaibatsu and the govern-ment. As Scalapino (1967) remarks,

> large number[s] of new industrial leaders ... were men of the old bushi class and consequently men whose political predilections and personal friendships – not to mention economic security – lay with the government. With Meiji political and economic elites extremely small in numbers, with the latter fre-quently selected by the former and having a similar background, close per-sonalized contacts were most natural.[6]

At this early date, Japanese industry was highly centralized, with the key finan-cial-economic controls held by the government and the zaibatsu. Although small and medium-sized businesses played an important part in overall production, they depended heavily on the zaibatsu and government. Indeed, the zaibatsu were the ultimate recipients of tremendous economic and political power, and symbols of Japanese capitalism.[7]

For example, the zaibatsu benefited considerably from various aspects of the mass privatization of state-owned enterprises at the end of the nineteenth century. The great zaibatsu families were virtually the only entities with pockets deep enough to participate extensively, and their close political connections, and the government's financial exigencies, made for bargain prices. Most privatization prices were far lower than the Meiji government's capital outlays in establishing them (Kobayashi, 1985: 64–65). However, many state-owned enterprises were in dismal shape, and although many privatized enterprises subsequently encountered serious difficulties, the Japanese government rarely provided direct subsidies. At the same time, the state did provide generous tariff protection and other indirect assistance to ensure the success of the privatized enterprises. Regardless of the government's intention, many privatizations turned out to be windfalls (Morck and Nakamura, 2005: 385–386).

Since agrarian power came in the form of votes, and was therefore concentrated in the Lower House, rural interests generally lacked the political power of the zaibatsu. Thus, the zaibatsu, which garnered political favors from the oligarchs through their financial influence, frequently prevailed when conflicting urban–rural interests arose, such as nominating premiers and legislation affecting the financial system.[8] For example, right through the 1920s the Genrō would always nominate business-friendly premiers. One early example is Yamagata's premiership, which began in November 1898. He allied with the Jiyūtō group of the Kenseito (the precursor of the Kenseikai pro-business party and created by the cooperation of the Jiyūtō and Shimpōtō parties) and made a bargain with them which helped align the political parties to the swelling numbers of business owners (Umegaki, 1988).

The frequent corruption scandals further illustrate the close business–political relationships. Zaibatsu businessmen were constantly making personal gifts to party leaders and high government officials. The initiative in cases of corruption did not always rest with the business community; in fact, there were many instances in which politicians collected a forced draft from businessmen and used it for personal purposes or to bribe legislative representatives. There were multifarious ways in which oligarchic leaders obtained personal funds, including outright monetary bribery, shares in the company, and loans written off. Exposés such as the Textbook Scandal, which brought the arrest of about 150 people, ranging from lowly examiners of texts to prefectural governors, illustrate how widespread corruption was in government (Scalapino, 1967: 265).

A secondary factor influencing close business–government relations was the electoral system for the Lower House of the Diet. Under the electoral rules of 1900 and 1925, voters in each district were given a single nontransferable vote in selecting from among multiple candidates. This system was initially devised by Yamagata to keep parties as weak and fractious as possible (Ramseyer and Rosenbluth, 1995: 45). The idea was to force any party seeking to win or maintain a legislative majority to field multiple candidates in most districts, thereby creating severe intra-party competition and thus be less likely to act coherently in the Diet.[9] Under this kind of electoral system, candidates must rely on their own personal reputation rather than that of the political party to which they are affiliated. Accordingly, they must develop a loyal base of supporters, which was accomplished by distributing pork (e.g., subsidized loans). In postwar Japan, the ruling LDP used government-dispensed pork, cash and in-kind gifts, and bureaucratic services. In prewar Japan, the parties used very similar tactics, but oligarchs, not the popular political parties, controlled the purse strings.[10] In return, businesses would offer money to fund their campaigns, and bribes, as discussed above (Duus, 1968: 19–24). Mitsui, for example, was a strong backer of the Seiyukai Party, while the Kenseikai Party was supported by Mitsubishi.[11]

Labor

In the prewar period, labor had almost no influence on the financing decisions of large firms, nor on the financial system more broadly. Although labor gained some concessions during the interwar period, when it was strongest, the most significant legislation which would have legally protected labor unions, the Labor Union Bills of 1926 and 1927, was never passed by the Diet. However, the Labor Disputes Conciliation Law was passed in 1926, which established rules for conciliation committees composed of representatives from labor, management, and the public (Garon, 1987). Hope was renewed with the first election, in 1928, under the Universal Manhood Suffrage Law of 1925. This pushed the Lower House of the Diet in a reformist direction, as an alliance developed between the more liberal party, Kenseikai/Minseitō, and the labor movement (the Seiyūkai being on the conservative side of the aisle). With a growing labor movement and an inchoate Communist Party calling for the "state management of credit,"[12] the conservative Cabinet minister Tanaka, who had been appointed in 1927, used force and repression to weaken labor.

The new prime minister, Hamaguchi, came to office in July 1929 and sponsored a new labor union bill. At the same time, austerity measures were imposed to fight the downturn in the economy (with pre-Keynesian economic policies such as devaluing the yen which led to lower wages and higher unemployment), and contributed to an increase in labor union membership, reaching a prewar high of 7.9 percent in 1931. All of this alarmed employers who mobilized to fight any new pro-labor legislation (Garon, 1987: 168). Businesses advised Minseitō leaders that the union bill stood in the way of continued industrial support for the Cabinet's economic policies. This forced many party members to reconsider the costs of defending the bill, and ultimately Hamaguchi bowed to the demands of big business. A more conservative version of the bill was eventually passed by the Lower House, but was subsequently defeated in the House of Peers in 1931 (Garon, 1987: 184). This ended any hope of favorable legislation for labor until after World War II.

Because of the importance of labor unions' success in bargaining with owners in the postwar period, it is useful to trace the origins of its company-specific unions. Following World War I, the government made plans to set up works councils, which led zaibatsu affiliates to experiment with various kinds of company unions. To draw workers away from cross-firm (horizontal) trade unions, an increasing number of employers discussed wages, hours, and working conditions within factory councils in the latter half of the 1920s (Garon, 1987: 169–170).

Factory councils were partly inspired by top Japanese businessmen visiting the United States in 1921 and 1922.

> They were most impressed by talks with corporate executive and Republican Party leaders in the United States. Herbert Hoover, then secretary of commerce, warned against recognizing industrial unions because workers thus organized would surely emerge victorious. Elbert Gary of U.S. Steel lectured his Japanese guests on the evils of collective bargaining and the virtues of his firm's factory councils.
>
> (Garon, 1987: 170–171)

From rhetoric of the Japan Industrial Club in 1930 and 1931, Garon finds that factory councils were also promoted to prevent trade union legislation. Figure 4.1 illustrates unionization rates in Japan, underscoring their weakness in the prewar era compared to the postwar period.

Because Japan was still poorly democratized, social legislation did not focus on broader segments of the population or on those most in need of help. The welfare state was not introduced with the intention of easing the plight of those most negatively affected by industrialization. Social rights were granted from above by a bureaucratic elite to specific groups or were introduced with the aim of stabilizing certain client-like ties between bourgeois parties and specific interest groups, including the business community (Manow, 2001a).

With labor remaining weak during the prewar period, a public pension scheme (the Employee Pension System (EPS)) was not introduced for blue-collar workers until 1941 (and extended to white-collar workers in 1943). The main motive for its introduction was to accumulate capital for the war

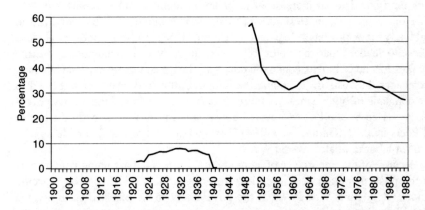

Figure 4.1 Unionization rates, 1921–1988. (source: Odaka (1993). For prewar data see also Garon (1987)).

Note
Rate of unionization = number of union members/number gainfully employed in non-agricultural/forestry sectors.

effort. The EPS required a long qualifying period for an individual worker (20 years) before the first pension would be paid out. This provision served the aim of capital accumulation, since under a fully or partially funded system like the EPS, funds grow with the length of the qualifying period. Thus, as Martin Collick has argued, the pension system was more of a "disguised war loan, rather than a major step forward in the creation of a universal pensions system" (Collick, 1988: 210).

Farmers

The agriculturally based economy of pre-industrializing Japan required numerous local banking facilities. As industrialization and commerce expanded, funds were diverted away from rural areas to new needs by branches of large banks. But because farmers lacked political influence, they lacked financing during the 1889 to 1937 period, with worsening conditions over time as industrialization progressed.

One of the first attempts to weaken local banking as firms exercised their growing political influence was with a bill in 1894, which sought to limit the entry of and competition among banks by imposing minimum capital requirements. It failed to pass the Lower House out of concern for preserving the number of small banks.[13] In 1896, however, the Bank Merger Act, to encourage mergers among banks, did pass the Lower House. It passed because it did not impose capital requirements, and only offered incentives for mergers, such as favorable tax treatment, but no penalties.[14] Again in 1902 and 1906, the Ministry of Finance submitted bills that would impose a minimum capital requirement, but each time the Lower House failed to pass it.

Given the structure of the political institutions, the Lower House could not propose and pass legislation that assisted small banks during downturns in the economy; they could only block legislation proposed by the ministers. For this reason the number of small banks fell over time, from 1,854 in 1901 to 1,537 in 1926.[15]

In 1924, the Kenseikai won a plurality of Lower House seats, and formed a majority coalition with the Seiyūhontō (a splinter group of the Seiyūkai). The Kenseikai had closer ties to big business involved in international trade and investment, while the Seiyūkai was closer to small business and farmers. Consequently, the former drafted legislation to create capital requirements that would disqualify many small banks. The bill passed and was scheduled to go into effect on January 1, 1928.[16]

By January 1928, only 790 of the 1,238 banks that survived the financial panic of 1927 met the new capital requirements. The Seiyūkai now controlled the Cabinet, but it lacked a legislative majority and thus could not repeal the Act.[17] By 1932, the number of banks dropped to 683, allowing large banks to increase their market share. For example, the 13 largest banks held 40.8 percent of total deposits in 1926, and the zaibatsu banks and Shibusawa's Daiichi Bank controlled 24 percent of all deposits. In 1931, the 13 largest banks held 58.9 percent of total deposits, and the big five controlled 38 percent (Hoshi and Kashyap, 2001).

The Seiyūkai gained a majority in the Diet in 1932; by this time, however, the military was calling the shots regarding the banking industry. Under military government, the Ministry of Finance shifted its goals from maintaining the stability of the financial system to centralized control. To this end, it sought to reduce the number of local banks to one per prefecture, and to ensure that local banks efficiently transferred their funds to the large banks in the cities (Zenkoku, 1989: 54–55). By 1938, there were only 377 banks.

Throughout the prewar period, small farmers generally faced a capital short-age and had to pay high loan rates; around 9.2 percent in 1929, compared with large firms' bond yields of 5.5 to 6 percent. Small firms also had very high bor-rowing costs relative to large firms during the interwar period – around 15 percent for short-term industrial loans in Tokyo in 1930 (Lockwood, 1954: 289). Lockwood attributes these high costs of capital to scarcity of capital, since it was being directed towards the larger enterprises.

Recall that Table 2 illustrates the relatively low volume of deposits and bank debentures for local banks during the prewar years in comparison to the postwar period when their political power increased dramatically: 3 percent of the total for the 1910 to 1930 period, compared to 18.5 percent for the 1950 to 1987 period.

Summary

Owners of capital won the early political battles at the time of writing the Meiji Constitution; it restricted access to policymakers to owners of the new commercial and industrial firms and to bushido leaders. Political institutions prevented labor and farmers (or the popular political parties) from meaningful political influence. The broad structure of Japan's Meiji and Taisho era financial arrangements reflects capital owners' dominant position, including: (1) pyramidal ownership which enables owners to reduce the transaction costs of financing by relying on securities markets without sacrificing control of the firms; (2) low government intervention (the contrast with postwar Japan makes this particularly clear); (3) low agricultural financing (a comparison to the post-World War II period also illustrates the change here); and (4) pensions were private, and offered by firms to keep valuable employees. Taken together, these financial system attributes correspond to an LME capitalist system that strongly catered to business owners.

France, pre-World War II

Like prewar Japan, France's Third Republic political institutions (1870–1940) also privileged the wealthy elite and excluded labor and farmers from exercising real political influence. The financial system likewise exhibited a strong reliance on markets, with little government intervention, and low levels of agrarian financing. The historical record is unclear with respect to corporate ownership patterns.

The financial system

Prior to the 1930s, France relied heavily on capital markets as the conduit by which money flowed from savers to borrowers, as described by Gueslin (1992):

> The crisis of the 1880s brought to an end the preliminary phase of banking development in France: it consolidated the position of the great credit institutions and generated a policy of management rationalization which was coupled in due course with an "industrial disengagement." It inaugurated the "golden age" of a finance-market economy. The crisis of the 1930s marked the end of this period. Using modern economic concepts with care, I mean by this that, throughout the period, banking credit remained more or less limited and the financing of the economy came about through the accumulation of savings: primarily as companies directly used parts of their cash flow, but also by the transfer of domestic savings via the financial market.[18]

For the period 1865 to 1913, Freedeman (1993) illustrates with several detailed industry-level case studies that "the issue of securities indicates a relatively efficient French capital market." Other sources corroborate this (e.g., Rajan and Zingales, 2003). During the 1920s securities markets became increasingly important, while self-finance became more important during the 1930s.[19] Table 4.3 shows the decline in stock and bond issues for corporations beginning in the 1930s, and its persistence to the end of the sample in 1964.

There was little government intervention in the economy, and agrarian financing likewise remained relatively low during the prewar period in comparison to the postwar era, as illustrated with the *logarithmic* scale indicating the value of state advances to the Crédit Agricole in Figure 4.2. Pension programs also remained underdeveloped. "Not until the Second World War and the wave of reform inspired by Beveridge was [France] ready to run with the social policy pack" (Baldwin, 1990: 106).

Table 4.3 French corporations' stock and bond issues, 1896–1964 (percent of gross domestic product)

Year	Stocks	Bonds	Total
1900	2.0	1.8	3.8
1913	2.6	2.9	5.5
1924	3.3	1.2	4.5
1929	5.7	2.6	8.3
1930	3.4	4.4	7.8
1938	0.6	0.3	0.9
1949	0.6	0.3	0.9
1954	0.6	0.8	1.4
1959	1.7	1.4	3.1
1962	1.4	1.2	2.6
1964	1.2	1.0	2.2

Source: Carré *et al.* (1975: 334).

Politics

To explain the structure of the Third Republic's financial institutions, it is necessary to understand the distribution of power among the key political institutions,
and groups' locus of power within them. I will also examine important political
battles that occurred during the Popular Front (1936–1938) to illustrate how the
Third Republic political institutions played a critical role in preventing meaningful changes to the structure of the financial system, despite strong popular
support from labor and farmers.

THIRD REPUBLIC POLITICAL INSTITUTIONS

The Third Republic was dominated by the Parliament, comprised of the Chamber
of Deputies and the Senate, with the Senate having the clear upper hand. The
Senate was designed to insulate the political system from the universal suffrage of
the Chamber of Deputies. Senators were elected indirectly by mayors and coun-
cilors of departmental and arrondissement assemblies, ensuring that they were
elected only by the privileged. Wealthy landowners were over-represented in the
Senate, and big businesses also wielded considerable influence through their direct
financial contributions to Senators and through the growing number of wealthy
industrialists. Labor, small business, and small farmers had almost no influence in
the Upper House; their votes were important to the election of Deputies in the
Lower House. Although labor did not emerge as an influential constituency until
after World War I, they did not acquire real political power in the Chamber of
Deputies until 1936, with the Popular Front, despite a brief surge in political
support with the Cartel des Gauches in 1924, which was more moderate and less
powerful than the Popular Front.

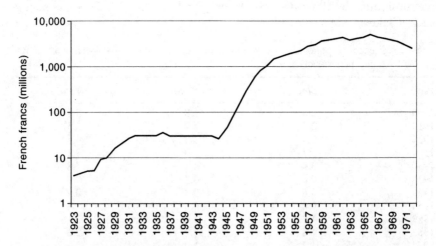

Figure 4.2 Value of advances from the state to the crédit agricole, 1923–1972. (source:
adapted from Gueslin (1984: 322)).

The Senate's power, relative to the Lower House, derived from its ability to veto any legislation passed by the Chamber, and its ability to delay legislation indefinitely. Similarly, although the formation of ministries was initiated by the Chamber, the Senate held the power to defeat them. Since the Senate held a veto on all bills initiated in the Chamber, the rural elite and big business acted as a veto-gate on the Lower House's more populist legislative initiatives, thereby preserving the status quo *laissez-faire* economy.

The president was elected indirectly by a joint session of the Senate and Chamber for seven-year terms. The president chose the president of the Council of Ministers (the technical name for the prime minister). The president could also influence the composition of cabinets (ministries). Ministries were responsible to Parliament, and had to command a majority there to survive.[20] Thus, the bureaucracy came under the control of the Parliament, and of the Senate in particular, which meant that the Senate could control the enforcement of legislation.

CAPITAL OWNERS

Kuisel (1981) aptly characterizes the political influence of business owners during the Third Republic when he remarks that "the weak republic ended up under the thumb of the trusts" (Kuisel, 1981: 178).[21] The law of 1867 formed the basis for the organization of French companies during the Third Republic.[22] By repealing the Commercial Code of 1807 that subjected the founding of a corporation to the consent of government, the new law permitted the corporate form of business organization (i.e., limited liability with a board of directors and shareholders able to influence management) without undergoing the lengthy process involved in government authorization.

Treaties promoting freer trade with Britain and Belgium in 1857 and 1862, which both possessed more liberal laws (i.e., easier rules for raising capital), necessitated the liberalization of French law as companies threatened to relocate or to start up in these neighboring countries. Consequently, in 1867, the government ended the need for Sociétés Anonymes (SAs) to obtain government authorization, leading to a dramatic surge in the creation of SAs, and to a mania in the raising of capital via the Parisian and regional stock exchanges (Freedeman, 1993: 5–14, 28); for example, the capital raised by newly founded SAs in 1881 topped any year for the period 1868 to 1914. This mania ended with a stock market crash in 1882. However, business influence on government is evident in the events following the crash, as business owners were able to stall and eventually anesthetize legislation to reduce abuses in the securities markets.

Following the crash, an extraparliamentary commission was convened to revise the law of 1867. The committee drafted a bill that satisfied the critics of the 1867 law, but which was anathema to much of the business community since it would greatly hinder the ease with which firms could raise capital on the exchanges.[23] The bill first went to the Senate, since Bozerian, who presided over the extraparliamentary commission, was also president of the Senate's committee to examine the bill.[24] It passed the Senate on November 29, 1884 without any significant changes.

More than a year elapsed between the vote of the Senate and the introduction of the bill into the Chamber of Deputies, which offered time for the public's anger to subside. While farmers, labor, and small firms exerted more influence in the Lower House, business remained an important interest group to many Deputies' political careers, such as Maurice Rouvier. In January 1886, the bill was referred to his committee in the Chamber. Before deciding how to act, the opinions of outside experts were solicited. The liberal/pro-big business view was best expressed by Antoine Jacquand, a lawyer and businessman, and a former president of the Chamber of Commerce of Lyon which, along with Paris, endured the greatest hardships from the mania. Jacquand strongly criticized the large number of provisions which could result in a company's being declared null, and against the financial liabilities and special criminal penalties that could be incurred by founders and members of boards of directors. The effect of such a law would "drive savings into foreign securities ... while our large financial industrial enterprises became the prey of adventurers who offered no guarantees other than their audacity and effrontery."[25]

In the Chamber of Deputies, only one member of the Chamber's committee favored the bill in the form passed by the Senate; overall, the committee aimed to soften the Senate's harsh recommendations.[26] The elections of 1889, however, brought the legislation to an end before the committee took any action.

Just before the elections of 1889, the movement for liberalization received a setback with the failure of de Lesseps' Panama Canal Company and the collapse of Secretan's attempt to corner the world's copper market, which brought down not only the Société Industrielle et Commerciale des Métaux, but also the Comptoir d'Escompte, one of France's largest deposit banks. To avert a general banking crisis, Maurice Rouvier, now Minister of Finance, met with Parisian bankers to find a way to save the Comptoir d'Escompte. The timely intervention of Rouvier and the Bank of France averted what might have become a serious financial crisis. To many, these latest casualties again pointed to certain weaknesses in company law, and dramatically illustrated the need for restrictive legislation.

Fears that such legislation would be passed appeared in 1890 when a new committee of the Chamber began to consider the Senate's bill. These fears soon proved to be unfounded, however. As with the 1886 committee, most of the members of the new committee were opposed to it.[27]

The short bill that eventually emerged, with some revisions in the Senate, became the law of August 1, 1893.[28] The law, which dealt with some of the more pressing problems, contained both liberal and restrictive provisions and did not fundamentally alter the ways firms raised capital. No further reform in company law occurred for almost a decade. Clearly, business had won the political battle and retained relatively liberal laws that allowed them to use securities markets for their financing needs.

After World War I, the Confédération Générale du Patronat Français (CGPF) was formed to represent the interests of big business to government, in reaction to the growing political influence of labor. Duchemin was president of the CGPF from 1926 to 1936, and in his book he outlined the philosophy of the CGPF which informed his annual addresses to Parliament.[29] While many issues caused divisions among firms from different sectors (e.g., especially regarding international trading arrangements), a key overriding philosophy governing the CGPF was the commitment to economic liberalism. Big business sought to ensure that the "classical laws" of *laissez-faire* governed the structure of the French economy. Liberty was safeguarded as long as the government refrained from controlling business and business agreements. This equated to ensuring that access to capital remained free from any government-imposed restrictions or manipulation, such as regulations affecting access to securities markets, as well as control over lending arrangements through various credit granting facilities (i.e., banks). While Duchemin articulated the interests of big business only after labor became a real political threat, he was merely expressing the sentiments that business leaders shared for many decades prior to the formation of the CGPF.

In sum, large firms' domestic political power played the critical role in France's market-oriented financial system during the Third Republic. International trade and capital flows were important to the extent that they gave large enterprises a credible exit option, which increased their influence in government. The political institutions ensured that business owners prevailed over populist political interests when battles ensued over financial regulations.

LABOR

Prior to World War I, unions and left-wing political movements had sporadic but largely negligible influence on firms and government. At the end of World War I, labor activity and union membership surged. On December 16, 1918 the Confederation of Workers (Confédération General du Travail (CGT)) issued a statement of the changes it sought in its Minimum Program, which formed the basis for labor's economic policy prescriptions during the interwar years. The main overriding objective was the implementation of *dirigisme*: "The working classes must manage the national effort" of reorganizing the economy by exercising "permanent" control over all branches of production.[30] While the document does not explicitly say that control over the allocation of credit, or of financial institutions, is how this will be achieved, it is nonetheless clear that this is consistent with its objectives. The Program advocated nationalization of key industries, which was to be implemented not by the state alone, but by mixed public corporations, administered by the representatives of producers and consumers (Lorwin, 1954: 52–53).

Elections in 1924 brought the Cartel des Gauches to power in the Chamber of Deputies – a coalition of the Socialists, Radicals, and some minor left-wing groups. It was a center–left alliance since the Radicals were centrist. Because of the strength of the moderate partners of the coalition, left-wing members were unable to push their policies through. However, the government did initiate the first "mixed companies" in 1924 in the reacquired territory of Alsace: the Compagnie de Navigation du Rhin and the Chantiers et Ateliers du Rhin. The government owned a minority share in both enterprises and participated in their management along with representatives of private stockholders. However, no real change occurred with regard to the financial system since labor lacked sufficient political power. They would have to wait until the Popular Front to attempt such fundamental reforms.

The most important feature of the Third Republic's agricultural economy was the rapid industrialization movement. From the mid-nineteenth century up until the 1930s, the national supply of credit went increasingly to firms participating in the Industrial Revolution (Gueslin, 1978: 29–44).[31] Consequently, farmers faced rising borrowing costs. To remedy this problem, the Law of November 5, 1894 created a nation-wide banking institution devoted to agricultural credit, which formed the foundation for the Crédit Agricole.[32]

One of the key problems with passing a law devoting capital to agriculture is that farmers would not have sufficient qualifications to establish credit and obtain loans, especially peasant farmers (Henry and Régulier, 1986: 9).[33] Studies conducted by the Minister of Agriculture to evaluate the effects of the 1894 law in 1896 and 1900 found that credit was granted primarily to the wealthy farmers since they could more easily guarantee repayment of the loan, and banks could more easily evaluate their creditworthiness (Henry and Régulier, 1986: 17). Thus, with the passage of the 1894 law, the rural elite successfully alleviated their initial credit crunch caused by growing industrialization and worsened by unforeseeable natural calamities; peasant farmers were left behind.

Agricultural elites used their political influence to great effect at the turn of the century. The number of regional banks grew from nine in 1900 to 98 in 1913, local branches grew from 87 in 1900 to 4,533 in 1913, and the number of bank accounts at these local banks grew from 2,175 in 1900 to 236,860 in 1913. The laws of 1899, 1906, and 1910 permitted the state to advance (i.e., redirect) money to the regional agricultural offices; the total advances from the state went from 612,000 F in 1900 to over 93.9 million F in 1913, comprising 45 percent of the total resources of the regional agricultural offices in 1900 and 74 percent in 1913.[34] Clearly, agricultural interests were exerting considerable influence over the state's finances.[35] Despite the high growth in the number of regional banks and local branches, only a select group comprising 2.9 percent of the active male agricultural population were members of one of these facilities in 1910 (Gueslin, 1978: 253).[36]

In 1920, the government consolidated the national agricultural credit system under the Caisse Nationale de Crédit Agricole, thereby increasing the availability of agricultural credit and sparking the creation of new agricultural cooperatives with the law of August 5, 1920.[37] This new institution gave agricultural finance a centralized national office, linking local and regional offices. Laws in 1928, 1929, 1931, and 1932 offered additional grants for medium- and long-term agricultural loans, which went predominantly to large landowners. The vast majority of small, peasant farmers did not and could not participate.

However, in terms of France's overall financial system, agricultural credit constituted a small fraction of total enterprise financing during the Third Republic. Comparing the volume of lending by commercial banks, which were primarily involved with funding big business, to that of the Crédit Agricole, illustrates that agricultural finance had only a small impact on the French financial system. Recall that at this time France depended to a large extent on capital markets, making farmers' financing a very small proportion of total financing indeed. Thus, although rural elites created and bolstered agricultural banks because of their political power, financing directed to the rural sector comprised a small fraction of the French financial system.

The Popular Front

The Popular Front, which was elected in 1936 to the Chamber of Deputies, was a temporary electoral alliance of those hit hardest by the depression: farmers, the middle class (including small business), and workers. This alliance included a coalition of Communists, Socialists, and center–left Deputies, the most numerous of whom were the Radicals (who represented small business and independents).

The Senate's composition, which had elections in 1935, was not altered by the Popular Front surge. The Upper House was still dominated by conservatives such as the rural elite and big business. Consequently, many bills approved in the Chamber were sent to Senatorial committees for further study, never again to see the light of day (Wright, 1964: 66). Big business and large landowners who dominated the Senate posed a considerable roadblock to the Popular Front's objectives.

In the two years prior to the Popular Front, members of the SFIO (the French Socialist Party) discussed various possibilities for reorganizing the state's finances to deal with the depression and to achieve their more fundamental goal of redistributing national resources and improving working conditions.[38] Henri de Man, a Belgian socialist who constructed a plan based on his analysis of the German experience and adopted by the Belgian Labor Party in December 1933, captured the attention of the French Left. De Man identified finance capital as the common enemy and he argued that no more distributive reforms, such as higher wages or cheaper credit, would occur without structural change, and that nationalization of key sectors should begin with the credit system.[39]

To achieve these ends, the Socialists proposed a Plan which would demand the creation of a National Economic Council, comprising representatives of big business, workers, directors and employees of banks, and representatives of the state. This organization would be responsible for the direction of credit and, in particular, control of the Bank of France. Nationalization of credit was pivotal to the Plan: "The socialization of credit is the condition of industrial socialization."[40] Two leaders of the CGT, E. Lefranc and J. Itard, further remarked:

> The nationalization of credit and the control of the banks ... the immediate effective control of key industries by the representatives of the collectivity

and the salaried workers ... these two structural transformations are necessary for the economy of this country to leave the capitalist stage and are only possible with the distributive reforms requested by the CGT.[41]

Controlling these two aspects of the economy would give labor the ability to implement the *dirigiste* economy that it had sought since it first proclaimed this objective in its Minimum Program. Control over credit, for the CGT, was the key to managing the economy. In the mid-1930s, "nationalizing credit" meant expelling private interests from the regents of the Bank of France (the largest shareholders who chose the regents of the Bank of France were called the "200 families" and almost exclusively represented the interests of big business) and using the central bank to control credit and investment. It also meant setting regulations for private banks, nationalizing semi-public credit institutions, and expanding their activities.

The Popular Front Program[42] included reforms regarding the banking profession, the sociétés anonyms (most businesses fell into this category), and the Bank of France.[43] With regard to the latter, the Program stated the following objectives:

> Removing the credit and savings from the domination of the economic oligarchy, by the Bank of France.... Enlarging the power of the governor, under the permanent control of a council composed of representatives of legislative power, or representatives of executive power and of representatives of the large forces of organized workers and industry, commerce, and agriculture.

With regard to agriculture, the Program sought to develop the Crédit Agricole and to support the agricultural cooperatives that would extend credit to small farmers who could not qualify for loans under the existing rules.

Legislative action regarding the financial system only occurred for the Bank of France, however. Many of the other proposed reforms never made it on to the legislative agenda (e.g., reform of the sociétés anonymes and the banking profession) because they would never survive the Senate. Popular Front representatives would have to wait until after the war for the conservative Senate to lose its power, thereby permitting labor to finally implement its agenda.

THE BANK OF FRANCE LEGISLATION[44]

Revision of the statutes governing the central bank had become genuinely popular by 1936 because of its role in financing business and agriculture, in addition to its more traditional central bank activities. After 1930 the bank had done little to attenuate hardship. It extended privileged credit to big firms but disdained small business and farmers and refused to help troubled local banks:[45]

> The Bank, it is said, has rested comfortably on its tradition. The discount is always more or less reserved for a limited and privileged circle. But today

things are aggravated.... Farmers, artisans, and small businessmen are not
... obtaining the smallest amount of credit, and are finding that this even
concerns the guarantees of access to credit in extremely difficult situations.... Who therefore receives the supply of credit, and offers the necessary guarantees for access to credit, other than those already found at the
head of the important enterprises and given considerable amounts of
capital?[46]

The Bank of France competed directly with private banks, which led to
involvement in at least one major bank failure. As a champion of deflation, the
central bank pursued a tight monetary policy and used its secret fund to influence
the press. Above all, for a central bank to be in the hands of a hereditary oligarchy that shut out other interests and on occasion forced its will on the government seemed anachronistic and anti-democratic to the Popular Front interests.

Blum and his Socialist finance minister Vincent Auriol justified reorganization on the grounds that credit policy should serve the national economy; there
should be an end to the bank's unrepresentative management and its discriminatory practices. But Blum and Auriol decided against nationalizing the bank given
the opposition of the Radicals, who feared allowing the government to dictate
monetary policy (Dauphin-Meunier, 1936: 199). Instead the two Socialist leaders
sought only to overhaul the bank's administration. They sponsored legislation
that replaced the regents with a new council and an executive heavily weighted
in the state's favor and democratized the shareholder's assembly. It was passed
on July 25, 1936 (the Blum government took office on June 6, 1936 making this
legislation one of the first to be passed). Only 77 Deputies, all from the Right,
opposed the legislation. The Senate passed the legislation as a way to appease
growing public anger, but prevented further legislation from altering other
important and related functions, such as allowing "open market" buying and
selling of securities, proscribing competition with private banks, or establishing
an agency to monitor the money and credit markets. Because the prospect of
getting more radical measures through the Senate was very unlikely, the Blum-
Auriol team tabled any further action, especially since public support for the
Popular Front's agenda was quickly declining. In the end, the reorganized bank
changed its policies very little; for example, in 1936 to 1938, the discount policy
was not liberalized.

Ultimately, Popular Front initiatives were stymied by the lack of political
influence in the Senate and the Executive. The political institutions entrenched
capital's power despite the surge in support for the representatives of labor and
farmers, and thereby preserved the pre-existing structure of the financial system.

Summary

In Third Republic France, owners of capital were the winners, and they dominated policymaking since the political institutions denied farmers and labor from
exercising meaningful political influence. The financial system reflects attributes

corresponding to capital owners' political dominance, including: (1) a reliance on securities markets to keep transaction costs low; (2) low levels of agricultural financing relative to farmers' economic and population importance; (3) low levels of government intervention, deferring to market mechanisms to work out economic and financial problems – even when there were serious problems, as in the 1890s or 1930s, popular interests could not surmount the political power of capital owners; and (4) the pension system – especially the public pension system – was undeveloped. While comprehensive data on the structure of corporate ownership are not yet available for this period, it would not be surprising to find that France's pyramidal corporate ownership emerged at this time, as in pre-World War II Japan, allowing owners to retain the benefits of ownership and control while also drawing on low-cost financing via securities markets.

Labor–farmer coalition wins: Mediterranean

France, post-World War II

Conservatives and Socialists had different visions for postwar France. The conservative neoliberal perspective was articulated best with Courtin's Program, which sought a return to the free market of the Third Republic. Socialists, by contrast, sought to implement the reforms articulated during the Popular Front – controlling credit via government-operated banks. Each viewpoint would have serious repercussions for the structure of the postwar financial system as well as for the broader political economy. Ultimately, labor in alliance with farmers (as the junior partner) would win the political battle by a wide margin and France would bolster industrial banks and agrarian financing to the detriment of the securities markets, promote high levels of government intervention, and a public pension program. I discuss the goals of the Socialists and Neoliberals at the end of the war before examining the measures passed by the provisional government affecting the financial system. I then review the contemporary financial system implications of these early laws.

THE SOCIALIST PROGRAM

While there were several visions for placing the management of the economy firmly under government control, André Philip had the broadest support from the Left, and for this reason de Gaulle appointed him the Comité Française de Libération Nationale Commissaire in charge of relations with the Constituent Assembly and the study of postwar problems.[47] In January 1944 Philip created several study commissions that brought together representatives of the external and internal resistance. He packed the Commission on economic problems with structural reformers from the Left. General de Gaulle received the Commission's report in July 1944 as the provisional government completed its preparations for its return to France (Kuisel, 1981: 173).

The Commission, and Philip, pressed for structural reforms within six months of the landings since the fervor for change would peak with the beginning of the new republic. Philip proposed comprehensive planning (and Keynesian counter-cyclical policies) to sustain full employment and economic development. He contrasted this mode of state management with the style of the prewar Parliament which had turned economic management over to experts in economic liberalism who "intervened only reluctantly in order to cure illnesses rather than prevent them, to salvage enterprises rather than organize them" (Philip, 1944: 4). No unit of production lay outside state management:

> From the moment one admits the necessity of planning, private sectors are no longer possible because no element of the economy should escape the plan. Direction could be achieved by more or less flexible methods. Certain sectors could be socialized, others directed, and still others simply super-vised. Nothing, however, would escape the impetus of governmental author-ity, which is responsible for the survival and grandeur of the nation.[48]

In a planned economy, he argued, certain producers were so important that they had to be nationalized so that the state could effectively control investment:

> Finally and in all cases, there is in a planned economy, certain highly essen-tial productions which, by their importance and by their repercussions on the whole of industrial life, the state must absolutely assure the direction of if it wants to exert effective control on all investments.
>
> It is therefore indispensable that, upon the return to France, the state takes direct management of *all modes of land, sea, and air transport, of the mines, electrical utilities, iron and steel manufacturers, chemical producers, the insurance industry and the banks*. The socialization of these important sectors will permit the state to have a hand on the sufficient instruments for effectively controlling investments and assuring the direction of the rest of the national economy [emphasis in original].[49]

For directing the private sector, Philip advocated rejuvenating the Comités d'Organization from the Vichy years, which he renamed "industrial groups." In addition, he proposed the creation of a National Economic Ministry as "a coordinating organ," whose primary purpose was to plan the national economy according to socialist guidelines. Accordingly, labor spokesmen sat on a host of regulatory and advisory bodies comprising the system of wages, prices, mater-ials, credit, and other economic controls.

THE CONSERVATIVE PROGRAM

In the debates following World War II on how to structure the French economy, René Courtin issued his report expressing the neoliberal (pro-business) perspec-tive, which was the main alternative to Philip's Socialist version. Courtin envis-aged a "return to the market, economic freedom, and free trade" that prevailed during the Third Republic (Kuisel, 1981: 171). His vision for the French economy ultimately turned upon investment. "Still more than an abundance of natural resources and raw materials the wealth of a nation derives from the importance of its equipment," declared Courtin.[50] The development of the stock of capital equipment depended on savings and investment. Do not look to the state, however, the neoliberal economist admonished: "the state has always been a wretched investor." Neoliberals sought to prevent the socialist agenda which would rely on state-run intermediaries.

It is amusing and revealing that with regard to the pro-market bias of Courtin's program, a socialist commentator remarked,

> For our part we shall consider the report that was submitted to us for our evaluation appropriate only in case our country submits to an American economic and financial takeover and if we want to maintain liberalism to its utmost and direct the economy only by financial means.[51]

But to determine which program would be adopted, we must consider these groups' political power.

SOCIALISTS AND THE FINANCIAL SYSTEM

In the immediate postwar environment, popular opinion accused big business of aiding the downfall of the French Republic. This anti-business sentiment pervaded the first years of the liberation. Labor was seen as opposing the Germans, and was celebrated as defender of the French Republic. The popular election held in October 1945 confirmed the leftward swing that had taken place in the electorate and enabled the Left to dominate policymaking in the new Constituent Assembly.[52] Before and after this election, laws were passed that gave power to labor "from below" on works committees, "in the middle" with representation on supervisory boards, and "from above" with the government control over industrial policy and financing via state-owned banks. While laws regarding works committees and supervisory board representation were passed (resembling the German mechanism of industrial relations), the preferred tool used during the postwar period was the control from the central government with state-owned banks. This became critical to the structure of France's postwar financial system, and the organization of the broader capitalist system.

On February 22, 1945, a law was passed to realize the old trade union demand for a voice in management by the establishment of labor–management planning committees. These works committees would become obligatory in all firms with 100 or more workers, which included 7,000 to 8,000 firms employing about 2.5 million workers (out of a total of 1,800,000 firms and 12.5 million wage earners; agricultural workers were not included (Pickles, 1953: 54). Made up of elected representatives of employees, presided over by the employer or plant manager, the committees were given control of plant social welfare work and consultative powers in production and *economic decisions*. The legislation fell short of the left-wing representatives' hopes, who wanted works committees to be compulsory in all establishments employing 50 workers or more – however, this was achieved with the act of May 16, 1946, adding 750,000 more workers – and who would share in the running of firms instead of merely being consulted about management. With the 1945 Act, workers had the right to be informed of the amount of profit made and could make suggestions regarding the use of these profits (special provisions applied to limited liability companies). A committee was empowered to inspect the books before the annual general meeting and to call in an accountant to help members to understand the points at issue. This was resented by right-wing members of the Assembly and by employers. The act of May 16, 1946 also provided for the inclusion of delegates from Works Committees on the boards in an advisory capacity.[53] A later Act imposed an obligation on the employers to consult (not merely to inform) them before putting into force decisions regarding the general running of the firm.

"From the middle" France has two types of boards of directors which firms can choose from (Will, 1969). The first type, which is more common, is single tiered, as in the Anglo-American system; it is from the early 1940s. The board elects the président directeur-général (PDG) who is like a CEO but is more powerful. He or she has the sole right to represent the company and is the only person who can delegate this power. Single-tiered boards mostly consist of outside directors, who are shareholders and representatives from financial institutions with which the firm has transactional relationships. As in the Anglo-American model, the board determines business policies, which are then carried out by the PDG and management.

The second type of board, in effect since 1966, has two tiers, as in Germany. The conseil de surveillance is like the German supervisory board except that employees do not have the right to representation. However, one unique feature of the French system makes it more akin to the German one with single-tiered and two-tiered boards, and workers' representatives have the right to attend board meetings as observers in all companies with at least 50 employees. The conseil de surveillance appoints the directoire, who have responsibility for the management of the company. One of the members of the directoire is designated président de directoire by the others (Will, 1969).

"From above," the nationalization of banks occurred shortly after the election of the Constituent Assembly in October 1945. The scope of nationalization was limited, however, because de Gaulle, who was sympathetic to big business, was able to postpone action for 15 months, allowing the fervor of the liberation to subside. He then used his authority to circumscribe the nationalization of credit so that investment banking was excluded. After his resignation, the MRP (Popular Republican Movement, or Christian Democrats) – the party most closely associated with him – succeeded in persuading his successor, Gouin, to confine nationalization to a shortened list of sectors and then fought, with some success, to limit the measures within these sectors (Kuisel, 1981: 208).

The banking act that was eventually passed on December 2, 1945 completed the process begun by the Popular Front of eliminating private interests from the

Bank of France, and nationalized the major commercial banks.[54] All representatives from the Left and Center voted for it (461 out of 494 representatives from mainland France voted for the law; 442 from the Left and Center, and 19 from the Right; 33 on the Right voted against). The law structured French finance for the postwar period and gave the government greater influence over the course of postwar economic development by placing the volume and allocation of credit firmly under its control. The legislation established three agencies in charge of the financial system: the National Credit Council (CNC), the Bank of France, and the Control Commission. The CNC set the basic guidelines for credit policy, which were executed by the Bank of France. The CNC was headed by the Minister of Finance, as appointed by the prime minister, and comprised representatives from the government and from various sectors of the economy. As a result, the delegation of authority granted the legislature with ultimate control over the financial system. The CNC had a broad range of responsibilities, including credit policy, establishing detailed regulations on bank interest rates and commissions, creating rules on entry or merger applications, imposing modifications on the financial and legal structure of banks, and levying sanctions on banks which violated its directives.

The Bank of France would enforce the policy directives of the CNC, and share policymaking powers through the governor of the Bank of France, who would be ex-officio vice-president of the CNC. The third agency, the Control Commission, would exercise technical supervision over banks' loan and investment operations. It would also supervise the banks to ensure compliance with all bank regulations, including regulations issued by the other two agencies. The Bank of France would be represented on the Control Commission by the governor of the Bank of France, who would also be president of the Control Commission.

The law nationalized the four largest deposit banks (these held around half of all banks' assets and were the only banks with nationwide branch networks) and extended minor regulations over private investment banks. The largest insurance companies were also nationalized. The deposit banks and insurance companies came under control of quadripartite governing boards (consumers, employees, managers, and government) (Alhadeff, 1968).

The left-wing coalition in the Assembly overwhelmed political resistance to these measures by business interests which tried to obstruct or shape the legislation by exerting influence on the MRP. Business had lost its prewar national employers' federation, the sympathetic political parties of the Third Republic, and most of its friendly press. By mid-1946 the most significant structural reforms were enacted. The second Constituent Assembly that met in the summer and fall did not even discuss any further measures.

PENSIONS

The MRP supported white-collar employees' resistance to an all-inclusive pension system. "Though in favor of reform, the MRP preferred social security organized through a plurality of insurance carriers or funds outside the state's control"

(Baldwin, 1990: 167). Nevertheless, small, poor farmers achieved an inclusive pension program with workers in the 1950s. Other groups were eventually included too (Baldwin, 1990: 253–268). Farmers pushed the system towards a universalistic pension scheme that eventually emerged in the 1970s. While a universalistic pension scheme was slow in arriving in postwar France, it was always publicly administered, depriving securities markets from an important source of liquidity.

AGRICULTURAL FINANCING

With the new provisional government, small farmers now enjoyed political influence more closely reflecting their proportion of the population; there was no longer a Senate to block their legislative initiatives. The Crédit Agricole remained intact at the end of the war despite laws from 1940 to 1943 permitting the state to use the Crédit Agricole's financing capabilities for wartime use. The ordinances of October 17, 1944 and October 20, 1945 sought to attract prisoners from during the war, or those deported and recently repatriated, to rural employ by offering favorable credit terms. The law of May 24, 1946 likewise targeted young people between the ages of 21 and 35 with subsidized loans. In 1946 there were 661 loans totaling 140 million Francs; by 1959 there were 168,000 loans totaling 914 billion Francs for these young rural workers (Henry and Régulier, 1986: 74). The total value of medium- and long-term loans made by the Crédit Agricole grew from 630 million Francs in 1950 to 13 billion Francs in 1963.[55] While the extensive subsidies and favorable credit terms were necessary following the war to deal with food shortages, the continuance of these generous benefits beyond the immediate postwar shortages illustrates that other political motives were at play (Kuisel, 1981: 187).

Postwar evolution and contemporary implications

The political strength of labor after the war was institutionalized with the Constitution of the Fourth Republic, adopted in October 1946. It assured everyone the right to "take part in collective bargaining to determine working conditions and in the management of enterprises."[56] With this new constitution, the Assembly gained control of government, while the Senate was relegated to a less powerful position.[57]

With the founding of the Fifth Republic in 1958, the new constitution moderated the power of the Assembly, granting co-equal power to it and the Senate. However, with regard to the balance of political power between the executive and legislature, Huber (1996) illustrates that the president is more influential with regard to foreign policy, and Parliament is more powerful when it comes to domestic economic policy.[58] Thus, farmers and labor would retain much of their newfound power over the financial system. Consequently, government intervention would remain high, publicly administered pensions would dominate, assets would become and remain specific, and agrarian financing would increase and remain disproportionately high.

FARMERS

French farmers have maintained considerable political influence during the post-World War II period for several reasons: (1) constituency size; (2) political mobilization; (3) popular sympathy to environmental and health-related issues; (4) neocorporatist influence; (5) over-representation; and (6) voter heterogeneity leading to the exercise of a critical swing vote.

Even after many years of urbanization and economic modernization, farmers were the fourth largest occupational group in France in the early 1990s.[59] But more important than the number of active farmers (the statistic usually cited) is the size of the broader agricultural community, which Hervieu (1992) calculated to be 17 percent of the electorate, including active farmers, retired farmers, spouses of farmers, voting-age children of farmers, and former farmers now in other occupations.[60] In addition to these groups, rural residents have strong common interests with farmers, since cutting farm subsidies, for example, would "trigger a perverse multiplier effect" accelerating the exodus of rural merchants and thus impairing the quality of life. Firms making up the agribusiness (e.g., traders, storers, food processors) likewise have a huge stake in the fate of farmers.[61]

A second factor contributing to French farmers' political power is the membership density of the farmers' union – the FNSEA – which is more than twice as high as that of the labor unions (54.5 percent for the farmers' union versus 23 percent for the labor unions).[62] The nature of farming issues bolsters reliance on the FNSEA since, as the owner of his own business, a farmer must deal with a wide range of service needs which require organizational assistance. And because many farmers possess relatively low levels of education and income, and work in isolated settings, the FNSEA acts as a useful guide through the maze of regulations related to farming as well as providing access to financial resources through its close relationship to cooperatives and semi-public organizations, such as the French Chambers of Commerce (Keeler, 1996: 135). In addition, in recent years the farmers' union has effectively elicited public support by appealing to concerns over the environment and farmers' role as custodians of the rural areas as well as protecting consumers against the potential risks of genetically modified crops from America.

A fourth factor contributing to French farmers' unusually strong political influence is the state's need for collaboration with an interest group in the agricultural area; no other economic domain features such numerous, small, and inaccessible production units. Consequently, state officials are highly dependent on their interest group clients for information on which to base policy and for staff assistance at the local level to assure the effective implementation of complex programs. Thus, France has developed neocorporatist group–state relations in which the agricultural ministry grants official recognition to the FNSEA and provides it with exclusive access to state decision-makers at the national level, devolves power for the administration of certain policies at the subnational level, and offers special subsidies designed to facilitate the FNSEA's performance of its quasi-official roles. In short, the FNSEA does not simply "lobby" state officials, but instead tends to "comanage" the affairs of the sector (Keeler, 1987: 6–16, 256–259).

Farmers also have a disproportionate chance to be elected officials and are over-represented in many elections. France has more local administrative districts (36,487 communes) and thus more sparsely populated rural districts than any other European state. As a result, an unusually high number of French mayors have been active farmers.[63] Since members of the French Senate are indirectly elected by an electoral college in which 95.5 percent of the votes are cast by members of the communes' municipal councils, it is not surprising that farmers are over-represented in the national Upper House as well.[64] Farmers are also over-represented, albeit to a lesser degree, in the departmental general councils (Keeler, 1996).[65]

Although the number of farmers elected to these various representative positions has declined over the years, as one would expect with the rural exodus, it is important to note that the degree of their over-representation has in fact increased. For example, the percentage of farmers among the mayors has declined from 56.4 percent in 1953 to 28.5 percent in 1989, but the ratio of representation (the percentage of mayors who are farmers divided by the percentage of farmers in the active population) has increased during those years from 2.1 to 4.6. By the same token, the percentage of farmers in the Senate has declined from 24.8 percent in 1959 to the current 14.3 percent, but the ratio of representation has increased in that time from 1.2 to 2.0 (Keeler, 1996).

Finally, in comparison to Germany, French farmers are considerably more diverse socioeconomically. The spread between farm sizes and types is much larger in France than in Germany. During much of the postwar period, German farms have tended to be small and medium-sized and heavily capitalized. French farms display a wide range of farm types, ranging from modern farms in the northern plains to backward farms in mountainous regions barely permitting their sharecropper operators to live on a subsistence level (Averyt, 1977: 38). And with the exception of a lower communist vote and a higher centerist vote, French farmers' voting patterns have generally resembled those of the rest of the electorate (Averyt, 1977: 24). This allows them to use a critical swing vote during elections, which political parties pay handsomely to court.

French farmers' choice of government support – between raising farm prices and increasing subsidies for farm products (including subsidized lending) or via grants directly to farmers to modernize their operations, as in Germany – illustrates how economic policies have preserved their influence. The large, efficient farmers use the high costs of production of the technically backward small farmers as an argument for high price supports. And the small farmers have generally supported a price policy because structural reform usually meant, in addition to modernizing medium-sized farms, retirement grants to farmers with very small plots. Thus the large and small farmers have little real interest in modernizing policies and have maintained "the fiction of a farming community" that has similar needs in all its parts (Averyt, 1977: 28). This has helped to preserve farmers' electoral importance, and by extension increase the pressure brought to bear upon the government.[66]

As a result of these numerous ways of preserving their political influence, farmers have benefited from financial policies that cater to rural areas. Between 1950 and 1963, Crédit Agricole medium- and long-term loans rose from 630 million Francs to 13,000 million Francs.[67] This expansion has continued as the bank has financed, with considerable government subsidy, the technical and infrastructural modernization of the countryside. Figure 4.2 (shown in the section of pre-World War II France) illustrates the tremendous increase in government assistance to the Crédit Agricole during the postwar period in comparison to the prewar era. Government assistance continued to increase until the early 1960s when the pro-business Gaullist government took power. Despite the leveling off in government support, Crédit Agricole loans continued to grow. In addition, the balance of deposits increased tremendously after the war as a result of a rapid expansion of its branches and favorable deposit rates. By 1959, the deposits of the Crédit Agricole represented about 11.2 percent of total deposits in the French banking system. Comparing this to its deposit base in the prewar era illustrates the enormous change (Table 4.4).

While the Crédit Agricole has expanded its services, its core business has remained the agricultural sector.[68] Indeed, Crédit Agricole has considerably increased its services to farmers in comparison with the prewar period, corresponding to farmers' far greater political power (Carré *et al.*, 1975: 337).

LABOR AND LARGE FIRMS

Following World War II, the pattern of financing of large firms resembled that of Japan – both countries had large firms that were uncompetitive relative to their main foreign rivals (German and British firms for France, American firms for the Japanese). Consequently, governments in both nations bolstered banking services that could collect household savings, with the government then directing these funds, via public and semi-public banks, to industries and firms of importance to the nation's industrializing strategy. International trade and capital flows increased as firms in both nations made inroads into foreign markets (and as foreign firms made inroads into the French market in particular). This, in addition to rising debt levels during the 1970s, placed strains on the government's willingness to continue the high levels of subsidized lending as it pursued macroeconomic prudence. With

Table 4.4 Composition of deposits in France (in millions of contemporary francs)

	Total deposits (1)	*Crédit agricole (2)*	*(2)/(1)*
1913	18581	4	0.0002%
1920	64249	27	0.0004%
1930	156705	999	0.006%
1937	180105	1297	0.007%
1959			11.2%
1975	1246.5 (billion FF)	147.9 (billion FF)	11.9%

Source: Gueslin (1992). For 1975 see Bayliss and Butt Philip (1980: 127).

many large firms also having become competitive as a result of the "miracle growth era" of the 1950s and 1960s, they could now seek financing from international capital markets. The stagflation and oil crises of the 1970s caused a backlash to the right-wing government in France, and led to the unprecedented success of the Socialists in the 1981 election. Initially, they nationalized banks (and many large firms) to direct funding to industry so as to preserve employment levels, and to assist firms in trouble (directly controlling 96 percent of all deposits!) (Zysman, 1983). A large part of their economic program was paid for by borrowing; they gambled that these funds would make growth possible again, but the economy became saddled with unsustainable debt levels. The growing cost of borrowing and debt payments led to measures to reduce public expenditures and to raise revenue which included privatizing the newly nationalized firms via share sales to private individuals and institutions (Hall, 1986).

However, the manner in which the government implemented these privatizing policies remained consistent with the Left's desire to preserve firms' long-term focus, which helped to ensure employment stability. This was achieved primarily by shifting from state-directed financing via banks to a pattern of cross-shareholding (similar to Germany and Japan) in the latter half of the 1980s. But since the 1990s, many French firms have moved towards an Anglo-American model of corporate financing. For example, Morin (2000) points to the tremendous increase in foreign share ownership, a large portion of which consists of North American institutional investors, which went from 10 percent in 1985 to 50 percent by 2001. This has led to the unraveling of share ownerships, heightened takeover activity, and placed a new emphasis on shareholder value among CEOs.

But why has France been unable to adopt German co-determination, especially as works councils have existed since World War II, and labor is represented on corporate boards? The distinctive features of the statist model of wage bargaining in France, in contrast to those in both liberal and coordinated market economies, did not induce unions and employers to develop strong firm-level organizations to support their sectoral wage negotiations. Given their weakness and traditional reliance on public intervention, "union officials could gain more from episodic political mobilization, designed to attract the attention of the dirigiste state, than from patient negotiations in their narrow arena" (Levy, 1999: 243). French unions had little to gain by developing their ability to promote in-firm discussion with employers, since they could do better by waiting for the inevitable public intervention. Employers' associations, which also knew that the likely outcome of any negotiation would be determined by the government, focused on developing their expertise in labor law rather than developing the collective capacities necessary to acquire information from member firms about their in-firm negotiating practices, so as to circulate best practices and coordinate company actions (Culpepper, 2003).

The prominent role the state played in strategic coordination left these arrangements vulnerable to the "move to the market" of the 1980s, which saw the decline of state intervention across Europe; firms and workers found themselves without the support for strategic coordination on which they once counted.

As a result, institutional change has been more dramatic in France than in the liberal or coordinated market economies of Northern Europe. The retreat of the state left the trade unions in a weak position, and firms have taken advantage of the opportunity to move wage bargaining towards the firm level, reduce job security, and render work relations more competitive (Hall and Thelen, 2009).

This has led to an extended period of transition in which labor and capital are still searching for a stable equilibrium. The state continues to assert its authority over French firms on labor's behalf despite this apparent shift towards the market. For example, in recent years, to discourage hostile takeovers and to prevent the layoffs that frequently accompany them, market conforming as well as state intervention mechanisms have increased. In reaction to recent hostile takeover attempts, such as Alcan's takeover of Pechiney (which subsequently shut down numerous Pechiney sites despite repeated pledges on jobs), PepsiCo's reported intentions to acquire Danone in 2005, and Mittal Steel's successful bid for Arcelor in 2006 (Mittal Steel is a Dutch incorporated firm managed from London by the Indian billionaire, Lakshmi Mittal; Arcelor had around 30,000 employees in France), France has granted companies the right to use "poison pill" defense strategies.[69] Shortly after Mittal Steel's bid, Dominique de Villepin, the prime minister in January 2006, made a statement against hostile takeovers which was reminiscent of de Gaulle's support for national champions, by espousing a new "economic patriotism."[70] And it was Sarkozy, the polarizing French politician who is both decried and praised for touting the benefits of American capitalism, who fiercely condemned Mittal's acquisition of Arcelor, describing it as a "waste." In his manifesto in his bid for the French presidency in 2007, he announced his resolve to block foreign takeovers, declaring that "Europe must not be the Trojan horse of globalization reduced to circulation of capital and goods, but must ... protect people within globalization."[71] In addition to the use of market conforming tools like the poison pill, in early 2006 French authorities declared the right to veto or impose conditions on takeovers in 11 "strategic" industries, despite objections from the internal market commissioner of the European Union, Charlie McCreevy.[72] On top of this, in March 2006, de Villepin outlined fresh plans to boost employee share ownership and to use the Caisse des Depots et Consignations (CDC), the biggest institutional investor in the CAC-40, to ward off foreign takeovers. De Villepin said, "We need to consolidate the capital of companies and protect them against hostile operations." He explained that "fragmented share capital" was a big risk for the independence of French companies. The CDC has been branded as the "armed wing" of the government, a reputation boosted in 2003 when it subscribed to rescue rights issues at France Telecom and Alstom, in support of state-backed bail-outs.[73]

Of further interest to the politics of corporate ownership in France is the influence of the *agricultural sector* to blocking hostile takeovers. The French reacted very strongly, and appealed to nationalist sentiment in order to block PepsiCo's rumored interest in Danone, while little was said when Taittinger, the venerable Champagne maker, fell to an American company, Starwood Capital – an American real estate and private equity group. The difference in reaction is likely due to

Danone's strong ties to the politically powerful agricultural sector (dairy farms in particular), which provoked immediate and vociferous reactions from President Jacques Chirac, Prime Minister Dominique de Villepin, and Interior Minister Nicolas Sarkozy.[74] Evidently, labor and agriculture remain at the forefront of the political battles affecting corporate finance even 60 years after the initial bargains over the structure of French capitalist institutions were constructed.

SMALL FIRMS

Small firms were not a critical player during the initial postwar bargains. Unlike their small firm counterparts in Japan or Germany, French small firms do not have political institutions that magnify their political influence (via the electoral system in Japan and the decentralized politics of Germany). Consequently, they have suffered from a lack of organizational assistance. Since the early 1980s, the state has attempted to boost lending to small firms, though these attempts have met with frustration and ineffectiveness.

Neither equity markets nor a more competitive banking environment has provided adequate assistance to France's capital-starved SMEs, according to the French government's own assessment.[75] And the failure of France's liberalizing reforms in the 1980s and early 1990s has dragged the state back in. Government authorities have attempted to fill the void by proposing plans that combine tax breaks, exemptions from social security charges for new hires, and low-interest loans. Three programs administered by the Ministry of Finance have been particularly important and have achieved modest success (Levy, 1999).[76]

One is an unsecured state loan for small businesses experiencing difficulty administered by the Comité Départemental de Financement Industriel (CODEFI). CODEFI's basic mission is to convince reluctant bankers or investors to commit additional resources to near-bankrupt companies that are deemed salvageable. The state offers loans with very generous repayment terms and requires no collateral to bait private investors.

A second privileged financial channel for SMEs is the Société Française de Garantie des Financements des Petites et Moyennes Entreprises (SOFARIS). This was established in 1982, and offers guarantees on bank loans to SMEs. The lending institutions typically pay a commission of 0.5 percent, and SOFARIS pledges, in return, to reimburse 50 percent of the loan should the client default.

The third program for SMEs consists of low-interest loans for expansion and investment through the Crédit d'Equipement des PME (CEPME), which was created in 1981 to administer the state-subsidized loan program (Levy, 1999: 281). After recovering from financial difficulties, the CEPME was merged with SOFARIS into a single agency, the Banque de Développement des PME (BDPME) in 1997. The official rationale was to create a kind of one-stop service for small businesses, combining the low-interest loans of CEPME with the loan guarantees of SOFARIS. However, the private sector has been skeptical of this program, since state backing of selected SMEs creates moral hazard opportunities and raises the chances for political opportunism.

The difficulty with creating effecting SME financing institutions within France illustrates how political institutions that concentrated power in the hands of state officials, and which lack political accountability at the local level in addressing SMEs' needs, has led to persistent difficulties for offering effective, low-cost financing comparable to that found in Germany or Japan.

Summary

The new political situation following World War II led to a very different financial structure. Labor and farmers emerged as the political victors, and the political institutions secured their newfound power with control over domestic economic policy located in the Lower House. Consequently, the financial system fostered specific assets via a strong reliance on bank lending and concentrated ownership, a dramatic increase in agricultural financing, and the considerable expansion of the public pension system. But of most importance is the dramatic increase in state intervention. Farmers' support for nationalizing the commercial banks after World War II and for government intervention created heavy reliance on state institutions for the administration of the economy. While farmers may not have been directly involved in deciding the distribution of lending to industrial enterprises from these state-owned banks, they were supportive of the state's capacity to administer funds (since they benefited from funds being redirected to agriculture). This created an overreliance on the state to manage the economy, with wide-ranging implications (Hall, 1986; Culpepper *et al.*, 2006). For example, although labor implemented works councils and held seats on many firms' supervisory boards, institutions controlled by Paris were repeatedly relied upon to resolve conflicts and provide services. Thus, when the state removed itself and capital became increasingly important in the 1980s, labor faced difficulties in preserving a reliance on patient capital. Yet pensions remain publicly oriented, the state still exerts influence over firms to preserve employment stability, and French firms retain concentrated ownership – so France is unlikely to turn into an LME like the US or UK. Rather, it is in transition. Other Mediterranean economies with similar reliance on the government have faced comparable difficulties to varying degrees (e.g., Italy), which depend on alternative institutions for mediating the transition (e.g., decentralized power in Italy to the benefit of SMEs).

After World War II, French labor successfully implemented changes from above, in the middle, and from below. But the French case usefully illustrates that corporate finance was primarily determined from above. Labor could have utilized their positions from below and in the middle, but chose to rely on the government's power to intervene. Certainly, concentrated ownership existed, but this did not determine corporate strategy nearly as much as the government's control over key financial institutions and instruments. Indeed, the French case shows that understanding corporate strategy may critically depend on considering the range of forces affecting corporate strategy that are exogenous *and* endogenous to the firm. That is, it is important to keep corporate governance in perspective, since the broader regulatory environment can have a more substantial influence on corporate strategy.

Conclusion

In pre-World War II France and Japan, owners of capital won political battles against labor and farmers because the political institutions denied them from implementing their preferred policies. Prewar Japan was less democratic than France as a result of its reliance on the oligarchy (Genrō and Privy Council) and with the emperor being the supreme leader. This granted capital greater influence insofar as it denied labor and farmers to a greater extent than France. But the difference is small, since capital was dominant in both countries. Owners of capital could easily block the proposals of popular interests, thereby preserving the status quo *laissez-faire* policies. Pre-World War II Japan modeled its constitution on Germany's pre-World War I version, so it should not be surprising that markets were well developed; in essence, political institutions restricted access to those with enough money to buy influence, and in this regard, France's Third Republic Constitution was similar. The importance of these political arrangements was clearly tested during the Popular Front, when popular will capitulated to capitalists' power despite pressure for reforms arising from the difficulties of the Great Depression. Thus, before labor and farmers could change the institutions of capitalism, they would need to alter the political institutions. This occurred after World War II.

While more change is possible with the majoritarian electoral system in France, the difficulties in changing, as well as the direction of the change, demonstrate the importance of the initial bargains when political and financial institutions are (re)created. Indeed, the broad contours of financial systems are determined at these critical junctures when political and economic institutions are created anew by bargains struck between the dominant interests. When institutions do change, they are constrained by the pre-existing structure (e.g., France could not become like Germany in the late 1980s).

That the basic structure of the political and economic institutions was determined at the last critical juncture (when the constitution was created, and new rules of the game were established for economic actors) is clearly illustrated in these cases. In addition to the Popular Front test, modern French difficulties in adjusting to globalization's pressures illustrate how the institutions created after World War II constrain the scope of possible change. In the prewar period, during the last great era of globalization, France did not face political difficulties, since the political-economic institutions catered to capitalists' interests; labor and farmers lacked political influence. As mentioned, the key test came with the Popular Front when pressure for change mounted from popular interests.

5   Social contract

Inclusive CME: post-World War II Japan

In this chapter, I examine the financial outcomes when landed interests, labor, and capital have similarly powerful bargaining positions, as in post-World War II Japan. Immediately following the war, labor's power swelled. Despite early support for unions, American Occupation authorities soon did an about-face as they sought to stymie increasing communist influence. Within five years of the end of the war, Japanese labor had become weaker than its German counterpart, especially in the political arena. It was during this period of flux that bargains over financial institutions were struck.

Farmers' power also vaulted to new heights following the war: land redistribution as well as several institutional mechanisms – the electoral system, increasingly malapportioned representation, universal male suffrage, and the executive–legislative balance – cemented Japanese farmers' unprecedented political power. Unlike labor, they held on to their new gains, and bargained over the structure of the nation's financial institutions from a position of strength. Indeed, farmers have played a critical role in Japanese postwar financial architecture in two ways: (1) immediately after the war they pushed the financial system in a direction that privileged intermediation through government-operated banking facilities; and (2) as a key actor within the consensus political system, they have wielded sufficient power to veto changes to the status quo (which they helped to create immediately after the war). With financial institutions complementing one another (Table 3.2), farmers' capacity to influence the initial structure of one, or more, of these institutions has constrained the possibilities for the rest of the financial system. And insofar as Roe (2003) finds that long-term financing arose as a stable complement to employment stability, but not necessarily as a result of labor's bargaining power, farmers may fill the causal void

Relative to the prewar period, the power of owners of large firms suddenly diminished and became constrained by the rise of these groups and the institutions that cemented the new distribution of political power. Occupation authorities came to their rescue, however, by weakening labor's bargaining position and pushing for outcomes that would be beneficial to business owners.

The altered political circumstances correspond to changes in the variables under consideration: asset specificity, corporate ownership, government intervention, agrarian financing, and pensions. Asset specificity became far more specific in the postwar years as a result of: (1) the new keiretsu intercorporate ownership structure which complemented labor's successful push for greater employment stability and enhanced role in corporate governance; (2) government involvement in collecting deposits via the postal savings bank, and then lending these to industry via the Fiscal Investment and Loan Program (FILP); and (3) pensions became more public, more encompassing, and larger, with private pensions structured to maintain firms' reliance on patient capital. Financial support to agriculture likewise increased via attractive savings arrangements, subsidized lending, and government-funded projects. Together, these financial outcomes correspond to Japan's inclusive style of CME capitalism.

Japanese capitalism – resulting from labor–farmer–capital owner compromise – has exhibited traits of other capitalist systems that emerged from bargains struck between just two of these actors. It became interventionist like France (a labor–farmer coalition), but has also borne similarities to the coordinated market economy of Germany (a labor–capital coalition). Although not commonly noted, Japan also resembles the US's capitalist system (a capital–farmer coalition) in terms of its diffuse intercorporate ownership structure, which gives managers more power and regard to rural overrepresentation. Is it a coincidence that these traits of Japanese capitalism resemble those of other bargained capitalist outcomes? Or, do these similarities emerge naturally – and expectedly – from the bargains struck among the key players following World War II?

I first describe the origins and character of the postwar financial system. Next, I detail the structure of the political institutions, the role and interactions among the key interest groups, and the impact of the US Occupation during this critical postwar period. I then briefly summarize the evolution of the Japanese financial system during the postwar era in the wake of these institutional changes, emphasizing how political institutions have since preserved the bargains and constrained the particular evolutionary trajectory of Japanese capitalism.

The postwar financial system

The post-World War II financial system developed a strong reliance on specific assets via patient capital from main bank lending, government-led financing (via savings collected by the postal savings bank and then lent out via FILP), and the development of interfirm ownership. It also adopted stronger government intervention than that found in Germany, and greater agricultural assistance – resembling France in both respects. The pension system likewise supported the use of patient capital for corporate financing by turning private pension funds into an internal financing option, as in Germany, and via public pension funds that were also used for lending by the FILP. Here, I document the emergence of these financial system attributes following the war.

SPECIFIC FINANCIAL ASSETS

When the war with China began in 1938, a series of laws were passed to put the allocation and control of finance firmly under government control, resembling similar actions performed by other countries during World War II (e.g., France, Germany, and Italy). To this end, banks were consolidated. The 424 ordinary banks at the end of 1936 were reduced to just 61 in 1945,[1] and savings banks fell from 69 in 1941 to just four in 1945. Table 5.1 shows the sources of external funds for industries, demonstrating the concentration of banking that occurred and the increasing reliance on banks for external finance.

During the war, the government passed legislation encouraging the concentration of and reliance on bank financing, and discouraged equity and corporate bond financing which funneled savings towards the purchase of government bonds to help finance the war effort.[2] The stock exchanges suspended trading before the war ended and remained closed until May 1949. Corporate bond markets were eventually reopened in 1949, but both the stock and bond markets were tightly controlled, and their use limited (Hoshi and Kashyap, 2001: 75–77). Consequently, the relations formalized by the munitions companies system of World War II (where a bank is assigned to a particular firm) lasted well into the postwar period. Even after 30 years (1974), 79 percent of 157 munitions companies from World War II still had close ties to their designated wartime financial institution (Hoshi and Kashyap, 2001). Occupation period policies helped to cement these relationships since the designated institution was typically involved in a firm's postwar reorganization.

Although banks dominated financing during the war, this did not mean that Japan's postwar financial system would necessarily remain banking oriented. In both the US and UK, banks were heavily relied upon during the war, yet markets came to dominate corporate finance shortly after the war ended. The political situation in Japan following the war was critical to the continuance of the wartime bank–firm relations.

Because American General Headquarters (GHQ) viewed the business elite within Japan as having been strong proponents for the war effort, they sought to eliminate the zaibatsu – thereby ending the dominance of a small group over a

Table 5.1 Sources of external funds for industries, 1931–1957 (percentage distribution of total)

Year	Total (¥ million)	New share issues	New bond issues	Net new bank loans
1931	361	56.5	29.92	13.57
1935	1,199	68.06	2.17	29.77
1940	7,653	38.42	7.96	53.63
1945	50,405	6.11	0.64	93.24
1950	512,898	6.22	8.48	85.3
1955	676,471	14.12	3.92	81.95

Source: Bank of Japan, *Statistical Annual* (1960).

large number of firms – and attempted to decrease concentration by limiting the size of any one firm within its industry (Hoshi and Kashyap, 2001: 68–71). Zaibatsu dissolution was originally envisioned to include 83 companies, but in the end only 30 firms were dissolved. The others were required merely to eliminate their holding-company structure. The zaibatsu financial institutions emerged from the process completely unscathed. However, the prewar structure of the zaibatsu – characterized by holding companies, layers of subsidiaries, and family stock ownership – was largely ended (Hoshi and Kashyap, 2001: 68).

The deconcentration effort was even weaker; only 18 companies, out of an original 325, were broken up under the Deconcentration Act (Hoshi and Kashyap, 2001: 68–71). In the end, dissolution and deconcentration efforts were weakly implemented, permitting the evolution of zaibatsu into keiretsu through share purchases to form horizontally integrated alliances across many industries. The major keiretsu became centered around one bank, which lent money to the keiretsu's member companies and held equity positions in them. Each main bank exerted considerable influence over the companies in the keiretsu and acted as a monitoring and bail-out entity. This cross-shareholding structure proved especially useful for preventing hostile takeovers in Japan, especially by foreign (American) corporations, and fostered the use of patient capital.

GOVERNMENT INTERVENTION

The postwar banking-dominated system was given a substantial boost by the early concentration of government-directed investment in heavy industry. Capital scarcity and the necessity of rebuilding basic infrastructure led the government to directing available credit, via banks, to essential industries which helped cement bank–firm relationships. During the immediate postwar years (1945–1949), direct credit controls were used. The Reconstruction Bank played a crucial role in rebuilding Japan's basic industries, and by late 1948 it had become by far the largest supplier of capital for the coal, iron and steel, fertilizer, electric, shipping, and textile industries. As of 1949, the total loans made by the bank amounted to 74.1 percent of the total investment of all industries, and 84 percent of the bank loans were concentrated in the aforementioned industries (Yamamura, 1967: 28).

The Reconstruction Bank was disbanded in January 1952 owing to its inflationary consequences – it raised funds largely through bond issues monetized by the Bank of Japan. Consequently, government officials moved to the use of postal savings to fund government-targeted industries via the Fiscal Investment Loan Program (FILP), which was finally consolidated in 1953 (Figure 5.1). The Japan Development Bank, as an entity within the FILP, replaced the functions of the Reconstruction Bank in 1951, and devoted 84 percent of its total loans to the coal, iron/steel, electricity, and shipbuilding industries in the years 1951 to 1955 (Broadbridge, 1966: 32–33). Thus, the early concentration of investment in these sectors, coupled with the powerful position of the city banks, produced an industrial and financial pattern which led to close linkages between firms and banks (Hoshi and Kashyap, 2001).

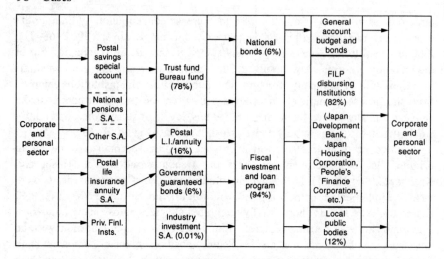

Figure 5.1 The Fiscal Investment and Loan Program (source: Calder (1990: 34)).

In addition to the Reconstruction Bank and the Export-Import Bank for financing large firms, several institutions were created within the FILP to assist the financing of small firms. In 1949, the People's Finance Corporation (PFC) was founded to lend funds primarily to extremely small enterprises. And in 1953, the Small Business Finance Corporation (SBFC) was created to provide loans as investment funds and long-term working capital necessary for modernization and rationalization. More closely linked to the industrial policy process than its counterpart PFC, the SBFC concentrated on lending for purposes which relate specifically to government policy objectives, such as pollution control, energy conservation, and productivity enhancement. It was intended to insulate small business finance from competing big business demands at the Japan Development Bank, through which many small firms had previously been funded. The activities of the Central Cooperative Bank for Commerce and Industry, which was founded in 1936, also grew considerably in the postwar period. It provided finance mainly to business cooperatives and their members, especially those located in geographically concentrated industries, such as pottery, silk weaving, small-scale shipbuilding, and flatware. Similarly, the Environmental Sanitation Business Finance Corporation emerged in 1967 to provide funds for guest-houses, coffee shops, and bathhouses; these firms are strategic gathering spots in urban communities and prospectively importance locations for undertaking various types of political activity.

Government intervention was bolstered by the postal savings bank, which offered very attractive deposit account treatment and which catered to those living in the countryside owing to its numerous branches. Postal savings have succeeded as a result of government support in four areas: licensing of new financial products, tax treatment, administrative cost support, and the expansion of post office branches. The attractiveness of the financial products it offers has been important to its rapid expansion. One highly attractive product is the ten-year fixed-interest deposit without penalty for early withdrawal. These deposits have few analogues either in the Japanese financial system or elsewhere. They carry comparatively high interest rates for Japanese financial instruments and can serve as collateral for housing and other loans (it is possible to temporarily withdraw the bulk of the principal without impairing the high, long-term guaranteed interest of the account). Second, until 1988, postal savings accounts were tax exempt, although there was a ceiling on permissible deposits. However, there has been little effective control over the proliferation of multiple accounts. Third, the postal savings system in Japan also benefits by having its operating costs subsidized from the interest income flowing from Trust Fund Bureau lending. Finally, the network of post offices across Japan has proliferated rapidly during the postwar era, with over 23,000 branches by the mid-1980s, orders of magnitude greater than those of even the largest banks, which were constrained by Ministry of Finance (MoF) restrictions from expanding as rapidly. The Dai Ichi Kangyō Bank, Japan's largest, had, for example, only 379 branches in late 1988. Internationally, Citibank had 2,900 branches while France's huge Crédit Agricole had 10,620.

Commercial banks have received far fewer benefits than the postal savings system; even the concessions they received came with a discriminatory time lag during which the postal savings system was able to gain market share at the expense of the banks. For example, although postal savings were accorded tax-free status in the early postwar period, banks did not receive this for even a portion of their deposits until 1952. In addition, the private banks have never been allowed to offer financial products as attractive as postal savings bank deposits or to freely develop the sort of huge national branch network that postal savings enjoys (Calder, 1990).

AGRICULTURAL FINANCING

In addition to attractive deposit treatment by the postal savings bank, the Norinchukin Bank has provided extensive lending subsidies to farmers, and Japanese public works spending has increased substantially for rural areas.

The postwar agrarian lending structure began when, in 1943, agricultural associations and cooperatives were amalgamated into a single system of national, prefectural, and village farm organizations. All farmers and landowners were required to join. In the same year, the Central Bank for Industrial Cooperatives became the Central Bank for Agriculture and Forestry (Norin Chuo Kinko, or Norinchukin) (Mulgan, 2001). These came to occupy a central role in the administration of agrarian finance in the postwar period as the banking arm of the Nokyo (the postwar manifestation of the farm organizations begun in 1947).

The bank collects funds through a complicated three-tier system. At the lowest level, the *nokyo* offers savers deposit desks at 16,000 offices (only the postal savings system has more offices). These offices serve 5,612 cooperatives which, with several fishing cooperatives, deposit their savings with 47 prefectural, or county, agricultural banks called *shinnoren*. With this money, Norinchukin has been able to buy government bonds which yielded 6 percent to 7 percent, several points more than the interest it paid, giving the bank a comfortable spread. In return, the bank offered better interest rates than commercial banks and paid dividends.

The Agriculture, Forestry, and Fishery Finance Corporation also emerged in political response to interest group pressure, reacting against MITI's efforts to channel scarce funds towards industry. When the Japan Development Bank was set up in 1951, agriculture was initially accorded only a special account within it. But in 1953 the Diet established a separate agricultural finance institution so that agriculture would not be forced to compete directly for scarce government funds with the basic industries that were the JDB's fundamental clientele.

Pensions

Both public and private pension systems have promoted the reliance on specific assets. Public pensions, which are partially funded, have become an important source of public finance; together with postal savings, they are deposited in the Trust Fund Bureau, which gets distributed through the Fiscal Investment Loan Program, as shown in Figure 5.1. Private pensions have been used as a source of internal financing by firms and as a means for solidifying corporate ties.

The earliest pension plan, the Mutual Aid Pension, began in 1890 and was for military servants. It did not require individual contributions since it was funded out of general revenue. Later, it was expanded to include civil servants. The main public pension scheme covering private sector employees, the Employee Pension, began in 1941. It was introduced to accumulate capital for the war effort, and so it required a long qualifying period for an individual worker (20 years) before the first pension would be paid out. The National Pension, created in 1959, acts as a type of residual pension for those not covered by the Employee Pension System or Mutual Aid Pension – notably farmers and employees of small firms. The Employee Pension and National Pension comprise the bulk of public pension funds, which are deposited with the Trust Fund Bureau, along with postal savings.

Private pensions have come to play an important role in Japan's financial system in two ways. First, in cases where private pensions are book reserve plans (begun in 1952), firms indicate pension liabilities in their financial accounts but do not set aside money in a separate fund to cover future liabilities as with "funded pensions." The attraction of book reserve plans is that they provide firms with an internal source of working capital, which acts as an important source of "patient capital" for such firms (Manow, 2001a).

Funded corporate pensions, known as the Tax Qualified Pension, offer a second method for covering private pension liabilities. These were created after the public pension system in 1962 to provide tax benefits for private pensions and form the basis for Japan's modern private pension system. In 1966, another private pension, the Employee Pension Fund, was established which allows firms to manage a portion of their employees' pension funds. Together, they comprise the bulk of private pension funds in Japan. Funds in these programs not managed by the firm are managed by banks or life insurance companies. Because both types of companies have been highly concentrated, the MoF can actively guide their investment decisions to promote industrialization by instructing these financial institutions to invest in public projects and to lend to key sectors. These funded private pensions, like book reserve plans, have provided a source of "patient capital" in two ways. First, in exchange for the right to manage a corporation's pensions, life insurance companies have often invested directly in the corporation whose pension business it received. Life insurance companies did not pressure the companies in which they invested for profits, in part because these companies were not owned by shareholders but rather by their clients, collectively known as mutual companies. Over time, life insurance companies became some of the largest equity holders of Japanese corporations. A second way of creating patient capital has been through the banking system. In anticipation of liberalizing reforms in the 1960s, the government, corporations, and banks feared foreign competition and the takeover of Japanese banks. In response to this threat, the MoF coordinated the purchase of bank shares by life insurance companies and trust banks. As banks were also owned by friendly patient capital, their lending to corporations was shielded from the demands for short-term gains (Park, 2004). So, although pension funds' equity investments are higher in Japan than in Germany (Davis, 2001), this has not led to the kinds of short-term performance pressures faced by firms in the US and UK.

Summary

Following the war, firms relied heavily on patient capital via private banks and government lending; likewise, intercorporate ownership prevented shareholders from exerting short-term performance pressures on managers. Government intervention through FILP and the structure of the public and private pension programs further contributed to the reliance on patient capital. The mechanisms for diverting funds to rural areas were also established in the immediate postwar years. Why did Japan's postwar financial system undergo such numerous and fundamental changes?

Politics

The political situation in Japan following the war enabled managers of large firms to make a bargain with labor that led to patient corporate financing (although labor was politically weaker than its German counterpart). After the war, Japanese farmers became very strong politically (much stronger than German farmers and likely stronger than French farmers), with several reforms to the political institutions cementing their newfound power. I first discuss the reforms to Japan's political institutions that contributed to farmers' (and small firms') greater power and labor's weaker influence relative to capital owners. I then look more specifically at the political power each actor wielded immediately following World War II and the consequences for the nation's financial institutions. Finally, I consider how these financial bargains, which were entrenched within new postwar political institutions, have shaped the evolution of Japan's postwar financial system.

POLITICAL INSTITUTIONS

Land redistribution vaulted farmers to a very politically powerful position following the war, comprising nearly half of the total electorate in 1950 (Mulgan, 2001: 304). With such an overwhelming proportion of the electorate, agricultural interests had sufficient power to elect Diet members outright and to propose and pass legislation. As the rural population declined, agriculture still retained considerable negative political power (i.e., the ability to ensure electoral failure if votes are redirected away from a candidate and to veto unfavorable policies), which was sustained by increasing malapportionment of electoral districts begun with the 1947 electoral law (Wada, 1996: 11). Table 5.2 illustrates the creeping malapportionment in both houses during the postwar period.

Following the war, American General Headquarters (GHQ) initially rejected Japan's prewar electoral structure (the single nontransferable vote, multi-member system) because they delivered it may have contributed to the rise of militarism (McCubbins and Rosenbluth, 1995). In its place, the GHQ introduced a proportional representation electoral system in 1946 in order to encourage new political forces as part of the democratization effort; this was also the favored electoral system of the Socialist Party. Because a large number of Socialist representatives won seats in the 1946 election (93 out of 464 seats), MacArthur, who was

Table 5.2 Differences between voting values in the least and most densely populated electorates, 1947–1990

Year	Ratio in House of Councillors prefectural constituencies		Ratio in House of Representatives constituencies	
	Least densely populated constituency	Most densely populated constituency	Least densely populated constituency	Most densely populated constituency
1947	1.25	: 1	1.51	: 1
1950	1.55	: 1	2.17	: 1
1960	2.39	: 1	3.21	: 1
1967	5.07	: 1		
1970			4.83	: 1
1980	5.37	: 1	3.95	: 1
1990	6.25	: 1	3.38	: 1
1998	4.98	: 1	2.40	: 1

Source: Mulgan (2001: 330).

worried about the growing communist threat, relented to Liberal Party leader Yoshida's request to return to the prewar electoral system (Cowhey and McCubbins, 1995: 37–38). The conservative Liberal and Democratic parties, which together comprised a Diet majority, revised the election law to reinstate the 1925 multi-member district system. Despite this revision, neither party did as well at the polls in 1947 as was expected, and the Socialists actually took the lead with 143 seats over 131 for the Liberals and 124 for the Democrats. The conservative parties, however, rebounded by the next election in 1949 and have retained majority control ever since.

Candidate-centered electoral systems such as Japan's multi-member district single nontransferable vote system (MMD-SNTV) create incentives for politicians to develop a loyal group of supporters by wooing them with pork in exchange for votes. Journalistic reporting as well as scholarly analyses (e.g., Cox and Thies, 1998, 2001) of Japanese elections invariably focus on individual candidates' support networks and the enormous sums of money needed to build and maintain them (Cowhey and McCubbins, 1995). In exchange for loyal electoral support, politicians offer favors via government regulations and through the bureaucracy (e.g., Fukui and Fukai, 1996). With regard to the United States, Fiorina (1977) explains that bureaucracies can be designed to create opportunities for legislators to intervene personally on the behalf of individuals or groups of constituents, thereby allowing legislators personalized, credit-claiming activities that can help build personal vote coalitions.

> The party in control of the government has, of course, a distinct advantage in creating personal vote coalitions for its candidates because it monopolizes policy and budgetary favors. As long as the majority party can pass its legislation through the parliament and can direct bureaucrats effectively, it can enact (or have bureaucrats implement) particularistic policies that facilitate the creation and maintenance of personal vote coalitions.
>
> (Cowhey and McCubbins, 1995: 44)

Some of these particularistic policies may include subsidized lending and other forms of financial assistance. To direct these financing favors to specific recipients, intermediaries are relied upon. In Japan, farmers and small business have benefited considerably as key members of these personal vote coalitions, and the close links between these groups and LDP politicians have contributed to LDP majority control in the postwar period.

These two political institutions – malapportionment and MMD-SNTV rules – have magnified the political power of farmers (the latter has also magnified small firms' political influence). In addition, the legislative–executive balance changed after the war, placing the locus of political power firmly in the Lower House of the Diet to the benefit of farmers, labor, and small firms. Moreover, Japan's consensual politics has helped to cement the financial institution outcomes created during this period owing to the numerous veto-points that preserve the status quo. What kinds of financial bargains have these actors compromised on?

FARMERS

In addition to land reform and political institutional changes (the electoral system, malapportionment, and a legislative bias), farmers' political power also received a boost from reform of the Nokyo in 1947, which enabled them to organize locally, and to be highly influential in electing representatives to government. Consequently, farmers received favorable deposit policies from the postal savings bank, subsidized lending via the Norinchukin Bank, and were beneficiaries of numerous government-funded projects. I briefly discuss these here.

Immediately after the war, land reform measures were introduced by SCAP officials, who feared that the revival of the tenancy system could lead to a relapse of authoritarianism or a communist insurgency among landless farmers. SCAP also viewed land reforms as critical to the democratization effort.[3] A dramatic restructuring of landholdings in rural Japan ensued. At the end of the war, tenants cultivated 45 percent of arable land; by 1950, tenants cultivated only 10 percent. Likewise, the number of farm families that owned 90 percent or more of their land increased from 1.7 million to 3.8 million.[4] Added to this was the reform of the cooperatives, which enabled farmers to organize and become highly influential in electing representatives to government. During the war, cooperatives were part of the Imperial Agricultural Association (IAA). As an instrument of government control over agriculture during the war, the IAA was tainted by authoritarianism in the eyes of SCAP officials, and in 1947 Occupation authorities ordered its dissolution. Under the Agricultural Cooperative Association Law (or Nokyo Law) passed in December 1947, local cooperatives were reconstituted as a private, voluntary organization – the Nokyo. As a result of their new legal status, the number of local Nokyo proliferated rapidly – from 4,256 in April 1948 to 27,819 by December 1948.[5]

The Nokyo Law allowed agricultural cooperatives to take deposits and to lend funds via the Norinchukin Bank – Nokyo's banking arm. Nokyo was also permitted to supply credit to local public organizations, banks, or other banking institutions.[6] Consequently, Nokyo garnered tremendous political and economic power at the local level. In addition, the cooperative banks collected government payments destined for producers. These government transfers, in turn, fueled the expansion of cooperative activities in other areas. According to a 1951 SCAP publication, "In most villages, general-purpose cooperatives now provide the primary credit, marketing, purchasing, processing, and other essential services used by farmers."[7] The framework for offering agricultural subsidies through cooperatives was established under the Land Improvement Law of 1949 and through the Law for the Reconstruction of Agricultural Finances in 1951. During the 1949 to 1953 period, subsidies more than tripled, bolstering the reliance on agricultural cooperatives as politically useful intermediaries.[8]

The political instability of the 1945 to 1950 period offered the agricultural cooperatives a golden opportunity to establish themselves as a potent political force at the "rice"-roots level. With 90 percent of all farm households represented by at least one cooperative member, Nokyo became the most important organization in rural Japan.[9]

There were frequent instances in which the position taken by Nokyo determined the success or failure of a given candidate. Furthermore, Nokyo executives made use of their vote-gathering capacities to enter and win national and local elections.[10] In short, cooperatives became an essential component of every rural politician's re-election constituency, and considerably enhanced credit availability to small farmers (Mulgan, 2000).

In order to receive the political support of the local cooperative, however, politicians had to distinguish themselves as advocates of agricultural interests. The surest way to secure the endorsement of Nokyo officials was through government largesse. Funds for paddy reconstruction, irrigation, and other pork-barrel projects carried out through the local cooperative were critical for rural political success. Between 1949 and 1953, agricultural expenditures increased from 5.9 to 16.6 percent of the national budget; direct subsidies and grants accounted for 50 percent of the Ministry of Agriculture budget. And in 1953, agricultural interest successfully lobbied to prevent the diversion of funds towards interest rate subsidies for industry with the Trust Fund Bureau Law, which set a floor of 6.05 percent on the lending rate of Trust Fund Bureau loans to government financial institutions, except in especially authorized circumstances (Calder, 1990; Sheingate, 2001).[11]

The massive growth of rural subsidies was partly due to party competition for farmers' votes since they comprised nearly half the electorate. Conservative politicians outdistanced their socialist rivals at channeling government resources to rural Japan, which ballooned as a result of the Korean War (1950–1953). A 1952 opinion poll reported that 77 percent of farmers favored the two conservative parties over their socialist rivals. By the time the various postwar parties combined in 1955 into the Liberal Democratic Party on the Right and Japan Socialist Party on the Left, the cooperative associations were a central part of the conservatives' electoral strategy and a main reason for subsequent LDP political success. As the LDP–Nokyo alliance solidified over the following decade, subsidies for local public works projects rose steadily (Sheingate, 2001).

LOCAL INTERESTS AND POSTAL SAVINGS

The key to the political influence of postal savings has been the special postmaster system – it has magnified the influence of farmers and small firms in particular.

Shortly after amalgamation of the Liberal Democratic Party in 1955, the special postmaster system was sharply expanded, and systematically linked with conservative politics as the LDP tried to establish a nationwide organization to consolidate its precarious hold on power.[12] The special postmastership was the only civil service appointment in Japan available without competitive examination, other than the repair of rare books. In addition to lucrative perquisites such as space rental fees, postmasterships allowed the subsequent appointment of family members as assistant postmasters. Consequently, the special postmasterships became a highly attractive form of patronage, which the LDP moved aggressively to control and to then dispense. The combination of an extremely broad grass-roots base, and the deep roots of these post offices in their local communities, made them useful political tools. The commissioned post offices became especially effective politically because their proprietors were typically drawn from well-established local families, because they were often linked to the support associations of local politicians, and because these post offices were traditional gathering spots in small local communities, well suited to informal building of political ties. In this sense, they complemented the Nokyo in helping the LDP representatives build local support coalitions among farmers and small firms, and in dispensing pork to retain their loyal support. In addition, post offices were far more important deposit-taking institutions for rural households than private banks, since the latter restricted their services to the cities. Throughout the postwar period, postal savings have remained the most important source of funds for the FILP, comprising between 30 to 40 percent of its total funding source annually (with postal insurance making up an additional 10 percent; Cargill and Yoshino, 2003: 59).

LABOR AND CAPITAL BARGAIN

Although scholars have discussed the postwar bargain elsewhere (e.g., Gilson and Roe, 1999; Jackson, 2001), I recount it here as a necessary part of understanding the labor–farmer–capital owner compromise.

While government intervention, bank influence, and intercorporate ownership increased, with labor playing a stronger role in corporate strategy and organization via each of these routes compared to its prewar position, it was weaker than its German counterpart. This would grant firm owners, and managers in particular[13] (as a result of intercorporate shareholding), greater influence over corporate strategy and financing decisions. For example, Japan's postwar enterprise-based unions, company-linked benefits, and loyalty to the firm were influenced by American employers' anti-union "American Plan" and "welfare capitalism" during the 1920s. As a result, Japanese firms could take greater advantage of financing opportunities available from capital markets from the mid-1970s onward.

The labor movement surged immediately after the war. In December 1945, 380,000 workers were members of labor unions, swelling to 900,000 in January 1946. The prewar Sodomei, or Japan Confederation of Trade Unions, was revived by Social Democrats and other moderate left-wing organizers in August 1946, and soon numbered 855,000 members. In late August, communist activists organized the Congress of Industrial Organizations (Sanbetsu Kaigi), which had 1,630,000 members. Another national organization, the Japan Congress of Trade Unions (Nichiro Kaigi), and a number of independent enterprise-wide federations of local labor unions in large multi-plant companies such as the steelmaker Japan Steel Tube (Nippon Kokan, or NKK Corp.) were established as well.

Nosaka Sanzo, a leading communist, published "An Appeal to the Japanese People" which served as the basis for the Emancipation League (formerly the

Anti-War League), founded in 1944. The League's program was couched in moderate language so as to appeal to a wide audience, but among its key policy prescriptions it advocated "maintaining and strengthening state control over banks" (Colbert, 1952: 64). The program served as the ideological basis for a large segment of the postwar labor movement. The more moderate socialists, in 1946, proposed a system of state control of key industries (Colbert, 1952: 88), as well as the establishment of a Supreme Economic Council to determine general economic policies, subsidiary councils for each industry, and at each level of planning or supervision trade union representatives, as well as representatives of business and government, would participate. The long-term financial program of the Socialist Party called for the socialization of all banks and insurance companies, entailing the establishment of a Banking Control Committee to be headed by the finance minister and to be responsible for the utilization of funds. In addition, it proposed that half of each banks' managers would be selected from among its employees (Colbert, 1952: 90). The resemblance to France's postwar socialist policies is striking.

At first, American General Headquarters (GHQ) actively promoted labor unions, but as the Cold War began and the communist threat increased, GHQ modified its policies. After ordering the cancellation of the General Strike on February 1, 1947, General MacArthur directed Prime Minister Yoshida to hold a general election in April in order to alleviate social unrest. The Japan Socialist Party's (JSP) subsequent election victory brought Japan's first socialist government to power (Koshiro, 2000); they won a plurality of seats, but the right-wing combination of Liberal and Democratic parties prevented any effective left-wing legislation from being passed. GHQ became increasingly worried about the rise of communism and the growing strength of labor, so as of July 1948, national civil servants were deprived of the right to strike via a change in the National Civil Service Law.

The election on January 24, 1949 shattered the Socialist Party, whose seats fell from 143 to 48 in the Lower House, while the Communist Party was strengthened, winning 35 seats and nearly 10 percent of the vote. The overall result, however, was a swing to the Right and Yoshida became premier of the new post-election government. Yoshida now moved the anti-union struggle into high gear. This took two forms: (1) extensive subversion of left-wing unions from within, via "democratization leagues" or *mindō*; and (2) an "anti-inflationary" policy, one of whose chief features was wholesale dismissal of militant workers.

The implementation of the Dodge Plan led to firings and layoffs on a huge scale, causing the elimination of a large sector of the militant Left, and to the reorganization and strengthening of oligopoly capital. Although the Dodge Plan involved expanding big industry and therefore employment in big industry, the reorganization was used carefully to weed out militant workers and to weaken the union movement. In 1949 alone, 435,465 workers were dismissed from their jobs, and around 300,000 more in 1950. In the same period, the number of unions declined by over 5,500 and union membership fell by 880,000. The government purges were accompanied by direct promotion of the anti-communist *mindō* (Halliday, 1978: 217–220).

As the old workers' union (Sanbetsu) and the left were gravely weakened, the Yoshida government, the Employers' Federation (Nikkeiren), and GHQ worked towards a new union coalition based largely on the *mindō*. The new federation, Sōhyō, was founded in July 1950, immediately after the purge of the Japan Communist Party and the start of the Korean War. As the head of Sōhyō wrote in 1965: "the history of the foundation of Sōhyō is closely connected with the fight against the domination of the Japanese trade unions by the Communist Party" (Halliday, 1978: 220). Just after the formation of Sōhyō, Sanbetsu membership dropped to 47,000, and in 1953 it went down to 13,000. The Federation was dissolved on February 15, 1958. Sōhyō's domestic platform and the wrecking of the Sanbetsu were a major victory for business in imposing the seniority wage system and intra-enterprise unions (Halliday, 1978: 220).

To retain the loyalty of the remaining workers, managers offered them lifetime employment (Price, 1997: 253). Labor wanted to have influence over the form of corporate financing, making it long term to suit its employment stability goals. However, labor was weakened, and its economic initiatives were stymied by America's intervention to quell the growing communist threat. But, as Gilson and Roe (1999) assert, "Because labor retained potential political influence despite the fact that managers recovered workplace authority in the early 1950s, the government wanted [the lifetime employment] bargain [forged in the wake of the labor strife of the late 1940s] to remain stable." Indeed, the postwar constitution contains a "right to employment" clause that commits government policy to full employment, and legal norms of lifetime employment arose through active courtroom struggles of unions against abusive dismissals of labor activists during the 1940s and 1950s. Japanese courts required employers to show "just cause" for the dismissal of regular employees, since dismissals were (and are) normally considered an "abuse of right" that shifts the burden of proof to employers. Thus, firms have had to exhaust alternative measures of reorganization and employment adjustment, thereby strengthening union involvement (Hanami, 1989). Furthermore, employment security has been supported by effective cross-class alliances with business to make political demands for state support of jobs and employment adjustment in declining industries (Kume, 1998). Subsequently, the government would intervene by forcing delegated main banks to bail out weak affiliated industrial firms (Aoki, 1994). Thus, lifetime employment began and endured as a political bargain, with long-term financing arising alongside it as a necessary component of that bargain.

Summary

Farmers were important to the creation of the FILP, postal savings bank, and the pension system; each of these influenced the early bias towards patient corporate financing. Of course, farmers also increased agricultural financing and bolstered government intervention in the economy. Insofar as Roe (2003) finds that long-term financing arose as a complement to employment stability, but not necessarily as a result of labor's bargaining power, farmers may fill the causal void through their creation of various intermediation channels that fostered patient lending arrangements. Because financial institutions tend to complement one another (as seen in Table 3.4), once these long-term financing mechanisms were in place, they reinforced this long-term orientation in the broader financial system.

The post-occupation evolution

While Japan became interventionist like France, it has coped with globalization more successfully owing to the intrafirm labor–capital bargains, as in Germany.

As capital's position has improved with globalization, Japan's capitalist system has moved in the direction of the United States in some ways (the size of its equities market), although certain laws and regulations give more of a role to labor than in the US, and Japan's institutional structure preserves many of the differences (e.g., less diffuse ownership, which helps labor's employment stability). This is in contrast to Germany – the country to which Japan is frequently compared – where labor has entrenched its power more firmly via the structure of the political institutions, but which lacks farmers' political influence.

Here, I discuss how political institutions (and the manner in which they magnify or diminish actors' power) have constrained and biased the evolutionary path of the financial system.

FARMERS

During most of the postwar period, Japanese government's agricultural spending has been higher than that of any other major industrialized nation (Calder, 1990: 235). This spending has come in the form of a variety of specialized programs designed primarily to cater to the constituent interests of Japan's Dietmen from rural or semi-rural districts. For example, Calder (1988: 236) finds that in early 1983, 195 LDP Dietmen, or 68.2 percent of the ruling party members in the Diet, were members of the LDP's Agricultural Committee – the highest participation rate on any LDP committee.[14]

Following the capital shortage and system of directed finance during the Occupation, the postwar electoral system created incentives for politicians to favor local support groups with "pork"; consequently, there has been a clear and pronounced bias towards local government expenditures and financing institutions that cater to local business such as farmers and small firms, including the mutual loan and savings banks, credit associations, rural financial associations, and the Trust Fund Bureau.[15] The increasing proportion of funds for small business may be seen in Tables 5.3a and 5.3b.

The mutual loan and savings banks (or *sogo* banks) are large lenders to small businesses (wholesale, retail, and construction firms). The credit associations are similar to credit unions in Western countries; their capital comes from fees paid by association members, and deposits and lending are offered primarily to members. Their operations are highly localized and target the same clients as the

Table 5.3a Changes in the shares of total employable funds of Japanese financial institutions, 1955–1980

Institutions	1955	1960	1965	1970	1975	1980
City banks	33.1	29.7	24.9	22	19.3	16.5
Local banks	16.1	15.5	15.5	14.1	13.5	12.6
Long-term credit banks	4.6	5.1	6.1	5.7	5.7	4.8
Trust banks	4.4	7.6	6.9	7.3	7.2	7.2
Mutual loan and savings banks	5.7	5.8	7.2	6.1	6.2	5.7
Credit associations	4.0	5.1	7.5	8.1	8.2	7.7
Rural financial associations	5.3	4.4	7.1	7.9	8.0	7.4
Insurance companies	3.5	4.6	6.0	7.1	6.6	7.1
Trust Fund Bureau (postal savings)	11.6	10.3	8.8	10.6	13.1	17.4
Others	11.7	11.9	10.0	11.1	12.2	13.6
Total	100	100	100	100	100	100

Source: Bank of Japan and Bronte (1982: 15).

sogo banks. Rural financial organizations comprise institutions serving farmers (the Nokyo: agricultural cooperatives), fishermen (the Gyoko: fishery cooperatives), and foresters (Shrinrinkumiai: forestry cooperatives). Nokyo are by far the largest of the three.[16]

The high level of agricultural spending has been largely due to an unusually wide range of subsidies. In fiscal 1984, for example, approximately 15.5 percent of Japan's extraordinarily high subsidy budget went to agriculture, to support nearly one-third of the 1,500 line items subsidized in the national budget as a whole. And subsidies comprised around 60 percent of the Ministry of Agriculture's annual budget. Most of these funds are designed to cater to the constituent interests of Japan's large number of Dietmen from agricultural or semi-agricultural districts. And a large fraction of Japan's heavy public works spending (four times the share of GNP which public works represent in the United States and twice the share in France) is concentrated in the countryside, providing part-time work for farmers (Calder, 1989).[17]

SMALL FIRMS

In addition to policies amplifying small firms' lending via private banks and cooperatives, government-funded institutions catering to small business (via the FILP) have expanded their activities considerably in the postwar period. For example, the People's Finance Corporation, founded in June 1949, lends primarily to extremely small enterprises. By 1986, the PFC's annual loan volume was nearly that of the Export-Import Bank of Japan, with no-collateral loans its major financial product. This system of no-collateral loans is without analogue in the industrialized world, and enabled the PFC to grow explosively in the 1970s.

Table 5.3b Changes in the shares of total employable funds of Japanese financial institutions, 1985–2005 (hundreds of millions of ¥)

Institutions	1985	1990	1995	2000	2005	% change 1985–2005
City banks	14.4	29.4	26	25.8	29.5	104.8
Regional banks	14.3	23.6	26.8	28.1	28.9	102
Trust banks			1.8	2.6		
Long-term credit banks	0.6	1.5	1.1	0.8		
Financial institutions for small business[a]	9.3	15	19	20	20.9	124.7
Financial institutions for agriculture, forestry, and fishery[b,c]	9.9	14	18.5	18.8	22.6	128.2

Source: Bank of Japan online statistical database.

Notes
a Includes Shinkin Banks, Shinkin Central Bank, Shoko Chukin Bank, Credit Cooperatives, Shinkmuni Federation Bank, Labor Credit Associations, and the National Federation of Labor Credit Associations.
b Includes Norinchukin Bank, Agricultural Cooperatives, Credit Federation of Agricultural Cooperatives, Fishery Cooperatives, and the Prefectural Federation of Fishery Cooperatives.
c Excluding data for fishery cooperatives and the prefectural federation of fishery cooperatives, the change from 1985 to 2005 is 133.4%.

Government lenders to small business have grown in importance – by 1990, the two government financial institutions originally seen by strategists as the heart of government financial operations; the JDB and the Exim Bank were only the fifth and sixth largest recipients of FILP funds. They were dwarfed in scale by other politically inspired banks devoted to housing and small-business credit (Calder, 1990: 320; 1993).

Beyond directly supplying credit, the Japanese government also facilitates extensive credit guarantees to small businesses that borrow from private banks through the Small Business Credit Insurance Corporation, created in 1985. The scale of this is huge, comparable to the total loans made by the other small business lending institutions. In addition to the government banks, a complex structure of ambiguously defined off-budget public "units" expanded rapidly during the 1960s. A few of these new creations had clear strategic objectives, but these were few in number and received relatively little funding. The vast majority of the new entities supported by the FILP – receiving 94 percent in 1990 of total FILP funds not allocated to the government banks described above – specialized in supporting the operation of local post office (25 percent of funding), construction (21 percent), local government (20 percent), and pension subsidies (18 percent). The overall objectives of these institutions were primarily political (Calder, 1993).

The smaller banks were treated even better, despite heavy funds demand, for example, the access of the city banks to new funding sources was strictly limited; regional banks during the 1955 to 1973 period were allowed to expand their branching network three times as rapidly as were the city banks, despite having a lower demand for loans (Calder, 1993).

LABOR AND CAPITAL

In the postwar period, large firms remained politically powerful, but lost their monopoly on influencing financial policy because of the newcomers to the political stage. Capital shortages during the immediate postwar period, which fostered the continuance of wartime bank–firm relationship financing, were exacerbated by the US placing extensive orders with Japanese firms in its war with Korea, begun on June 25, 1950. Both of these circumstances forced industries to rely heavily on bank lending.[18]

However, firms remained reliant on banks even after these situations improved as a result of the government's economic strategy (via MITI) to improve Japanese firms' competitiveness, especially with regard to American firms (Johnson, 1982). From 1953 to 1961 the direct supply of capital by the government to industry (as opposed to its indirect supply via overloans) ranged from 38 percent to 19 percent. Financial institutions such as the Japan Development Bank and the Export-Import Bank of Japan served government needs for channeling funds into politically favored industries especially during the 1950s and 1960s.[19] The city banks were the dominant providers of funds during 1955 to 1975, consistently supplying over 60 percent of external funds acquired by the firms (Hoshi and Kashyap, 2001).

Summary

During the period 1952 to 1973, Japanese bond and equity markets suffered from regulations discouraging their use. Bond yields were generally kept lower than at market-clearing rate, deterring investors from buying bonds. Equity markets suffered from low levels of individual wealth following World War II, postwar inflation and land reforms which wiped out most wealthy business families and landlords. Moreover, interest payments on debt financing were deductible, offering a further disincentive to equity financing. Equity and bond issues that did occur were subject to rationing according to government-determined priorities (Hoshi and Kashyap, 2001).

From the mid-1970s onward, Japanese firms began turning to capital markets with increasing frequency to meet their financing needs, first in London and then returning to Tokyo as Japanese banks began offering competitive investment banking services (Rosenbluth, 1989; Hoshi and Kashyap, 2001). However, the cross-shareholding patterns that preserve a longer term corporate strategy remained intact. Indeed, modern Japan continues to display institutional rigidities emanating from the bargain struck after World War II. Gourevitch and Shinn

(2005) attest, "Among the major industrial countries, Japan seems the least responsive to the supposed Darwinian pressure of international capital flows in forcing governance reform toward the shareholder value model." Dore (2000) echoes this sentiment: "Japanese savings are going to remain more modest in proportion and to find their way into the global economy through bank lending, rather than through asset managers operating in secondary markets all over the globe." This reliance on banking is consistent with farmers' heavy political influence (aided by that of small firms) and their support for (and ability to veto changes to) numerous government-sponsored lending institutions, notably those associated with the FILP (since postal savings are directed through it); indeed, small farmers in Japan do not wish to see their savings flooding out of their control and into the international marketplace (draining out of the interior to urban centers, as small American farmers likewise feared in the early twentieth century). They retain a strong interest in propping up the banking system, and resisting a "move to the market."

Recent developments in the corporate sector reflect the general resistance to change, and the implementation of new mechanisms to defend it. For example, in reaction to takeover battles heating up in the past few years (e.g., Livedoor's bid for Nippon Broadcasting System in 2005), civil servants from the economy, trade, and industry ministry (METI) are advancing "right plans" – i.e., poison pills – as part of a new set of corporate takeover rules.[20] When METI crafted its guidelines, it broadly defined four categories of "harmful bidders," including greenmailers (a strategy used to generate a large amount of money from attempted hostile takeovers), asset strippers and those wishing to engage in "scorched-earth" management.[21] The four tests outlined by METI show the focus is on corporate interests in the wider sense rather than purely shareholder interests according to Julian Pritchard, partner at Freshfields, Bruckhaus Deringer, a leading law firm. In this regard, although a takeover may be in the interests of shareholders, it may fail to pass METI's four tests. As further evidence of protecting the post-World War II bargain, in late 2006, the government began encouraging companies to buy each other's shares as a protective measure against hostile takeover attempts.[22] In the first half of 2007, more than 15 percent of listed companies (over 300) installed poison pill defenses.[23] And on September 6, 2007 the government implemented the most radical overhaul of Japan's inward investment regulations in 16 years with another barrier against foreign takeovers that imposes tough controls on non-Japanese acquisitions of more than 10 percent of domestic companies which have technology that can be used in weapons systems. They replace a non-specific technology protection regime with a list covering 137 products including technologies involving titanium, batteries, and semiconductors. The rules will apply for the first time to bluechip companies, such as Nippon Steel which has advanced titanium technology, and electronics groups, such as Sony, Toshiba, and Sharp owing to their semiconductor and battery interests. Foreign observers are concerned that the new rules would be used to block politically sensitive foreign takeovers, rather than to protect national security.[24]

Conclusions

The German and Japanese political economies have resembled each other during much of the postwar era, with long-term employment stability complementing patient financing. These countries' institutions were created under the watchful eye of the United States in both cases, which intervened to prevent labor's direct control over the financial system, as emerged in France. But they do not match each other perfectly. Of particular importance is the role of Japanese farmers. They have contributed significantly to sustaining the institutions and policies of the country's coordinated market economy with favorable deposit rates, and other perquisites, via the postal savings banks. This led to a high accumulation of funds for the government, which were used to finance industry, and saved these firms from turning to securities markets and diluting their ownership. This helped Japanese firms build and sustain their intercorporate ownership structures (and which contributed to managerial power). Thus, through their important role in the creation of the FILP, and the policies of the postal savings bank, farmers have contributed to Japanese firms' reliance on patient capital. And insofar as Roe (2003) finds that long-term financing arose as a complement to employment stability, but not necessarily as a result of labor's bargaining power, farmers may fill the causal void through their creation of various intermediation channels that fostered patient lending arrangements. Because financial institutions tend to complement one another (as seen in Table 3.4), once these long-term financing mechanisms were in place, they reinforced this long-term orientation in the broader financial system. Indeed, farmers have played an important complementary role to labor. Farmers have created mechanisms external to the firm that preserve a reliance on bank lending; Japan's financial system, and the forces that preserve it, cannot be properly understood without considering farmers' important role (and subsequently joined with the support of small firms whose power was magnified via the electoral system). Indeed, incorporating farmers into an understanding of Japan's financial system helps to explain how and why it is different from Germany, or the US, or France – countries with bargains between two actors.

6 Urban vs. rural cleavages

When farmers battle against a political power-sharing coalition of labor and capital owners, rural–urban cleavages emerge. When farmers win, an agrarian CME arises, as exemplified by the early nineteenth-century United States. Local banking facilities are expected to dominate. As the economy industrializes, increasing government intervention is expected to occur along with corresponding pressures for the diffusion of corporate ownership. These latter two features are examined in the context of the twentieth-century case. Moreover, pensions are unlikely to emerge in an agriculturally based economy, since it is only with the advent of industrialization and the labor movement that pressure for them arose, at which point farmers would form a coalition with labor in favor of publicly administered pensions.

When labor and capital owners win, the classic example of a CME develops, as in post-World War II Germany. Financial assets are expected to be more specific than the LME cases, though more general than the Mediterranean or Agrarian or Statist CME cases as a result of pressure for concentrated corporate ownership, pensions that exhibit public and private elements, a centralized banking system, and indirect (or muted) government intervention. In this chapter, I discuss these two cases.

Farmers win: rural case

United States, early nineteenth century

The early US financial system is an excellent example of what happens when farmers control the policymaking machinery of government. In most countries, farmers' political influence has been heavily muted by the arrangement of the political institutions. In pre-World War II France and Japan, and Imperial Germany, small farmers lacked political power since the Upper House, where the elite's power was concentrated, could block, or override, the Lower House's initiatives where farmers were represented. In other countries, such as the UK and Canada, other groups (e.g., business owners or foreign powers who generally acted on behalf of their commercial interests) were politically powerful enough to force a compromise with farmers. In few instances have farmers dominated political institutions as much as they did in the early nineteenth-century US. In addition, American industrial/manufacturing firms (primarily in the northeast) were small enough that they did not oppose the emerging bank-dominated financial structure. As a result, regulatory power over the American financial system was largely determined at the state (local) level, with wide-ranging financial system implications, including the fragmentation of the banking system, and the eventual diffusion of corporate ownership in the twentieth century (Roe, 1994).

The financial system

In the early US, stock markets were of negligible importance. In the industrial northeast, where markets were most likely to emerge to meet the financing needs of the growing manufacturing sector, Lamoreaux explains that, "At that time, scarcity of information and the modest scale of enterprise had combined to keep credit markets localized and financial institutions small" (1991: 539). New England's banks were a primary source of funding for New England industrialists, and relationships between bankers and the owners of commercial enterprises determined lending decisions; in many cases, the officers and directors of the banks were their principal borrowers (Lamoreaux, 1994). The rest of the country, which was dominated by agriculture, likewise relied on lending from banks.

Banking regulation was primarily determined at the state, rather than the federal, level. Failed attempts at national banking can be explained by identifying the dominant interest groups and their reasons for opposing it. In doing so, it will become clear that the early United States was an agrarian coordinated market economy, in which close relationships between local banks and the clients to whom they made loans characterized the nature of the economic landscape.

The founding of the United States was unusual among developed democracies because farmers were the unquestionably dominant economic group at the time, and they wielded *real* political power. In many other countries that had democratic rules of some sort (often not until later in the nineteenth or early twentieth century after industrialization had begun, at which point workers and capital also began exerting significant political influence), small farmers' political power was heavily muted, since the Lower House, to which they frequently elected representatives, could usually be overridden by other branches of government that were more sympathetic to the interests of capital. This makes the early nineteenth-century United States a particularly useful case for examining financial system outcomes when farmers clearly dominate politics.

The dominance of local (state) interests over the federal government was reflected in the government's first three attempts at chartering a national bank. In the first instance, the Bank of North America was chartered by the Confederacy in 1781 to help finance the Revolution. It was the first commercial bank in the United States, and was soon forced to abandon its controversial national charter to take up business as a state-chartered bank, first in Delaware, and later, in 1787, in Pennsylvania (Hurst, 1973: 7).

Despite constitutional and political controversies surrounding the federal chartering of a nationwide bank, the first Bank of the United States (BUS) was founded by Alexander Hamilton in 1791. It was delegated with performing a variety of specific tasks (marketing government debt, collecting government revenues, subsidized lending to the government). Despite its considerable success in performing financial services for the federal government, its 20-year charter was not renewed in 1811 (Calomiris, 2000: 46). The war of 1812 led to the chartering of the second BUS in 1816 to raise badly needed funds for the federal government. Subsequent controversy over whether the bank constituted a national monopoly (particularly with regard to its dual roles in lending and currency issuing) caused its rechartering to be vetoed by the President, and not overridden by Congress, in 1836 (Schweikart, 1988). Consequently, from 1836 until 1863, there was no federal government presence in the chartering of banks.

Politics

The federal government's institutional structure led to the devolution of regulatory authority to the state level with regard to banking. This dominance of states' rights was preserved by Congress in three ways. First, elected officials to the House of Representatives depended on the support of local groups in their home constituency for re-election, comprised largely of farming interests during the early nineteenth century. Consequently, members would support legislation that assisted local farmers, including the preservation and strengthening of local banking facilities, placing the regulatory authority of them at the local level, and defeating efforts that could erode this financial structure (e.g., interstate bank branching). This accountability to the local constituency stands in contrast to some other countries' electoral systems where voters must choose between party lists, as opposed to a specific representative for the local district, which lessens the need for individual politicians to cater to local interest groups.

Second, the Senate helped to preserve farmers' power by granting every state the same number of senators. This would later lead to considerable malapportionment in favor of rural states, which would give agricultural interests sufficient political power to block changes to the banking system, and preserve the status quo as constructed in the early nineteenth century, and as detailed by Roe (1994). This was not of great importance to the banking system of the early nineteenth century, but it would become highly important in preventing changes to it in the twentieth century.

The third way in which Congress helped to keep banking regulations set at the local level was by its influence over Supreme Court nominees who were frequently selected for their support of states' rights. As a result of this emphasis, the Supreme Court did not extend constitutional protection to banking as an activity involving interstate commerce, thereby opening the way to state regulatory prohibitions on bank activities across and within states during the nineteenth and most of the twentieth century (Calomiris, 2000: 68).

While farmers dominated the political and economic landscape of the nation, cleavages did exist between different regions. Regional groupings included southern plantation owners and slaveholders versus smaller northwestern farmers versus a small but growing industrialist population in the northeast. The nature of their economic activity led to preferences for different banking structures. In the south, wealthy slaveholders favored branching since the dominant form of collateral in the antebellum period was slaves rather than land (Kilbourne, 1995); there was little advantage from bonding the banker to a particular locale, as other non-slaveholding farmers would prefer. In the antebellum Northeast, branching restrictions were not an important constraint on the dominant economic class – merchants and industrialists – since they benefited by the creation of charter rents to the extent that they could use their control of banks to improve their own costs of credit. In the northwest, the middle-class farmer would carry the day with variations on location-specific banks (unit banks). In the mutual-guaranty systems of Indiana, Ohio, and Iowa (where banks joined a small cooperative network that offered mutual protection, self-regulation, and enforcement), farmers received many of the benefits of branching (particularly lower interest rates and lower risks of bank failure), while retaining the advantages of location-specific bank capital. Other banking systems of the northwest opted simply for unit-free banks (anyone willing to abide by a common set of state regulations could open a unit bank); none authorized free entry in the form of branch banks (Calomiris, 2000).

The pro-unit banking agricultural states of the northwest tended to dominate the congressional committees that controlled banking regulation. They accomplished this via congressional "horse-trading" over committee appointments (Calomiris, 2000: 68–69). Since the northeast was the region for which competition for seats would have occurred (between the south and the northwest), northwestern representatives won out since representatives from the northeast preferred to trade their seats to members who also opposed slavery. And once slavery was abolished, unit banking gained further political support from southern farmers.

Another interesting facet of early American banking that resembles later CME capitalist systems (with extensive labor power) is the intervention by the government in the banking system. In the period before the Panic of 1837, state governments were frequently involved in the ownership and governance of banks. And generally speaking, the more heavily a bank was involved in agricultural lending, the more public involvement it had. Banks set up to provide commercial loans in economically established areas fell closest to the private end of the continuum (Calomiris, 2000: 43–46; Hoffmann, 2001: 75). Existing explanations attribute this intervention to the public's mistrust of concentrating financial power in the hands of private bank owner; however, the heavy involvement of the state in determining geographic and functional credit distribution in addition to bank regulation suggests that underlying political interests were at play. Additional research in this area would likely offer interesting results illustrating the nature of political interests influencing how government decided which, and where, unit banks were chartered, as well as the distribution of credit throughout

a state (similar to the way in which the post-World War II French labor government directed credit to specific industries partly as a way to ensure employment
stability).

In the antebellum period, pensions were unimportant, although they did come
to prominence as a result of the Civil War (Skocpol, 1992). These were administered by the government, and were purely redistributed from current taxes. Thus,
they did not facilitate the development of securities markets by being placed in
the hands of private pension funds.

Summary

The early nineteenth-century US financial system was banking-oriented, with
direct government intervention in favor of agricultural interests and a corresponding bias towards agricultural financing, and nonexistent pension funding.
In sum, the early US financial system displays the key attributes of an agrarian-
oriented CME. Relationships dominated the organization of economic activity,
with political institutions amplifying the political power of local farmers and
small business.

Capital and labor win: urban case

Germany, post-World War II

The origins of German capitalism may be located in its industrializing period in
the late nineteenth century. But after World War I, labor gained considerable
political influence which led to democratic changes to the country's political
institutions (with the Weimar Constitution), and to changes regarding certain
elements of its financial system, including corporate governance rules. However,
the peace and stability of the interwar period was short-lived, denying the new
political arrangements from having a meaningful impact on the country's financial system. Not until after World War II did Germany's financial institutions
reflect attributes that resulted from a second bargain struck between labor and
capital, with political institutions cementing these outcomes and delimiting
change in the following decades.

The bargain struck between labor and capital after World War II provided the
political basis for the perpetuation of Germany's banking-oriented financial
system, though with important differences to its prewar architecture. Following
World War II, Germany became somewhat more banking-oriented via an ele-
vated reliance on bank lending and proxy voting (but less bank-oriented than
France), witnessed moderately increased government intervention in the
economy with banks acting as policy allies of the federal and especially the
Lander governments (though with less intervention than in Japan or France),
modestly increased its financing of the agricultural sector (modest in comparison
to Japan and France), and expanded its pension system (both public and private)
in ways that preserved the reliance on patient capital. These financial system

changes correspond to the following key changes to the political system: a postwar bargain between labor and capital; more political power for labor, farmers, and small firms via a stronger legislature; a consensus political system which would make formal regulatory changes difficult as a result of numerous veto-points; and more decentralized political institutions via Lander-based representation in the Bundesrat, to the particular benefit of the Mittelstand (small and medium-sized firms).

I first discuss changes along the key dimensions of Germany's financial system from its pre-World War II structure to its post-World War II form, including the banking system, government intervention, securities markets, agricultural financing, and pensions. I then explain how changes to the political power of the key groups representing land, labor, and capital shifted the financial system on to a new path, and how political institutions cemented these bargains. Finally, I consider the contemporary implications.

The financial system

Following World War II, the financial system became more banking-oriented, government intervention increased, agricultural financing increased (though more mildly than postwar France or Japan), and public pension programs were expanded. Overall, post-World War II Germany's financial system embodied features characteristic of a coordinated market economy, with relationships among actors central to its organization.

THE BANKING SYSTEM

German banking has largely been Lande-based since German unification in 1871, mirroring Germany's fragmented political structure. During the Nazi era, banking came increasingly under the control of the national government; however, the institutionalization of decentralized political power following World War II put the regulation of banking – particularly savings and cooperative banking – back in Lander hands. To understand the structure of German banking following World War II, it is useful to briefly trace its evolution since Germany's rapid industrialization period.

In the nineteenth century, enterprises' growing demand for financing from industrialization received a boost with German unification, which gave way to the commercial banks building continuous financial relations with large firms. Thus was born the German tradition of the "house bank," which featured prominently in Gerschenkron's work. However, as Guinnane (2001) argues, the savings and cooperative banks were also of great importance to Germany's economic development. The commercial banks (or "house" banks) focused on the large firms, the savings banks focused on small firms, farmers, and craftsmen, and participated in government projects, and the cooperative banks tended to lend primarily to the Mittelstand (small and medium-sized firms, including craftsmen and farmers).

Industrialization intensified pressure on the Mittelstand to modernize production, with capital demands outstripping the available supply of finance from savings and cooperative banks. This, and other pressures, led savings and cooperative banks to form regional associations that could offer liquidity relief to members, as well as to lobby Lander governments on relevant policy proposals (Deeg, 1999). Mirroring the fragmented political structure in the wake of its unification in 1871, the regulation of Germany's savings and cooperative banks was almost completely determined at the Lander level. Indeed, not until 1931 did the German government implement its first comprehensive national banking regulations.

As industrialization proceeded apace, the commercial banks extended their branching network out of urban centers to increase their deposit base for lending to meet the financing demands of the large industrial enterprises. Consequently, credit began to be diverted to urban areas and financing began to be deprived from the Mittelstand firms. For this reason, Lander governments passed legislation allowing savings and cooperative banks to compete more effectively with commercial banks by adopting some of their universal banking services (e.g., by allowing the creation of central clearinghouses to carry out interbank transfers, to hold securities on deposit, and to implement checking accounts). By the 1920s, the hierarchical model of the commercial banks (with lending services conducted in the cities and with deposit-taking branches in the interior) and the association model of the savings and cooperative banks (with multiple banks forming a cooperative arrangement to assist one another) reached their mature form, and the basis for competition among these groups at the local, regional, and national levels was in place (Deeg, 1999).

During the Great Depression, commercial banks were hit hardest. The banking commission charged with making policy recommendations after the crisis argued that the overextension of credit on easy terms to large firms by commercial banks – and to the detriment of small and medium-sized firms – was one of the causes of the 1931 crisis, and led to Germany's first comprehensive national banking regulation.[1] Subsequently, the 1934 Imperial Bank Sector Law was enacted, which reconfirmed the right of the savings banks to exercise commercial banking activities, and the government focused on preserving liquidity in the banking system by redirecting capital away from large firms towards the Mittelstand. The major commercial banks would not reach the same equity capital levels of 1913 until well after World War II; the savings and cooperative banks, by contrast, reattained their 1913 equity levels by the late 1930s. As the vast majority of savings deposits were held by the cooperatives and savings banks, they became the primary intermediaries of war finance. By sustaining their favorable asset growth into the postwar period, savings and cooperative banks began the postwar era in a relatively favorable position relative to the big commercial banks (Deeg, 1999).

To prevent the concentration of financial power, the allies broke the three big banks into a total of 30 independent regional banks and attempted to implement a US-style financial system. But as the Cold War intensified, Allied policy

towards the new Federal Republic was increasingly concerned with reconstructing a successful economy. Thus the banks were allowed to gradually reconsoli-
date, a process completed by 1957 (Deeg, 1999).

GOVERNMENT INTERVENTION

Following the war, close relationships between the banks and the government
developed largely because the Lander were seeking a bank that could help them
administer the vast number of reconstruction programs, as well as serve their
general financial needs. The savings banks were largely willing to accommodate
them because they needed scarce capital, and because it would reduce the proba-
bility that Land governments would establish a competing bank for these functions. Cooperative banks also served as an important channel through which
state funds (including Marshall Plan funds) flowed to rebuild the Mittelstand.
This relationship strengthened the position of the savings and cooperative banks
with government officials, to the benefit of these banks and their clients. Moreover, the new political institutions decentralized political power and gave the
Lander considerable regulatory authority over the banking sector.

The Kreditanstalt für Wiederaufbau (KfW) (Reconstruction Loan Corporation) was also established to pump money into the German economy from the
Counterpart Fund (set up to handle Marshall Aid). The KfW was used to supple-
ment the resources of the ordinary commercial banks. The managers of the KfW
generally followed the advice of the commercial banks about where to invest
since they were the most knowledgeable about where funds were most needed,
and the officials of the KfW sought to complement the banks rather than direct
or compete with them. Practically speaking, the KfW's influence was quite
limited since the total amount of money involved was not very large; it averaged
3.5 percent of gross investment during the 1949 to 1953 period (Shonfield, 1965:
277).

From the mid-1950s onward, the KfW focused on bottlenecks which commercial banking tended to overlook. In this regard, it would take a longer view
of the probable return on an investment than would an ordinary commercial
lender. For example, it focused on areas requiring special assistance under the
government's regional development schemes (Shonfield, 1965: 278–282). This
style of government intervention – via the KfW – is emblematic of the government's broader interventionist strategy; it largely stayed out of direct influence
on investment and simply supported or complemented rather than directed or
competed with the private sector.

SECURITIES MARKETS

Germany's securities markets developed alongside the growth of the industrial
enterprises and the commercial banks who worked with them in the late nineteenth and early twentieth century (e.g., Fohlin, 2005; Franks et al., 2006). In
contrast to the US where equity was sold to a wide swathe of individual share-

holders, equity was sold in blocks by family owners and then bought by other corporations – which led to a system of corporate pyramids and intercorporate holdings – or, to a lesser degree, outside investors (Franks *et al.*, 2006).

As a result of the stock market crash in the early 1890s, and banking failures in Berlin in 1891, the German government passed the Exchange Act of 1896. The act assisted the development of the securities market by making the underwriters and promoters of share issues jointly liable for any false statements in a company's prospectus (Emery, 1898). These measures benefited the large universal banks which operated as jobbers (a middleman who exchanges securities between brokers) on the stock exchange as well as promoters of securities. As a result, banks traded on their own account as well as making markets in securities, creating the potential for both conflicts of interest and monopoly.

> A very interesting result of these practices is the development of the banks as independent markets for securities.... In this way an increasing volume of business is being done outside the exchange, and this is greatly stimulated by the restrictions the new legislation puts on exchange trading. The exchange in so far declines in importance, and the large banks through whom this business goes become increasingly influential.... The recently published bank reports for the year 1897 show a material gain over 1896 in the earnings of the large banks from commissions.
>
> (Emery, 1898: 311, 319)

Companies became dependent on banks for access to securities markets, and banks abused their role as custodians for minority shareholders to their own benefit (Franks and Mayer, 1998). So, although de jure measures assisted the development of securities markets (e.g., Securities Exchange Act of 1896), de facto practices discouraged many investors from using them and led to their underdevelopment.

In the early 1930s, stock markets were widely held by the Nazi government to have exacerbated the financial crisis through the investment of capital in "speculative" instead of "productive" purposes, and severe restrictions were subsequently placed on them (Vitols, 2001).[2]

After the war, German authorities continued to discourage the use of stock markets as a source of capital for industry.[3] Consequently, the number of companies listed on the stock exchanges declined throughout the postwar period until the late 1980s and new equity issues were infrequent. Company debt came almost completely through long-term bank loans instead of bonds (Vitols, 2001: 187).

With regard to corporate governance, bank ownership of large firms increased incrementally during the first half of the twentieth century, reaching a peak in the 1940s. Intercorporate ownership accelerated in the 1930s, while individual ownership declined over the first half of the century (Franks *et al.*, 2006). After the war, banks and corporations became the major controlling shareholders of large firms which is significant owing to the postwar changes in corporate governance that granted employees more influence, and because of the Allied attempts to dismantle family ownership even further, with banks subsequently filling the vacuum. Consequently, bank and employee influence over corporate decision-making (via intercorporate share ownership) became substantially greater in the postwar years. Moreover, banks' role as policy allies of the government, in which labor had a substantially louder voice, contributed further to employees' influence on corporate strategy and organization.

Even though internal financing may matter more as a source of financing for German firms than bank lending (Edwards and Fischer, 1994), this form of financing helped preserve the existing reliance on patient capital (by preventing the need to meet shareholders' quarterly earnings expectations).

PENSIONS

After the war, pensions across Europe became more universalistic, following the surge in labor's political power (Baldwin, 1990). In Germany, however, most groups opposed the Allied powers' pension program, thereby delaying the adoption of a universalistic pension system until the late 1950s, although a public pension system was implemented.

In the prewar period, pension programs were constructed for separate groups, such as workers, farmers, and independents (farmers, artisans, shopkeepers, liberal professionals such as doctors and lawyers) (Baldwin, 1990: 96–99, 186–187; Manow, 2001a: 110–118). After the war, the Allies attempted to implement universalistic pensions in order to raise much needed fund to rebuild the country. They sought to incorporate a large swathe of the population in the scheme in a clearly redistributive fashion, but without subsidies, and forcing the system to finance itself without state assistance and with a reduction in benefits. Consequently, independents and white-collar employees could not agree to the clearly redistributive nature of the scheme. Workers also objected owing to the low benefit levels that the Allies proposed in comparison to the previous subsidized system, and farmers wanted a separate program for their own group, since the proposed plan would lead to higher contributions relative to payouts received. This fragmentation prevented the adoption of universalistic pensions, though public pensions remained the preferred administrative structure. Consequently, pensions in Germany were not extended beyond the working class during the Occupation.

Later, solidaristic reforms to the pension system were implemented, beginning with agricultural pensions in 1957, with clear redistributive outcomes. Reforms (in the form of subsidized support) were introduced by the Christian Democrats as a result of their fear of losing political support among independents – particularly farmers. The inclusion of additional groups served to cement the existing rules of the public pension system that were laid down in the years immediately following World War II, and increased the size of the public pension system. The Adenauer pension reform in 1957 brought a substantial expansionary step in welfare state spending. Expenses for pensions increased in real terms by 27 percent in 1957 alone. Mainly due to the pension reform, social spending as a share of total public spending jumped from 55 percent in 1955 to 59 percent in 1958. Total pension expenditures doubled in only three years, from 6 billion Deutschmarks in 1955 to 12 billion Deutschmarks in 1958. Moreover, corporate pension fund reserves have generally been retained by the companies as working capital and therefore have not entered the financial system (Vittas, 1978: 66). This, combined with generous pay-as-you-go public pensions, has led to a low demand for securities (Jackson & Vitols, 2001).

SUMMARY OF KEY FINANCIAL CHANGES

Five changes to the structure of the financial system following World War II are noteworthy: (1) a greater reliance on bank lending; (2) stronger bank and inter-corporate ownership, both of which led to an increase in labor's influence over corporate strategy and organization; (3) modestly increased government inter-vention in order to disburse funds to reconstruction projects through banks, bol-stering the reliance on the banking-oriented financial system; (4) mild expansion of agricultural financing; and (5) the swelling of public pension programs, espe-cially from 1958 onward. These changes correspond to the new distribution of political power among key groups following the war – particularly labor and capital – and reflect the manner in which the postwar political institutions cemented changes to the financial system. Each of these financial system changes contributed to an economic system organized by long-term relations between economic actors, mirroring the general adoption of a coordinated market economy.

Politics

How did these changes to the financial system occur? Labor, farmers, and owners of capital bargained over their structure and intended consequences. Once in place, political institutions biased and delimited changes to the financial system (and the broader capitalist system) in the postwar period.

INTERWAR PRELUDE

Germany's Weimar Constitution was one of the most liberal and democratic documents of its kind in the twentieth century in terms of allowing numerous parties from across the political spectrum to gain representation. The Parliament was made up of two layers – one represented the whole nation (the Reichstag) and made whole-nation decisions, while the other represented regions (the Reichsrat). Politicians were elected to the Reichstag through proportional repre-sentation electoral rules that allowed extreme parties to win seats, and with uni-versal suffrage for all people over 20 years of age. The Reichsrat represented regional governments within Germany, such as Prussia, Bavaria, and Saxony. The president could appoint the Chancellor with the support of a majority in the

Reichstag (generally a coalition involving the Social Democrats). The constitution was genuinely democratic, after the false democracy of Kaiser Wilhelm II, which formed the basis for Japan's Meiji Constitution.

The development of a revolutionary council movement,[4] and the role of Social Democratic politics and unions in the Weimar Republic led to the anchoring of co-determination in the Weimar Constitution and the passage of the Works Councils Law in 1920. The law mandated the formation of works councils in all commercial and public establishments with over 20 employees to be made up of a parity between elected blue-collar and white-collar employees. The supplementary law passed in 1922 allowed the Works Council to also send a maximum of two employee representatives to the supervisory board. The laws had many features of the contemporary German model: the obligation towards peaceful cooperation of the Works Council in the interests of the firm, the separation of collective bargaining from the activities of Works Councils, and co-determination rights in the personnel affairs of the firm. Works Councils served the dual purpose of protecting and representing the interests of workers while supporting the business interests of the employer. They spread to around half of all plants with over 50 employees from the mid-1920s onward. Most employers opposed the passage of the Works Council Law; however, pragmatic cooperation developed in many firms. The Weimar experiment was interrupted before co-determination could find solid footing, and, upon seizing power, the Nazi Party destroyed all autonomous labor organizations through arrests, confiscation of property, and dissolution of the organizations.

POST-WORLD WAR II LABOR–CAPITAL BARGAIN

Immediately following World War II, German unions demanded labor participation "from below" (i.e., at the shop-floor and plant level), "in the middle" (in the company boardrooms), and "from above" (via national as well as state-level economic planning agencies which were to guide – if not totally control and/or own – the major segments of the German economy, as in France). The bargaining position of workers improved considerably after the war, partly due to the continent-wide reaction to fascism and World War II, and partly as a result of the Allies' sponsorship of industry-wide labor unions. The Allies were able to sweep away the most segmented labor movement in the world, comprising trade unions divided by occupation, politics, religion, and industry, and replaced them with single trade unions for each industry, capable of agreeing and enforcing wage bargains with industry employers' associations.

This labor-friendly postwar environment enabled unions to revive their post-World War I victories "from below" with Works Councils and "in the middle" with codetermination; however, they failed to make headway "from above" largely owing to the start of the Cold War. While it would be wrong to blame the Cold War alone for the freezing of progressive reforms during the late 1940s, there can be no doubt that this geopolitical development represented a formidable obstacle to labor's goals. This led to a considerable strengthening of capital owners' interests as a result of American and British influence. In France, where Allied influence was absent, labor succeeded in exercising influence "from above" with the nationalization of the main commercial banks which were then used for directed lending to industry.

The resurrection of Works Councils was institutionalized by the Works Constitution Act of 1952. Like their interwar predecessor, these councils are elected by all blue-collar and white-collar workers in a plant and are designed to give labor the right to participate in and receive information about the management of the shop floor (O'Sullivan, 1998: 7). The Codetermination Act of 1951 granted workers parity representation on the supervisory boards of enterprises in the coal, iron, and steel industries (i.e., an equal number of shareholder and worker representatives), a dramatic increase in representation from the interwar period. The Act also stipulated that the labor director in these companies – a member of the management board – could not be appointed against the wishes of the worker representatives. Co-determination was closely related to the project of political democracy and was an attempt to prevent the political abuse of economic power that occurred under the Nazis, particularly in war-related industries. In other industries, however, workers were denied equal representation.[5]

As Streeck (1989: 131) observes, the impact of strong worker representation in German firms has led them to

> have long-term profit expectations and performance standards and high intangible investment in marketing and research, which pays only over a long period.... The emphasis on production as opposed to distribution, as institutionalized in both the finance and the industrial relations systems, corresponds to a pattern of high value-added manufacturing, which in turn is conditional upon high skills and cultivation of a continuously employed work force.

Among these firms, "financial strategies are conservative, with current profits and Hausbank credit being much more important sources of capital than equity" (Streeck, 1989: 123). For example, with regard to the automobile sector, bank representatives sit on all five supervisory boards, either as shareholders or representing the proxy votes for shares they have on deposit. Each manufacturer has a long-term standing relationship with one bank, which serves as its Hausbank. During times of difficulty, banks will intervene, as during the VW crisis of 1974 when the Deutsche Bank was crucial to stimulating reorganization by threatening, in a supervisory board meeting, to withhold further credit and let the company go to the receiver (Streeck, 1989). In this regard, labor and banks together have a significant stake and potential for influence over firms in the automobile sector.

Many large family-owned firms that were broken up by the Allies after the war reformed later. For example, by the 1970s, three of the old steel dynasties (Krupp, Klockner, and Thyssen) had reappeared as world leaders in their industry. In the case of IG Farben, however, three major successor companies had been established (Hoechst, Bayer, and BASF) by 1953, each of which survived. In all these cases, the influence of the controlling families was held back long enough by the occupying powers to allow Germany's unique voice-based corporate governance founded on employees and banks to put down roots (Buck and Tull, 2000: 127). Nevertheless, cartel-like arrangements persisted, which were viewed favorably by labor. As Karl Hardach writes:

> The continued existence of mild cartel-like arrangements partly reflected the fact that, throughout Germany's industrial history, the academic and governmental attitude toward economic concentration in general, and cartels in particular, had in principle never been one of hostility. Quite in contrast to the Anglo-American view, which connected competitive markets with equilibrium and monopolistic situations with indeterminacy and disorder, it was held that unrestricted competition was "destructive" and that cartels were an "element of order." Apart from special-interest groups favoring cartels and largely apathetic and unorganized consumers, labor unions usually expected better job security from cartels than from unrestricted competition, or regarded the former as an intermediate stage in the industrial evolution toward socialism, while small producers frequently viewed cartels as protection against being competitively beaten down or swallowed up by larger firms. If one does not subscribe to the demonization of economic bigness and industrial concentration as an act of faith, there is indeed precious little evidence that in the long run cartelization exerted detrimental influence upon growth of the German economy.
>
> (Hardach, 1980: 148)

While state-level intervention in German industry is not as common as in some other European nations, it has occurred, with labor having an important voice here as well. With regard to the process of industrial adjustment among firms in the steel and coal sectors in the Ruhr, "Major changes in the organization of production ... were shaped by a corporatist bargaining process involving the unions, the federal and Land governments, firms, and the banks" (Deeg, 1999: 126).

In summary, German labor reached a bargain with capital owners after World War II which pushed corporate strategy towards high value-added manufacturing, which in turn is conditional upon high skills and the cultivation of a continuously employed workforce. This corporate strategy has led to the development of, and sustained a reliance on, a long-term relationship with a Hausbank as well as other forms of corporate financing that minimize short-term pressures (e.g., self-financing). In this way, German labor succeeded in creating a relationship-based system of corporate finance. However, their forced bargain with capital during the Allied occupation prevented them from achieving state-level control over finance and industry, and limited the government's intervention in the economy. But with the support for a social market economy under the Lubke Plan, labor has been able to modernize the economy and reduce its reliance on the agricultural sector. While they failed to achieve universalistic pensions after the war, following the initiatives of their union counterparts elsewhere in Europe, public pension programs remained the method of coordination, with a more universalistic program eventually arriving in 1958.

FARMERS

In view of Germany's historically decentralized political system, one might expect farmers to be politically influential, as in the US. However, they were politically weak in the pre-World War I era because political institutions located their political representation in the weak Lower House of the legislature. In the post-World War II period, when political institutions granted German farmers political influence commensurate to their population size, they were politically weaker than their French counterparts for several reasons: (1) the Allies were mainly focused on generating cooperation between labor and capital, thereby depriving farmers from a seat at the bargaining table; (2) West Germany lost its agricultural heartland to East Germany and a large rural electorate along with it; and (3) German farmers have been more homogeneous in their voting patterns (mainly CDU-CSU, with some Free Democrats in the Protestant north), denying themselves the benefits of wielding a critical swing vote, which their French counterparts used to great advantage. With the exception of a lower Communist vote and a higher centerist vote, French farmers' voting patterns have generally resembled those of the rest of the electorate (Averyt, 1977: 24). German farmers also lacked the political power of Japanese farmers because they did not comprise such a large fraction of the electorate (nearly 50 percent in Japan after the war), nor did they get the same degree of over-representation in the Upper House as American farmers.

German farming did improve after the war, achieving political successes and improvements to their economic situation. Politically, the legislative–executive balance of power tilted towards the legislature after the war, following the Allies' desires to weaken executive authority, as well as populist desires to achieve a more equitable distribution of power among the federal institutions of government. Political power in the federal government also became far more decentralized, with the Lander wielding greater political influence through the Bundesrat, thereby granting more influence to local interest groups over domestic economic policies, including banking and agricultural programs.

In addition to these institutional improvements, the German Farmers' Union (Deutscher Bauernverband – DBV) was reconstituted in 1948 (after having been dissolved during the Nazi regime), and by 1951 the DBV had officially become the centralized and exclusive representative of farming interests in West Germany. The development of the DBV coincided with the re-establishment of medium- and short-term credit facilities for farmers in 1948 through the Raiffeisen bank, which actively supported the DBV (Andrlik, 1981).

However, the bargain struck between labor and capital to rebuild and modernize the economy took priority, and led to the depopulation of Germany's rural areas as new jobs were created in industry, and through efficiency-enhancing reforms to agriculture. For example, the Land Consolidation Act of

1953 – initiated within the context of the Lubke Plan which aimed to rebuild and modernize the economy – sought to reduce the number of farms through consolidation, and to make them more efficient through rationalization and mechanization (Wilson and Wilson, 2001: 41–46). The important 1955 Agricultural Act likewise sought to increase agricultural productivity and efficiency with similar kinds of programs (Neville-Rolfe, 1984). While these were framed as agricultural assistance programs, they served to reduce the agricultural population and move people into industrial jobs.

Push factors leading to rural depopulation under the Lubke Plan were complemented by pull factors as a result of economic growth during the 1950s and 1960s. By providing ample job opportunities for farmers wishing to leave the land as a result of wider changes in the West German economy, 40 percent of the people working in agriculture in 1949 had left the sector by 1963. By 1970, the agricultural working population in Germany was half that in France (Neville-Rolfe, 1984: 59).

This loss of the agricultural electorate, complemented by both the government's focus on rebuilding the country's industrial base, and its decentralized political institutions, created opportunities for the Mittelstand to fill the political vacuum at the Lander level and to reap considerable economic benefits.

POLITICAL INSTITUTIONS

Germany is a federal parliamentary democracy. Members of the Lower and Upper Houses, the Bundestag and the Budesrat, are elected with proportional representation. The Upper House, the Bundesrat, is fairly strong (less so than in the US, but more than in other European countries) and owes its power to the directives of the Allied Occupation Powers as well as to pressure exerted by various member states which suffered under Hitler. Three key features of post-World War II Germany's constitution have shaped the structure of the financial system: (1) the decentralization of power to the Lander governments which has privileged local banking for the Mittelstand; (2) a more powerful legislature that leads to more power to labor, farmers, and small firms with important consequences for corporate governance; and (3) a consensus government with numerous veto-points that prevent substantial changes to the structure of the financial system once its institutions are created. Government by coalition defines the structure of West Germany's party system and this encourages incremental policy change (Schmidt, 1985). Coalition governments led by the two major parties are about twice as frequent as single-party governments, and oversized coalitions such as the Great Coalition of the CDU-CSU and the SPD in Bonn between 1966 and 1969 have occurred frequently at the state level (Katzenstein, 1987: 40). Schmidt concludes (1985: 44) that "the bargaining process within coalitions tends to exclude extreme policy stances and issues which are highly controversial between the partners, and therefore that conditions are conducive to the diminution of policy differences." As a result, the status quo, as determined by the initial bargains after World War II, is preserved.

Contemporary implications

Germany's consensus political institutions have helped to preserve the bargains struck after World War II, notably the reliance on patient financing for large firms. Some change has occurred, but mainly in ways that follow the biasing effects of the political institutions. In particular, the decentralization of political power has led to increasing support for the Mittelstand, although they did not have a substantial influence on the initial structure of the financial system. At the same time, the Mittelstand have benefited from farmers' political weakness (relative to French, Japanese, and American farmers) since they do not face strong competition for resources channeled through local (Lander) authorities.

During the postwar period, labor has been active in finding ways to improve workers' welfare and moderate dislocations primarily by negotiating through established corporatist arrangements within large firms, but also through state–firm coordination mostly with regard to small firms. In the early postwar years, government intervention with the aid of banks was conducted in ways that complemented the market, rather than directed it, as in France. For example, in the late 1960s, the Land government of North Rhine-Westphalia adopted long-term structural adjustment policies that attempted to steer and shape market processes by altering incentives for firms. This new activism was supported by the labor unions, although the government's planning efforts usually did not go as far as they preferred.

In the 1970s the Land government became more interventionist through the use of its Landebank – the WestLB. The Land government and the WestLB attempted to influence firms and the adjustment process in the region's most important industries – coal, energy, construction, and steel. This particular case, as discussed by Deeg (1999), is the most prominent example of how some Land governments directly intervened in industry via the German system of universal banking, with labor heavily influencing the policy objectives. As Deeg (1999) concludes, "The relationship between the WestLB and the Land government ... shows how the state has influenced the institutional evolution of the banking sector according to its own economic policy goals, up to the present."

Zysman (1983) also finds close collaboration among the Land government, banks, and labor with regard to providing regional assistance to shift resources out of declining sectors and into more competitive ones, particularly for small firms. The emphasis on finding competitive market niches for small firms in growth sectors, rather than favoring large projects conducted by large companies, is reflected in the substantial funds allocated to small businesses. And Zysman notes that this policy of aiding small business was pursued through both the Lander governments, and the federal government (via the Ministry of Economics).

In the 1980s and 1990s, the organization of the regional economy shifted away from large, autarkic firms towards one centered around the Mittelstand pursuing diversified quality production (DQP). DQP entails a shift away from mass-produced, standardized goods to more customized, high-quality goods produced in comparatively small batches. Success is achieved through intensified R&D in combination with higher skill labor (Deeg, 1999).

The banking system is central to the German system of DQP. By providing long-term loans and stable, long-term relations, banks enable Mittelstand firms to pursue long-term objectives. In this manner, firms in Germany avoid or minimize pressures to maximize short-run returns. The strong preference for short-term investment horizons inherent in equity market-based finance systems is unlikely to support all the kinds of investments needed for DQP, and is perfectly consistent with labor's employment stability objectives (Deeg, 1999: 113–114). Table 6.1 illustrates the increasing importance of banks for small firms.

In addition to increased banking by the savings and cooperative banks, federal and state banks have increased the availability of funds to SMEs, and offer subsidized rates. Most important among these development banks is the Kreditanstalt für Wiederaufbau (KfW), discussed earlier. Between 1982 and 1987, over 10 percent of all firms in the Federal Republic with annual sales between DM 5 million and DM 10 million received one or more KfW loans; this percentage climbs steadily with the size of the firm, reaching nearly 30 percent of all firms with sales between DM 50 million and DM 100 million. Indeed, "Government loan programs are so widespread that SMEs expect their banks to incorporate such loans whenever possible into investment financing packages" (Deeg, 1999: 118).

Gourevitch and Shinn (2005) see a variety of cleavages forming around corporate governance reforms (cross-class corporatist coalition versus left–right conflicts) as preferences change depending on the specific issue (some workers increasingly prefer transparent accounting to track their pension funds which has led to some equity market-enhancing reforms versus the desire to preserve employment stability via blockholding and long-term financing).[6] Consequently, various moves have occurred to liberalize Germany's financial system and its corporate governance system in particular. However, as Hall and Thelen (2004) remark,

> [they] see few reasons why the adoption of international accounting standards, independent directors and better protection for minority shareholders should have a major impact on corporate strategies or damage the corporate networks that condition the provision of capital in such nations, let alone impose changes in labor relations.

Where proposed reforms strike at the heart of existing firm strategies, there has been substantial opposition to them. For example, German delegates to the European Parliament blocked legislation that would have made hostile takeovers easier, and they are not yet a common feature in Germany or other coordinated market economies (Guillen, 2000). And the German takeover law of 2002 gives

Table 6.1 Numbers and share of volume of business[a] of various categories of German banks,[b] 1950–2006

Institutions	1950[c]	1960	1970	1977	1988	1996	2006
Universal banks	36.4	24.4	24.9	24.9	23.6	24.3	28.8
Big banks	19.1	11.3	10.2	10.4	8.9	9.1	18.1
Regional and other commercial banks[d,e]	12.8	10.4	10.7	10.9	11.4	13.1	8.8
Branches of foreign banks[d]	–	–	1.5	1.9	1.8	1.3	1.8
Private bankers[e]	4.5	2.7	2.5	1.7	1.5	0.6	–
Savings bank sector of which:	30.8	35.7	38.5	38.5	37.3	37.6	36.8
Regional giro institutions	10.8	13.5	15.6	16.5	15.6	18.1	22.8
Savings banks	20	22.2	22.9	22	21.7	19.5	14.0
Credit cooperative sector of which:	12.4	8.6	11.5	14	16.9	14.7	11.5
Regional institutions of credit cooperatives	3.7	2.8	3.8	4.2	4.6	3.4	3.2
Credit cooperatives[e]	8.7	5.8	7.7	9.8	12.3	11.3	8.3
Specialized banks	–	–	–	–	–	–	–
Mortgage banks of which:	5.9	17.2	13.6	13	13.9	13.5	12.3
Private mortgage banks[f]	–	5.8	6.6	8.2	9	–	–
Public mortgage banks[f]	–	11.4	7.1	4.8	4.9	–	–
Instalment sales financing institutions[e,f]	–	1.5	1.1	1.1	–	–	–
Banks with special functions[f]	–	10.2	8.4	6.5	6.7	9.6	10.5
Postal giro and postal savings bank offices[f]	–	2.4	1.9	2	1.5	–	–
Total	85.5	100	99.9	100	99.9	99.7	99.9

Sources: Monthly Report of the Deutsche Bundesbank, March 1961, April 1962, December 1971, August 1978, November 1996, June 2006; Deutsche Bundesbank (1989).

Notes
a Volume of business is the balance sheet total plus endorsement liabilities on rediscounted bills, own drawings in circulation discounted and credited to borrowers, and bills from the banks' portfolios dispatched for collection prior to maturity.
b Banks reporting for the Monthly Balance Sheet Statistics excluding the assets and liabilities of their foreign branches and building and loan associations.
c No figures available for number of banks in 1950.
d Branches of foreign banks included in regional and other commercial banks in 1950 and 1960.
e Category instalment sales financing institutions dissolved in 1986, and the 72 banks in it reclassified as regional and other commercial banks (42), private bankers (22), and credit cooperatives (8).
f No figures available for private and public mortgage banks, instalment sales financing institutions, banks with special functions, and postal giro and postal savings banks in 1950.

a company's managing board the right to issue poison pills as long as the supervisory board agrees. There is no need to consult shareholders directly. However, since supervisory boards represent shareholder and employees in equal parts, and since top executives cannot look forward to windfall gains, there is an inherent bias against hostile bids. While this law was one of the central legislative projects of the government under Gerhard Schroder, the new grand coalition government remains committed to it. And although Germany has one of the more liberal takeover regimes in continental Europe, its takeover rules are restrictive and discriminatory in comparison to the US and UK (there have been only two successful hostile takeover bids in Germany since 1995).[7] For example, in May 2006 Germany announced that it would reduce the threshold at which shareholders must declare a stake in companies to 3 percent from 5 percent, in order to make hostile takeovers more difficult.[8] Thus, it seems that Germany remains committed to the core of its established labor–capital bargain, and a reliance on consensus-based capitalism, despite a variety of liberalizing reforms around the edges.

Summary

The German case illustrates that decentralized political institutions alone do not lead to diffuse corporate ownership, or to the fragmentation of financial institutions, as in the US. Rather, identifying the relevant political interests, whose power is mediated by decentralized political institutions, is critical to understanding how fragmented financial arrangements emerge.

The postwar bargain was to the benefit of capital owners owing to Allied actions to construct a market economy that resembled the US/UK, and preventing labor from nationalizing banks and industry, as in France. While large firms have certainly succeeded in postwar Germany for a variety of reasons (e.g., miracle growth era, increasing trade with other European nations, an increasing focus on the Soviet Union which relaxed Allied attempts to enforce the deconcentration of industry and finance), the decentralized political structure has led to strong Mittelstand support.

But the postwar bargain between labor and capital leading to co-determination and Works Councils allows for a corporate strategy that endeavors to satisfy both labor and capital as the firm adjusts to the pressures of globalization. The institutional structure created following World War II has allowed this to happen, in contrast to France, where labor imposed its will from above, rather than seeking a mutually compatible strategy from below negotiated by both labor and capital. Consequently, the formal institutional mechanisms for generating and enforcing bargains between labor and capital are absent in France, which has led to capital asserting itself independently of employees' input in some ways, which then leads to the government having to subsequently moderate some of these actions, rather than labor finding a bargain within the firm.

Conclusions

The cases outlined above illustrate the importance of politics to the broad structure of the financial system, and in turn, the supply (and cost) of financing to
various actors. Where farmers dominate politics, as in the early nineteenth-century US, there are more local banks which are tied more firmly to the local community as unit banks. While it is a relationship-based CME, as in Germany, the
structure is very different. The agrarian CME is distinguished by its decentralized nature and the extent of authority devolved to local political jurisdictions;
the classic CME is much more urban-based with both labor and capital pushing
it in this direction, although the decentralized political institutions of Germany
compensate for its urban/centralizing bias.

Germany illustrates, in contrast to France, US, and Japan, the outcome when
farmers have limited political influence. While the financing arrangements of
Germany's large firms is turning more towards securities markets, the slowness
of this change illustrates the critical importance of the bargains struck among the
key actors when corporate governance rules were first established. Indeed, the
broad pattern of Germany's financial landscape and its evolution since World
War II are constrained by the political power of actors, the manner in which
political institutions mediate them, and the complementarities with other capitalist (and financial) institutions. Germany's coordinated market economy and the
way it adjusts to globalization (in contrast to France) as well as the privileged
financing of the Mittelstand are clear consequences of these early bargains.

7 Voice vs. property

In this chapter, I examine the outcomes when either labor dominates, as in post-World War II Austria, or when capital owners and farmers form a power-sharing coalition, as in the twentieth-century United States. Such cleavages lead to a battle between those who exercise political influence via their voice at the ballot box, and those whose power derives from the ownership of land or money.

Voice: labor wins

Austria

Austria is at the far end of the CME spectrum, with high government intervention, banking dominance with poorly developed securities markets, a government-administered pension system, and low agricultural financing. Politically, an initial bargain very favorable to labor was struck (while preserving a capitalist economy), with a consensus political system that makes change difficult.[1] It is consistent with the theory outlined in Chapter 2, the statistical findings discussed in Chapter 3, and with the France post-World War II case that Austria would nationalize the largest enterprises and that they would have the greatest amount of government, and bank, ownership as a result of labor's political dominance. Indeed, Austria has exhibited these traits throughout the post-World War II period. How did these arrangements originate, and why have they remained so stable? To answer these questions, I first examine the structure of the financial system, and then consider how politics shaped it.

Financial system

Austria's post-World War II financial system is characterized by extensive government intervention, banking dominance along with small equities markets, highly concentrated corporate ownership, government-administered pensions, and an agricultural sector of limited importance. Consistent with actions taken by labor-dominated governments in other countries (e.g., France), Austria nationalized many of its largest enterprises and major financial institutions after World War II.[2] While around 70 industrial enterprises and plants were selected for nationalization,[3] through banks' substantial direct ownership or indirect control of a large number of subsidiaries, the Austrian government can influence an even larger part of Austrian industry (Katzenstein, 1984).

Part of the initial motivation for nationalization was to direct funds toward the reconstruction of the basic material industries after the heavy damages suffered during the war (as in France where the Left was strong, but not in Germany or Japan where the Left was politically weaker). At the same time, nationalization helped to maintain some degree of Austrian control over these assets during the Occupation (particularly to prevent Soviet expropriation of them). As a result, nationalization was seen as beneficial to the Left *and* Right, since it helped the Left towards its goal of full employment, while the Right supported it in order to prevent the Soviets from taking the countries' industrial and related business assets. Further, nationalization was seen as temporarily expedient to the Right for the rebuilding of the economy, though the Left had longer term intentions with regard to managing the economy, as in France.[4]

The Soviet Union objected to the nationalization laws insofar as they applied to former German properties, but the other Allies were able to override Soviet efforts to block these laws. Nevertheless, the Soviet Union prevented their application in the Soviet Zone, and as a result, about half the enterprises there, including the entire petroleum industry, were kept from Austrian control until after the occupation ended.[5]

These initial nationalizations have had a long-term effect on Austria's economy. Since World War II, about two-thirds of the largest 50 firms have been owned and operated by the government; private firms have generally accounted for little more than 10 percent, and foreign firms for about 15 percent of the total. Overall, the public sector has been responsible for about a quarter of the jobs and net production value in Austria, and almost one-half of all investment decisions have remained in public hands. Despite numerous privatizations since 1947, state-owned enterprises remain an integral part of Austria's economy (Freeman, 1989: 172).

The extensive government intervention has led to several corporate governance features that put Austria at the far end of the CME spectrum, including: (1) Austrian firms have the highest ownership concentration among OECD countries; (2) the state and the banking sector play a disproportionately large role in corporate governance, especially for larger firms – the larger the firm, the more likely the largest ultimate owner is the state or a bank – while families dominate smaller firms; (3) a large fraction of banking and insurance companies are organized as associations in which municipalities play a dominant role, allowing government to exert influence on the corporate sector via these associations as well.[6]

Because the nationalized part of Austria's economy is so large and has not been represented on the stock market, the Vienna Stock Exchange has remained small and illiquid (Hankel, 1981; Freeman, 1989). The pension system, which relies almost exclusively on intergenerational transfer payments, has reinforced this situation. Under Austrian law, pension funds have existed only as of 1990, and institutional investment by pension funds is still of minor importance

(Gugler *et al.*, 1997). To compensate for the weakness of Austria's local capital market, public authorities have borrowed funds from international lenders and then channeled these funds to selected firms and industries (Freeman, 1989).

How did these financial arrangements emerge?

Politics

The origins of Austria's post-World War II politics may be understood best by contrasting it to the interwar experience. The breakup of the Austro-Hungarian Empire after World War I, and the difficulties of adjusting to a new economic situation (without an adequate agricultural and mineral base left to it and with the old trading relations of the relatively self-sufficient empire and customs union broken), coupled with devastating inflation in the early 1920s, brought the Austrian economy close to collapse. While financial support was granted through a League of Nations austerity program, high unemployment and political and social unrest ensued. As a result, Austria suffered from violent class struggle in the interwar period, culminating in the civil war of 1934 before annexation (Anschluss) by Germany in 1938. Austria emerged from World War II with its economy shattered. The loss of life and the damage to industry and transportation had decreased production to only one-third of its prewar level.

The Occupation, which lasted for ten years, divided the country into four zones. Under the terms of the occupation, the Soviets were granted the "full and unqualified title" to all German assets in eastern Austria; that is, the part of Austria under Soviet occupation. Consequently, the Soviet Union dismantled and removed much of the movable industrial equipment, while fixed installations were formally confiscated and put into production to serve Soviet interests. When the occupation ended with the signing of the State Treaty in May 1955, the Soviet Union had around 450 firms with 50,000 employees – around 10 percent of the Austrian industrial labor force – under its control. To reclaim these assets, the Austrians compensated the Soviets with oil, goods, and cash over eight years.

By contrast, the Western Allies invested considerable effort, money, and materials under United States leadership in reconstructing the Austrian economy.[7] Substantial aid came in the form of consumer goods, raw materials, and capital equipment between 1945 and 1955.

After the bitter interwar class struggles, exacerbated by relentless economic problems and one of the highest unemployment rates in Europe, elites of both political parties perceived Occupation as a consequence of their inability to reconcile their differences for the good of the country. Thus, with the defeat of the Nazis, both camps were determined to replace class conflict with cooperation (Traxler, 1993: 272).

The SPÖ (*Sozialdemokratische Partei Österreichs* – Austrian Social Democratic Party) ratified the moderate social democratic and anti-communist outlook of the newly elected SPÖ president, Renner.[8] The party rejected an alliance with the KPÖ (*Kommunistische Partei Österreichs* – Communist Party of Austria), endorsed cooperation with the more conservative ÖVP (*Österreicheische Volks-partei* – Austrian People's Party), and supported the rebuilding of a capitalist economy tied to the West.

The ÖVP also moderated its stance after the war, with many of its postwar leaders having developed personal relationships with socialist leaders during their time at Dachau. After the war, they advanced a program that was more sympathetic to social welfare policies. Under the party's "Programmatic Basic Principles" of 1945, "independence, private initiative and achievement in eco-nomic terms were complemented by social-political principles such as pensions and social insurance for all and an equal and just distribution of liabilities – taking special account of family circumstances" (Dyk, 1988: 74).

The first national election since 1930 was held on November 25, 1945. The ÖVP received nearly 50 percent of the vote and 85 seats in the Nationalrat (the Lower House or National Assembly), while the SPÖ received 45 percent of the vote and 76 seats. The KPÖ received only 5 percent of the vote and four seats.

To limit conflict among themselves, the coalition partners (the ÖVP and SPÖ) devised a system to divide not only Cabinet ministries but also the entire range of political patronage jobs in the government and nationalized industries based upon each party's electoral strength. This proportional division of jobs, called the "Proporz" system, became an enduring feature that would solidify Austria's consensus style of politics, and, once in place prevent substantial changes to the status quo.

Interest groups (particularly labor and business) and political parties cooper-ated closely in the years following World War II. Partnership was based on a compromise in which business supported the goal of full employment and toler-ated nationalization while unions supported efforts to promote growth and tied their wage bargains to productivity gains. This compromise was also based on a mutual perception of national vulnerability to world market and nonmarket forces (e.g., the Soviet threat) (Freeman, 1989). But ultimately, the compromise was very much in labor's favor, as compared to labor–capital comprises else-where (e.g., Germany and Japan).

Why has labor been so powerful in Austria despite the clear sympathies with the Allied powers (particularly the United States which bolstered capital's bar-gaining position in Germany and Japan after the war), and the ÖVP's electoral strength? Four reasons: (1) the ÖVP's center to center-left political and eco-nomic ideology following the war, as discussed above; (2) the weakness of private capital in the structure of Austria's economy, partly as a result of the nationalization of the country's largest enterprises; (3) the strong, centralized labor union; and (4) the consensus political institutions that have made changing the initial political bargains difficult. I discuss the latter three reasons below.

WEAK PRIVATE CAPITAL

Even including the larger nationalized firms, Austrian firms are comparatively small. For example, in 1973, establishments employing 1,000 or more accounted for 27.6 percent of total employment in Austrian industry, compared with 38.7 percent in West Germany (Aiginger and Tichy, 1982: 11). And when accounting for the fact that the largest enterprises are publicly owned, actors representing the interests of private capital are small indeed.

In Austria's main business association, the BWK (*Bundeswirtschaftskammer* – Austrian Federal Chamber of Commerce), internal decision-making is based on the "one person, one vote" principle, which puts small capital in a strong position. Indeed, economy-wide bargains reached by the BWK and ÖGB (*Österreichischer Gewerkschaftsbund* – Austrian Trade Union Federation) cover almost all private employment outside agriculture (around 90 percent of employees are within the scope of these collective agreements).[9]

Since small firms tend to orient their activities towards the domestic economy, protectionist interests prevail among Austrian employers, given the weight of small firms. As a consequence, not only has large, export-oriented industry been forced to set up a trade association of its own (*Vereinigung Österreichischer Industrieller* – Federation of Austrian Industrialists), but it is also "*extremely dependent on the support of labor's peak associations*" to defend its product-market interests in the face of small firms' protectionist demands (Traxler, 1993: 273; emphasis added).

Labor's hand is further strengthened through the nationalized industries. With their large size and their subordination to the government (and to labor via the ÖGB), public enterprises have dominated industrial relations and have long set the pace for improving pay and working conditions throughout the economy (Traxler, 1993). This structural weakness of capital, as a result of the country's small private sector firm size and large public sector, forces capitalists confronted with a strong labor movement to cooperate on labor-market questions.

STRONG UNIONS

The Austrian Trade Union Federation was founded in 1945, before sectoral unions were set up, with the political aim of preventing the kind of inter-union rivalry that proved so politically disastrous during the interwar years. As a result, Austrian unionism became the most centralized in Western Europe, with the ÖGB encompassing the entire country's union membership. Austria's dual system of worker representation, both through the unions and through factory councils at the plant level, has reinforced the centralized organizational structure and power of the union movement.[10]

The encompassing size of the ÖGB leads to a policy outlook that emphasizes the aggregate welfare of the nation, rather than distributive welfare gains common to the more splintered labor unions of other countries (Olson, 1965). Thus, they have adopted an extremely consistent position based on long-term cooperation with capital. The ÖGB's main goal has been to preserve employment by promoting economic growth, which also allows for increases in income without generating conflict with capital over income redistribution (Traxler, 1993: 282).

Labor organization and political influence is enhanced through the Chamber of Labor (equivalent to a Chamber of Commerce). The Chamber provides information, advice, and policy analysis on general economic and social problems that have a bearing on the union's stance in collective bargaining. Membership in the Chamber is compulsory for all employees, and this strengthens the position of the Austrian Trade Union Federation among those parts of the labor force otherwise difficult to organize. And because the candidates standing for office in the Chamber's internal elections frequently come from the main political organizations – primarily the socialist faction – active inside the ÖGB, the SPÖ generally occupies a dominant position in the Chamber of Labor. As the intellectual base for labor policies, the Chamber has helped ensure labor of formal and influential representation in all stages of the policy process since 1945. Indeed, the Chamber's voice is usually influential on all issues involving social welfare. Moreover, almost one-half of the SPÖ members of Parliament are union officials on either a full-time or part-time basis. This fusion of union and party leadership greatly strengthens the labor movement's political influence (Katzenstein, 1984).

The centralization of union membership and power, its attention to aggregate economic welfare in addition to political power being concentrated in Vienna, leads unions to heavily favor "the *centralized* exercise of influence on economic decisions at the national level over decentralized forms of codetermination within plants" (Katzenstein, 1984: 38; emphasis added). Nationalized firms have played a key role in this.

Because of the close integration of labor in the governance structure of the country, the nationalized industries make a concerted effort to create and preserve jobs and serve as leaders for Austrian industry with respect to pay and working conditions. For much of their history, Austria's nationalized industries have consistently protected jobs in the face of cyclical and structural changes in the economy. For example, in the face of globalization, nationalized firms have reduced their capacity far less and laid off far fewer workers than have private firms, local and foreign (Freeman, 1989).

Austria's nationalized banks have also played an important role in implementing "socially responsible" employment policies by propping up ailing firms among their subsidiaries as well as by bailing out some private firms on the brink of bankruptcy. Generally speaking, the government's policy is not to defend every job but to ensure that employment levels remain stable. Thus, economic change has been accepted as a way of life, but it has called for "a deliberate policy of compensation," with nationalized firms and banks having played a central role (Katzenstein, 1984: 40).

CONSENSUS POLICYMAKING

Three defining attributes of democratic corporatism undergird Austria's consensual style of policymaking: (1) a commitment to partnership among the nation's political parties and interest groups; (2) a relatively centralized and concentrated system of interest groups that facilitates bargaining; and (3) continuous and informal political bargaining among interest groups, state bureaucracies, and political parties (Katzenstein, 1984: 27).

In the immediate postwar years, parties and interest groups both sought to avoid a repeat of the conflict-ridden interwar period that led to economic and social crises, and ultimately to the Anschluss. This commitment to cooperative policymaking became institutionalized in the mechanisms used for determining economic policy. A central feature of this new consensus-generating model depended upon interest groups reaching mutually agreeable policies. To establish the legitimacy of these groups and the bargains they struck, membership in the economic chambers became compulsory for all working Austrians. As Katzenstein (1984: 59) notes, each working Austrian belongs directly to at least three economic interest groups, and often to at least two additional groups indirectly, depending upon the place of employment.

Continuous, informal bargaining helps to generate consensus among the groups. Because groups reserve veto-power over unfavorable policies, each side is forced to work within the constraints the other is willing to accept. Within the ministries (where political parties divide power according to the "Proporz" rules), bureaucrats act as intermediaries who facilitate intergroup bargaining and try to assure that the potential veto-power of each side does not lead to stalemate. As Katzenstein notes (1984: 65), "informal consultations and arrangement rather than formal legislation provide the instruments for many of Austria's policies." As a result, this process tends to prevent substantial policy change, and thereby preserve the status quo, once in place.

This process of continuous, consensus policymaking has reinforced the main aims of the initial bargains, including:

> the commitment of the business community to the goal of full employment as well as its tolerance of nationalization, on the one hand, and the union's pursuit of productivity-based wage bargaining untempered by efforts to achieve greater equality in the distribution of income and wealth, on the other.
>
> (Katzenstein, 1984: 72)

The consistent structure of the post-World War II financial system reflects the durability of the initial bargain within this consensus political system.

In recent years, the Austrian government's management of mergers and acquisitions reflects the strong influence of the nature of these post-World War II bargains; that is, labor's influence and the priority placed on the protection of jobs, even for conservative coalition governments. Indeed, government intervention has been common and politically motivated when considering the approval of foreign acquisition of Austrian companies. The failed takeover of Telekom Austria by Swisscom in August 2004 reflects Austria's interventionist role. As Karl-Heinz Grasser, the Austrian finance minister at the time, declared, the bid collapsed because Austria wanted to protect jobs, and other "national interests."[11] And Austrian political interests were strongly opposed to a Siemens takeover bid for VA Technologies only two weeks after the failed Swisscom bid, an Austrian engineering group, owing to worries about protecting jobs. However, this attitude was reversed in November after Siemens gave assurances to "use its ownership rights responsibly," and, more importantly, when the US firm, General Electric, became interested in bidding for VA Tech.[12] The government's influence over Austria's corporate sector was also in evidence when Voestalpine, Austria's biggest steel group, stepped in to rescue fellow Austrian company Bohler-Uddeholm from an unwanted foreign bidder, a day after the specialty steel producer rejected the overture of the British private equity fund CVC.[13] As pressure from foreign takeovers has increased, a former finance minister and leader of Austria's political and industrial elite, Hannes Androsch, has recently sounded his intention to institutionalize the protection of Austrian firms from foreign takeovers with the establishment of a private equity fund. The so-called Austro-fund would buy controlling stakes in firms such as Bohler (the potential sale of which triggered the debate), Wienerberge, the world's largest maker of clay bricks, OMV, an oil and gas company, Voestalpine, a steelmaker, and Lenzing, a maker of Cellulose fiber.[14] It is clear that attempted takeovers that could lead to the unraveling, or transformation, of Austria's traditional capitalist system have led to a backlash to protect it. While some change is inevitable, it seems that the core of Austria's economic structure is unlikely to be fundamentally or drastically altered.

Farmers

Austria's political institutions do not significantly increase farmers' political power via over-representation, or via devolution of political power to the local level. This is institutionalized via the weak Upper House (Bundesrat). The federal government is politically answerable to the Naitonalrat (Lower House) alone, and not to the Bundesrat (Upper House). Pelinka (1988) affirms that "Austrian federalism may be regarded as under-developed, and Austria [is] a federal state with strong centralizing tendencies."

Although Austria's Constitution provides that all matters not delegated to the federation shall be left to the provinces, in effect very few matters have been left to them (Gerlich, 1981: 215). Almost all important policymaking powers are exercised by the Federal Government. Not only are there no provincial courts of law, but matters of education, police, and fiscal and social affairs are mostly legislated in the Nationalrat. While provincial autonomy extends to such matters as regional planning, hospitals, and electricity, provincial administrative authorities generally execute laws under the supervision of federal authorities (Gerlich, 1981). As a result, farmers' power is limited. Since economic policy is primarily determined by labor and capital, agriculture has a very weak voice. Indeed, the initial postwar bargains nearly exclusively revolved around establishing labor–capital cooperation. The very low agricultural employment level during the postwar period (around 1 percent since the early 1980s according to the Austrian

Institute for Economic Research) reflects their relative weakness economically, and by extension through their economic interest group, politically.

Summary

While Austria is often portrayed as having achieved a corporatist bargain between labor and capital, it is, in fact, a bargain very much in labor's favor, relative to other countries with capitalist economies. Because labor dominates, it follows Olson's logic of caring about aggregate welfare, so it is in some ways more successful than other countries with strong labor, but which compete with capital for influence (e.g., France or Germany).

The financial patterns observed in Austria are generally consistent with the expectations of a statist CME, as articulated in Chapter 2, including: banking dominance, publicly administered pensions, small agricultural sector (and correspondingly low agrarian financing), and high government intervention. While often portrayed as being hands-off in its treatment of nationalized enterprises, labor's political dominance is evidenced by the union's power to negotiate state-sanctioned, economy-wide bargains. Also important is that the state, and banks, have been major owners of large firms, in contrast to Germany where the state is not nearly as important. Consequently, the structure and strategy of large firms is heavily influenced by government-sanctioned ÖGB–BWK bargains that generally favor labor, and through bank lending policies that are sympathetic to labor.

Property: capital owners and farmers win

Twentieth-century United States

The pattern of financial system legislation in US history is the result of a constant battle between local interests favoring fragmentation against those seeking to make financial institutions, and markets, centralized. As Chapter 6 discusses, farmers were politically and economically dominant in the early nineteenth century, and so banks organized themselves according to the particular needs of agriculture in each state. This preserved local banking. Moreover, commercial and industrial firms remained sufficiently small and so they did not push for interstate branching, although small universal banks did begin to appear in the northeast (Lamoreaux, 1991). As Calomiris (2000) explains, tension increased in the late nineteenth century with the second industrialization wave. Political pressure to alter the financial system mounted with the growth of railroads and industry, and the attempts to reap advantages from scale and scope economies (Chandler, 1977). Indeed, many of the US's modern financial institutions trace their origins, or important formative moments, to events in the late nineteenth and early twentieth century. But the political battles fought at this time illustrate the entrenched power of local interests – particularly farmers – who could prevent substantial changes to the status quo, as it applied to them.

The outcomes of key legislative battles illustrate the constant tension between farmers on one side, and big industry on the other. Labor was largely sidelined. While farmers and capital have shared power in other countries, the outcomes in the US are unique because its political institutions granted legitimate power to small farmers during turn-of-the-century industrialization. In other countries, political institutions denied meaningful political power to small farmers during the country's industrialization period, and thus permitted owners of capital to dictate the structure of the emerging financial system (e.g., France and Japan before World War II; Germany before World War I).

Roe (1994) offers an excellent historical account of how politics affected the evolution of the US financial system. He focuses on how populist interests, in combination with the US's federal political institutions, led to the fragmentation of a burgeoning, centralized banking (and broader financial) system in the early twentieth century. Securities markets later developed as a way to circumvent the inefficient and fragmented banking system in order to provide much needed financing to America's large industrial enterprises.

However, as Becht and DeLong (2005) point out, Roe's argument contains "two holes." First, Roe has a hard time answering why "politics" was so strong in corporate finance, yet weaker in labor–management relations. Second, Roe's argument has difficulty explaining why pyramids did not emerge in the United States as they did in other countries. In my view, both of the "holes" in Roe's argument are due to combining farmers and labor into one general "populist" category. This term is frequently used to refer to those with low incomes, but this is problematic since farmers and labor can have widely divergent preferences.

For example, in the May 1932 edition of the *American Federationist* published by the American Federation of Labor, William Green, the magazine's editor, remarks that "In the April [issue] were published a number of articles written by persons with special competence in the field of banking.... From these articles one conclusion stands out conspicuously: The need of a unified banking system." He goes on to say:

> There are about 20,000 banks in the United States chartered as state banks or national banks.... In practice this amounts to 49 different banking systems, as each state fixes amount of capitalization and practices required by all chartered.... Obviously, the first step toward raising general banking practices is to establish the authority of the Federal Government – then unified authority will close the escapes that have enabled banks to evade higher standards. The great preponderance of failures have come from state banks in rural communities.... To meet the problems of the small banks, a system of branch banks is proposed.

Green reiterates these points and emphasizes the preference for small country banks to become branches of large city banks in the April 1933 issue.[15]

Owners of capital were on the side of labor with respect to wanting more centralized banks. According to an editorial in the *Wall Street Journal* (December 13,

1932), entitled "Too Many Banks," "A reasonable and guarded expansion of branch banking will go far to overcome the conditions which a mushroom spread of little isolated banks has left behind it." It was clear to owners and managers of large American enterprises that financing costs would be lowered with large, universal banks that could meet all their financing needs, as in Germany. As Calomiris (2000: 265) convincingly explains, "the statistical comparison of German and American financial systems confirms qualitative historical and theoretical analysis that has linked universal banking to low costs of industrial finance."

In contrast to labor and capital, farmers and unit banks wanted to keep banks fragmented and local. As a result of the massive bank failures of the 1930s, the unit bankers' lobby was considerably weakened. As a result, farmers' political influence became critical to the preservation of local banking. Calomiris (2000) argues that farmers' success at preserving a fragmented banking system is partly due to farmers' capacity to lobby politicians; states with a greater abundance of wealthy farmers more effectively blocked new bank branching than those with poorer farmers, even when controlling for expected differences between southern plantation farming (who had reasons to favor a limited form of branching) and northern farming. While specific types of farming led to variations in the support for branched versus unit banks, generally speaking, farmers tended to favor local banks over branched city banks. The statistical evidence from House and Senate votes on the McFadden and Glass–Steagall Acts outlined in Chapter 3 is consistent with this view.

The key point is that labor and farmers were at odds over the structure of the banking system, and should not be combined into a single "populist" category. Clearly specifying these actors' preferences, and accounting for their differing political power, neatly fills Roe's "two holes," and remains consistent with his broader argument. The first "hole" about politics being important to corporate finance, but not to labor–management relations is easily answered from this perspective. Farmers were politically powerful, and they favored fragmented, locally oriented financial regulations. In other words, they wanted to prevent the emergence of large city banks with branches in the interior that could drain money away and deny them a valuable form of insurance, as discussed in Chapter 2. Farmers care little about labor–management relations. And because labor has been politically weak in the United States, they were unable to affect labor–management relations, and have been unable to offer sufficient political support to large city banks.

The second "hole," about the failure of pyramids to emerge, is also consistent with distinguishing between politically powerful farmers, and politically weak labor. In other countries where labor is strong (e.g., Austria and France), pyramids do exist. Left-wing parties (and their labor union counterparts) view them as useful for implementing labor-oriented policies across a wide range of enterprises. But farmers would not benefit from such concentrated financial and economic might. Indeed, such arrangements would be to their detriment as such oligopolistic power would almost inevitably lead to funds being drained out of the interior and put to more "productive" uses in urban areas (i.e., invested in projects with a higher return, particularly in a period of increasing industrialization), and raising their own costs of financing. At the same time, farmers were likewise concerned that the concentration of industry would lead to higher transportation and other business services costs for farmers, as large firms would take the best and cheapest resources, and charge customers (farmers) higher prices as a result of monopoly.

Farmers and the fragmentation of bank control and corporate ownership (and the prevention of pyramidal ownership)

In the early 1890s, railroads and industrial firms, usually owned by families or small groups of investors, suffered from price wars that cartels could not remedy, forcing them to integrate into groups. This wave of mergers and reorganizations was fueled by the economic collapse of 1893. Banks implemented these changes which contributed to their control over many railroads and industrials, via voting trusts or board representations.[16] The most important reorganizers were J.P. Morgan & Co. and Kuhn Loeb; these were private banks organized as partnerships and not subject to government regulation. Like their counterparts in Germany, they acted as investment bankers, commercial lenders, and activist institutional investors. Banks did not exercise control by micro-managing firms, but rather by overseeing financial matters (dividends, capital structure, and investment), appointing top managers, and using proxy votes to exercise control over them (Simon, 1998).

By 1912, 18 financial institutions sat on the boards of 134 corporations. Of these 18 institutions, five banks were dominant: J.P. Morgan & Co., First National Bank, National City Bank, Guaranty Trust Co., and Bankers' Trust sat on the boards of 64 financial institutions and 68 nonfinancial corporations. Together, these five banks controlled industrial assets (on behalf of others) representing 56 percent of the country's GNP (Simon, 1998).

Bank concentration and the perception that banker-directors encouraged collusion generated widespread criticism. Farmers, small business, and local bankers were the main groups that opposed bankers and giant corporations. As a result of mounting political pressure, Rep. Arsène Pujo spearheaded a Congressional investigation on the concentration of power in Wall Street in 1912. The Pujo hearings succeeded in tarnishing bankers' reputation and led to the Clayton Act in 1914 which clarified and supplemented the Sherman Antitrust Act by prohibiting stock purchase mergers that resulted in reduced competition. The Clayton Act helped counteract the concentration of ownership and economic power of big business and financiers; bankers in particular were targeted as the main culprits in fostering a financial/industrial oligopoly. But many felt it did not go far enough.

The stock market crash of 1929 and subsequent Depression renewed calls for political investigations of Wall Street and the banking industry. The Gray-Pecora Hearings, from 1932 to 1934, brought to light many misdeeds of commercial bankers and led to the enactment of legislation that would further reduce the power of big bankers, including the Securities Act and the Glass-Steagall Banking Act in 1933, and the Securities Exchange Act in 1934. In addition, pyramidal corporate ownership structures were targeted with the Revenue Act and the Public Utility Holding Company (PUHC) Act in 1935. In the utilities industry, holding companies became massive and highly concentrated. For example, in 1930, 90 percent of all operating companies were controlled by 19 holding companies. The strength of the holding companies was intensified by the existence of interlocking directorates. The Federal Power Commission commented that: "48 major projects fall under the control of 10 groups which service 12,487 communities with a population of more than 42 million. The community of interest between the 10 groups is evidenced by the fact that 19 directors or officers were directors in at least 2 groups."[17] It was this high level of concentration and control that led to demands for the regulation of utilities. The Revenue Act complemented and extended the PUHC efforts beyond the utilities sector by imposing extra taxation on corporations on the basis of size, and to thereby eliminate unnecessary holding companies.[18] Together, they weakened the big bankers and financiers and their control over corporations, and cemented the emerging trend of fragmentation that would come to characterize the structure of the American financial system.

As a result of weakening large financial institutions and improving protections for small investors, local interests – led predominantly by farmers – unwittingly created the conditions that would lead to a flourishing equities market as a way to circumvent the fragmented banking system, and place power over corporations into managers' hands.

Agricultural financing

Although the US is regarded as a non-interventionist state, an important exception should be made in the case of agriculture. Saloutos (1974) observes,

> Perhaps in no period of American history were the efforts of the federal government to resolve the almost unresolvable problems of the farm prosecuted with greater vigor and optimism than during the New Deal years. What administrators and politicians thought and did about the depressed state of the farmers more or less set the pace for policy making in the post-World War II decades.

For example, farmers' vast political influence enabled the creation of the Farm Credit Administration in 1933, which extended billions of dollars in loans to farmers and their business cooperatives. At the same time, the FCA improved the farm credit market through the leadership and competition it provided. Credit was made available at the lowest possible rate, enabling thousands of borrowers to obtain credit who would otherwise have lost their property through foreclosures. According to Saloutos, "The New Deal ... constituted the greatest innovative epoch in the history of American agriculture."

While farmers' capacity to initiate reforms may have subsequently declined, they retained the power to prevent changes to these reforms through several political mechanisms, including: their importance to many politicians' home constituencies; malapportionment which has granted farmers over-representation in the Senate; the voting rules of the Senate which require a super-majority to pass legislation and thus protect laws once in place; and via the capacity to influence the appointment of federal judges who can protect their interests.

Contemporary implications

Kroszner and Strahan (1999) argue that as the value of local banking relationships declined – as a result of ATMs, banking by mail and telephone, technological innovation and deregulation reducing transportation and communication costs, increasing sophistication of credit-scoring techniques that diminished the value of knowledge local bankers had about the risks of borrowers in the community – small firms that were the main borrowers from the small banks also probably became more likely to favor the entry of large banks into local markets, and led to the erosion of branching restrictions. However, an important factor overlooked by Kroszner and Strahan, and worthy of further investigation, is whether the consolidation of American farming into agribusiness also facilitated the removal of political roadblocks to interstate bank branching. The transformation of small farming into large agribusiness that could tap equity markets may have paved the way for the dismantling of the Glass–Steagall Act (with the Gramm–Leach–Bliley Act of 1999) and bank branching restrictions once so cherished by small farmers.

Summary

Much of the political economy literature on the development of the US financial system groups "populist" interests into a single category. But it is clearly critical to distinguish between labor and farmers as two low-income groups with distinct policy preferences. Doing this provides a clearer understanding of the politics that have created America's unique financial arrangements, and illustrates the importance of farmers' similarly unique political influence in the US (unique both because of its long historical roots, and because of the unique way in which America's federal institutions aggregate and preserve farmers' power). This simple, but important, distinction parsimoniously fills Roe's "two holes" while remaining consistent with the rest of his overall argument about the fragmentation of American financial institutions, and the emergence of diffuse corporate ownership.

Conclusion

It is clear that labor prefers the centralized control of a nation's financial institutions. Capital also favors a centralized, as opposed to a fragmented, financial system, but without the government intervention that labor would favor. Rather, capital prefers to reap the scale and scope benefits that large universal banks can provide both with regard to commercial bank lending, and with regard to investment banking. Ultimately, they seek financial institutions that reduce transactions costs. So although labor and capital favor centralized financial institutions, they desire them for different reasons.

Farmers, by contrast, clearly prefer local banking. When farmers form a political power-sharing coalition with capital, conflicting rural–urban tensions arise. However, capital has been able to find a way around this through the creation of capital markets in the US. This is in contrast to farmers and labor forming a power-sharing coalition with rural–urban conflicts likewise emerging; in the case of France, central control resulted, but it was used to redirect financing to the agricultural sector (via the Crédit Agricole, and via subsidies made directly to the rural sector by the national government). The US's political arrangements allowed for the rapid development of capital markets because capital became so influential and needed a mechanism to raise financing for rapidly growing industries. But remember: the US is highly unusual. Rarely do farmers wield such enormous political power in other countries before capital enters the political fray. Consequently, it is unrealistic to expect other countries' financial arrangements to resemble the US's when their politics are usually quite different. Trying to force them to adopt a US financial model may be like fitting a square peg into a round hole, and cause a variety of economic and social problems as a result.

Part IV
Conclusions

8 Key lessons

The critical importance of initial bargains

As countries industrialized, capitalist institutions took shape according to the preferences of those who had the political power to organize economic activity in the late nineteenth and early twentieth century. Over time, economic behavior formed ingrained and interlocking patterns of mutual expectations that became institutionalized (both formally and informally) and complementary. These capitalist institutions were preserved because stable political institutions prevented substantial alterations to them, once in place.

In some countries, however, these established practices were disrupted; the distribution of political power changed, creating an opportunity to re-create capitalist institutions that better served the socioeconomic goals of newly powerful interests. Laws were passed, and new institutions were created. At first, legal enforcement of the new rules forced actors to alter their behavior. Over time, these behavioral patterns again became institutionalized and mutually reinforcing.

As shown with the quantitative evidence and the case studies, the distribution of political power *at the time capitalist institutions were (re)created* has fundamental and long-lasting consequences.[1] And because most countries' institutions did not change after World War II (only five of the 15 countries considered changed their constitutions after World War II), the bargains struck during the pre-World War II period matter more for most countries than the bargains struck in the post-World War II period. At the same time, it is important to emphasize that the analysis is not incompatible with subsequent change, particularly as capital becomes more influential. Subsequent change is simply constrained by the pre-existing institutional structure. For example, the French Regulation School (Boyer, 1990) has argued that capital has supplanted labor as the dominant actor affecting the structure of national political economies. However, capital is sometimes inserting itself into countries with pre-existing institutional structures that lead to awkward fits, particularly in those cases where institutions were created with capital as a weak partner, as with agrarian (early nineteenth-century US), statist (post-World War II Austria), and Mediterranean (post-World War II France) capitalist systems. Many have pointed to the US's uniquely fragmented and inefficient financial system; indeed, the US economy has succeeded in spite of it (e.g., with many unit banks hampering the financing of corporations with industrialization in the nineteenth century: Lamoreaux, 1994; Calomiris, 2000). The French political economy has likewise faced considerable difficulties accommodating capital's increasing importance since the mid-1980s (first attempting to adopt German style institutions, then giving this up and continuing to search for an alternative solution).

Thelen (2004) discusses some alternative mechanisms by which institutional change can occur, but the key point, as these country examples illustrate, is that change is constrained by the structure of the pre-existing institutions, both capitalist and political. In addition, as Hall and Soskice (2001) argue, political economies continue to exhibit attributes of their pre-existing capitalist architecture, rather than transforming into Anglo-American replicas. For example, hostile takeovers are a key feature of LMEs, and are conducted with the sole purpose of maximizing shareholder value, and usually lead to layoffs. While CMEs have implemented various liberalizing (LME-style) reforms since the 1980s, in recent years they have adopted stiff resistance to hostile takeovers that would undo the core of the initial labor–capital bargain (and tilt the balance in favor of capital) with a variety of measures consistent with the country's pre-existing institutional arrangements: government intervention in Austria; market-conforming mechanisms such as poison pills in Japan and Germany; and a combination of market-conforming measures and state intervention in France, including the increased use of poison pills, boosting corporate ownership with funds from the state pension (the biggest institutional investor in France), and protecting certain "strategic" sectors from foreign acquisition. A key lesson is that understanding capitalism among today's wealthy democracies demands that we look back to the origins of the institutions and consider the political power of the key actors when they struck bargains over their design.

The importance of farmers

Identifying the key players is critical. While most discussions about modern capitalism focus on different types of firms, workers, managers, and owners, these studies do not consider where the contemporary manifestations of the institutions came from. Considering the substantial influence of institutional inertia on modern outcomes, it is necessary to examine the origins, and to consider which actors were most important in the early construction of capitalist systems. In this regard, farmers have played an integral role. Although they may lack the power to exert changes to the institutions of contemporary capitalism in wealthy economies, their influence is felt most strongly through the legacy of the institutions they were instrumental in creating, and by retaining the power to block changes to it.

In France following World War II, farmers offered political support for the increased level of government intervention in the financial system, and helped to create and support the expansion of what was to become one of the world's largest banks – the Crédit Agricole. In the US, farmers' political influence led to strong regulations protecting local banks and, through the US's decentralized political system, they contributed to the fragmentation of the American financial system. In Japan, farmers supported the postal savings bank, which became even larger than France's behemoth Crédit Agricole, and which fed large amounts of money to the government which was then lent to industry (through the FILP) and thereby helped to foster a long-term financing orientation among Japanese firms.

By considering the importance of farmers to capitalist outcomes among today's wealthy economies, we can understand better the influence they have on developing countries. Indeed, many of today's developing countries are only now establishing their capitalist institutions. China and India, for example, are at a point in their development that resembles the process many wealthy countries went through at the beginning of the twentieth century. And in these countries, the rural population is very large, and potentially very powerful. In China, for example, leaders are particularly worried about inciting a farmers' rebellion (as has occurred before in Chinese history) and so they must be sensitive to the effects that their policies have on their rural inhabitants. Thus, while understanding the role of farmers among today's wealthy economies is important to explaining the varieties of capitalism observed among this select group, it is of potentially greater significance to understanding the potential development paths of industrializing nations.

The importance of power-sharing coalitions

A novel understanding of modern capitalist outcomes emerges by considering the political power-sharing coalitions that farmers have formed with labor (as in post-World War II France), capital (as in the twentieth-century US), and with labor and capital (as in post-World War II Japan). For example, in France following World War II, farmers offered political support for the increased level of government intervention in the economy, and helped to create and support the expansion of what was to become one of the world's largest banks – the Crédit Agricole. In the US, farmers' political influence led to strong regulations protecting local banks and, through the US's decentralized political system, they contributed to the fragmentation of the American financial system. In Japan, farmers supported the postal savings bank, which became even larger than the Crédit Agricole, and which fed large amounts of money to the government which was then lent to industry (through the Fiscal Investment and Loan Program) and thereby helped to foster a long-term financing orientation among Japanese firms.

Political institutions delimit and bias change

Pre-existing political institutions tend to preserve the initial financial/capitalist bargains and delimit the scope for change. Consensus systems tend to preserve the pre-existing structure more firmly than majoritarian systems since they incorporate more interests into the legislative bargaining process, and grant more actors a veto over changes to the status quo. But even in majoritarian systems, other institutional mechanisms can help preserve the status quo, such as malapportionment in the United States or France, which preserves farmers' veto power.

In addition to preserving the status quo, political institutions also bias the evolution of the financial system in a way that favors whichever actors gain politically over time. For example, small firms in Germany benefit from decentralization, complemented by farmers' political weakness. And Japanese small firms have gained considerably as a result of the electoral system. In both cases, banks catering to small firms have grown in importance over time.

Financial complementarities: a holistic view of financial systems

It is important to take a holistic view of financial systems since any one component is constrained by others, including corporate governance, banking, securities markets, pension programs, and institutional investors. All of these tend to go hand-in-hand, mirroring the complementarities inherent in other areas of the broader political economy. They frequently derive from a common political origin (the bargain struck among the key interest groups), and their evolution biased by political institutions and the complementarities with other financial institutions. Looking at the financial system holistically makes the role of farmers even more important since, by influencing one part of it, they can constrain the structure of other parts of the financial system. The Japanese and US financial systems offer the clearest examples of farmers' importance to a nation's overall financial structure. And although globalization's market-enhancing effects have been felt across capitalist economies over time, these countries have nevertheless remained fairly stable in terms of their relative spatial position on the capitalist continuum.

Notes

1 Introduction

1 This is consistent with the characterization of financial systems by Allen and Gale (2000).
2 On the characterization of capitalist systems as CME or LME, see Albert (1993), Boyer and Hollingsworth (1999), King and Wood (1999), Hall and Soskice (2001), Streeck and Yamamura (2001), and Thelen (2004).
3 This has enabled German and Japanese automobile companies to focus more on higher quality production in contrast to their American counterparts who tend to focus more on high-volume production. Thelen (2004), among others, sees skills as a defining feature of different capitalist systems, but as explained here, the acquisition of certain kinds of skills is contingent on financing arrangements.
4 The public–private distinction between pension funds is somewhat simplified since private pensions can be long-term enhancing too, as in Germany and Japan where collected pension funds may be used in a manner similar to internal financing from retained earnings (Jackson and Vitols, 2001). Jackson and Vitols distinguish between market-based pensions (low levels of public pensions and externalized private pensions) versus solidaristic pensions (high levels of public pensions and organizationally embedded private pensions). Recent work has begun to explore connections between pensions and the structure of the political economy, including the links between pensions and industrial relations and between pensions and systems of finance (Ebbinghaus and Manow, 2001; Estevez-Abe, 2001; Jackson and Vitols, 2001; Manow, 2001a, 2001b; Park, 2004).
5 See, for example, Lewis (1950), Gerschenkron (1962), Myrdal (1968), Garvy (1977), Kornai (1979), Shleifer and Vishny (1994), Shleifer (1998), and La Porta *et al.* (2002).
6 See also Beck *et al.* (2003), and Levine (2005) for arguments which acknowledge that political institutions matter, yet which see legal traditions as being more important.

2 Theory

1 However, depositors' welfare is sometimes improved when depositors can form an organized group, such as farmers. For example, farmers in post-World War II Japan improved bank deposit policies through the postal savings bank.
2 Thus, although internally generated funds may be widely used (Corbett and Jenkinson, 1996, 1997), this does not necessarily reduce the extent of short-term pressures in diffusely owned firms.
3 See Gourevitch and Shinn (2005) for a discussion on the dual incentives that owners face over corporate ownership.
4 See Pagano and Volpin (2005) on parliamentary governments and concentrated shareholding.

3 Patterns during the twentieth century

1 For this reason, I exclude data for 1938 and 1999 from the analysis.
2 Each variable is multiplied by 100 before taking the ratio to avoid mathematical problems that occur with dividing numbers less than one.
3 Bank deposits data are from Rajan and Zingales (2003). For data in the post-World War II period, bank deposits exhibit greater than 95 percent correlation to bank lending (data for bank assets are from Beck *et al.*, 2001).
4 Germany and Austria changed their constitutions markedly after World War I as well, and this prior change is taken into consideration in the analysis of this chapter. Austria reinstated its 1920 constitution after World War II (along with the 1929 revisions to the president's powers) after it was replaced by an Austrofascist constitution of 1934.
5 The expert studies include Laver and Hunt (1992), Laver and Schofield (1990), Dodd (1976), Castles and Mair (1984), Laver and Budge (1992), Sani and Sartori (1983), Inglehardt and Klingemann (1976), Mavgordatos (1984), Bruneau and MacCleod (1986), Blair (1984), Kerr (1987), Taylor and Laver (1973), Browne and Dreijmanis (1982), and de Swaan (1973). Multiple expert studies are used to minimize the bias/subjectivity caused by relying on only one or two.
6 Of course, the specific dates at which nations' modern capitalist institutions were formed will differ for each country, but by constraining the sample to these wealthy countries, the variation in the timing is minimized.
7 Both variables are with respect to GDP, which drops out when taking the ratio of them.
8 The McFadden Act remained in effect until the Riegel–Neal Interstate Banking and Branching Efficiency Act of 1994, after farms had transformed into modern agrobusiness that would be more sympathetic to large financial institutions.
9 The Gramm-Leach-Bliley Act of 1999 repealed the Glass–Steagall Act, opening up competition among banks, securities companies, and insurance companies by allowing commercial and investment banks to consolidate. As with the repeal of the McFadden Act, farmers had transformed into modern agribusiness by this point.
10 Data for the value of farm production are from the *Yearbook of Agriculture 1931*: Gross income of crops and livestock combined, 1929: 977. This value is then divided by total state income; data for state income is from *State Personal Income: 1929–1987*, US Department of Commerce.
11 Data measuring states' manufacturing population are drawn from the *US 15th Census, 1930*; state population data are from the same source. The 16th Census corresponds to 1940, so the 15th Census provides more accurate measures for these variables.
12 Data on Capital's Value Added by Manufacture comes from the 15th Census of the US: Manufactures, Reports by States (1930). Wages data are from the same source.
13 Federal Power Commission, Holding Company Control of Licenses, Washington, 1933: ix.
14 Roy G. Blakey and Gladys C. Blakey, "The Revenue Act of 1935," *American Economic Review*, December 1935.

4 Class conflict

1 Sat-Cho is the abbreviation used by Japanese historians to designate the oligarchy of Satsuma and Choshu men who constituted the supreme governing power of Meiji Japan.
2 For detailed discussion on prewar Japan's political institutions, see Duus (1968), Matsunami (1979), Umegaki (1988), Banno (1992 and 2001), Ramseyer and Rosenbluth (1995).
3 Scalapino (1967) and Iwasaki (1921) offer descriptive historical accounts of the Genrō's power during this period.

4 Members of the bureaucracy were hand-picked by the oligarchy (Privy Council, Genrō, and House of Peers) until they changed the requirement to enter via a civil service exam, which simply changed it from an aristocratic clique to a university clique. The Cabinet ministers ran various departments of the bureaucracy, and the bureaucracy was responsible for implementing the laws.

5 For more detail on the prewar government, see Kishimoto (1988).

6 See also Yamamura (1997).

7 Regarding the Meiji era, Iwasaki (1921: 102) remarks,

> The way to get rich was to become the friend of some high officers in the government. Such friendships were frequent. For example, Marquis Inouye, the great Genrō and leader of financial reform, was an intimate of the Mitsui family. Marquis Okuma and the Iwasaki family, the steamship kings, are also closely associated. The connection between the government and big business in Japan is frankly admitted.

8 See Allen (1981: ch. 8).

9 See Soma (1986: 41–42). The system would not necessarily prevent a large party from gaining a solid majority (e.g., the LDP in postwar Japan), but it would be far more difficult to initially achieve it.

10 See, for example, Furushima (1951: 165–168).

11 Also backing the Seiyukai, though less faithfully than Mitsui, were the Yasuda and Sumitomo zaibatsu, along with the Asano, Ōkura, Kawasaki, Ōsaka Shōsen, Furukawa, Kuhara, Fujita, Hattori, Ōkawa, Fukuzawa, and Nakahashi groups. The Kenseikai, on the other hand, was also supported by the Shibusawa, Yamaguchi, Nezu, and Hara groups as well as the Tōhō Electric power and Japan Electric power companies (Hazama, 1997; see also Colegrove, 1929: 402).

12 This type of control was actually espoused by the right wing of the workers' movement. The more leftist elements did not raise comparable demands likely because they feared harsh penalties from the government, who cracked down very hard on labor in 1928. See Cole *et al.* (1966). For more on Japan's prewar Communist Party ideology, see Hoston (1986).

13 Ramseyer and Rosenbluth (1995: 104).

14 Ginkō gappei hō [Bank Merger Act], Law No. 85 of April 1896.

15 See Ramseyer and Rosenbluth (1995) on the number of small banks over time, and Bank of Japan, Honpō keizai tōkei [Economic Statistics of Japan] (Tokyo: Bank of Japan, 1935: 6–39); Shin'ichi Gotō, Honpō ginkō gōdōshi [History of Bank Mergers in Japan] (Tokyo: Kin'yu zaisei jijō kenkyūkai, 1973: 55, 93, 127, 211, 359, 377).

16 Ueda (1999: 39–40).

17 The law gave banks five years to meet the new capital requirements, but many banks were unable to do it, despite efforts by Seiyūkai members to help banks raise the capital.

18 Gueslin (1992) offers ample evidence that relative to capital markets, banks overall were not heavily relied upon in the pre-World War II era.

19 Bank financing also experienced a change from a reliance on private banking in the 1920s to public banking in the 1930s (Gueslin, 1992: 85).

20 During the Third Republic, Cabinet turnovers were very common. Between the time of the consolidation of the power of the French Republicans in 1879 and the fall of the Third Republic in 1940, France was governed by a succession of 94 Cabinets, with an average life of eight months. During the same period, there were 44 prime ministers, occupying the position for an average of 16 months. In Great Britain, during the period between 1880 and 1940, there were only 21 Cabinets, with an average life of almost three years, and only 11 persons served as prime minister, occupying the position for an average of more than five years. Of the 94 French Cabinets of the period, only eight remained in office for two years or more (none after 1928)

and only ten remained in office for between one and two years (Pierce, 1983: 21). While there was a great deal of continuity of personnel and of policy throughout the numerous Cabinets, the considerable instability of ministries contributed further to the dominance of parliamentary control.

21 See also Vinen (1991: 45–52), for a discussion on how small business was excluded from political power to the benefit of big business during the Third Republic.

22 That is, until the 1967 law under de Gaulle's right-wing government.

23 Pierre Mathieu-Bodet, a former Minister of Finance, offered an influential critique, who doubted if a good law could emerge in the atmosphere created by the crash. *Observations sur le projet de loi relatif á la réforme de la legislation sur les sociétés.* Offprint from the *Journal des economistes* (May 15, 1884).

24 The process-verbaux of the commission is in AN C5514. See also Arnault (1884); *Journal officiel*, Senat, Doc. Parlem., January 1884, annexe No. 72, pp. 1097–1113, contains the text of the bill.

25 *Examen critique du project de loi sure les sociétés par actions* (Paris, 1886).

26 *Revue des sociétés*, V (1887), p. 410; C 5426.

27 PV of the committee, séance du 5 fév. 1890, C 5514. Only two members of the committee (A. B. Brugnot and Comte Anatole Lemercier) favored the Senate's bill.

28 J. B. Sirey, *Recueil general des lois et des arrest, Année 1893*, pp. 569–577; Vavasseur (1894); and the report of Claude Chaussel de Coussergues, *Journal officiel*, April 10, 1893, Débats parlem., p. 531, text in *Journal officiel*, Doc. Parlem., September 1892, p. 970.

29 Duchemin (1940).

30 Minimum Program of the CGT.

31 Gueslin's book, *Les Origines du Crédit Agricole (1840–1914)* (1978), offers a very thorough account of the formation of the Crédit Agricole.

32 Since the beginning of the Third Republic, and for 50 years prior to the formation of the Third Republic with the Crédit Foncier organized under Louis Napoléon to finance mortgage loans backed by a state guarantee (according to Born (1983: 104), Napoléon was returning a favor to his supporters among the rural population), discussion had occurred regarding the formation of an agricultural credit institution to help farmers get access to capital, and also to help them deal with unforeseeable natural calamities such as worm and insect infestations, phylloxera which hurt wine-makers, drought, and excess humidity (Henry and Régulier, 1986: 6).

33 A related issue which delayed the passage of the law for about four years was whether to create popular banks which would cater to small businesses and individuals in addition to farmers, or to create a credit facility which exclusively served agricultural financing needs. Because many politicians opposed aiding labor, the latter option was finally passed with the 1894 law (Gueslin, 1978: 142). For passage of the bill, see *J.O. Sénat, Documents Parlementaires*, Annexe no. 43, op. cit., pp. 87–96.

34 There was considerable variation in the amount of money allocated to different departments, which was not in proportion to the agricultural population. Gueslin (1978: 320) suggests that some of the factors affecting the amount of money distributed to each department include such things as the dominant agricultural speculation at the time, the size of the farmer, and the politics of the agricultural office (local/regional).

35 Total loans grew from 1.9 million francs in 1900 to over 104 million francs in 1913.

36 According to the March 1911 census, there were 5,271,000 active male agriculturalists. At the end of 1910, the number of members of agricultural caisses was 151,621. See I.N.S.E.E., *Annuaire statistique de la France*, 1961, p. 11.

37 See Boussard (1990), and Ministère de l'agriculture (1981).

38 Debates surrounding these issues are discussed in Michel Margairaz (1972).

39 De Man described his position in *Au delà du Marxisme* (1927) and *Socialisme constructif* (1933). Peter Dodge also wrote a biography, *Beyond Marxism: The Faith and Works of Hendrik de Man* (1966).

40 Quote from J. Itard, in Margairaz (1972: 249).
41 LeFranc and Itard (1935). Emilie Lefranc was secretary of the Centre Confédéral d'Education Ouvrière (Institut Supérieur Ouvrier et Collèges du Travail) and professor of French language and literature. Jean Itard was a professor of mathematics at the l'Institut Supérieur Ouvrier, a militant socialist, and a union leader.
42 Dupeux (1959) provides a copy of the original Program (pp. 180–183).
43 The Program colorfully entitled the main section seeking reforms of the financial system, "Against the pillage of savings for a better organization of credit."
44 For reform of the Bank of France, see Bouvier (1973: 158–159, 178–190), Dromer (1978: 52–70), Dauphin-Meunier (1936). Examples of the Left's campaign against the bank are Aymé-Martin (1931), Delaisi (1936), and Hamon (3 vols, 1936–1938).
45 Bouvier (1973: 185).
46 J.O. Documents parlementaires, Chambre des deputes 1936, Annexe no. 664, pp. 1290–1306.
47 André Philip was a professor of economics who had investigated American production techniques during the interwar years and published a study of de Man in 1928. He was an advocate for socialist reform from the 1930s on.
48 Philip (1944: 6–7).
49 André Philip's report was published by the Parti Socialiste, Pour la Rénovation de la République, and entitled *Les Reformes de Structure.*
50 Courtin (1944: 41).
51 Commissariat à l'Intérior (1944).
52 An interim legislature preceding the ratification of a new constitution and the election of the National Assembly in October 1946.
53 For further discussion on the usefulness and powers of Works Committees, see ILO (1950: 186–188).
54 For information on the formulation and effect of this banking legislation, see Alhadeff's six chapters on French banking in *Competition and Controls in Banking* (1968), Wilson's *French Banking Structure and Credit Policy* (1957), the France chapter by Henry Germain-Martin in Beckhart's *Banking Systems* (1954), and Dupont's *Les Contrôle des Banques et la Direction du Crédit en France* (1952).
55 INSEE, Annuaire des statistiques (1986).
56 See Wright (1948) and Lorwin (1954: 104–105).
57 See Rioux (1987). For parliamentary control of the executive and ministries, see Petry, in Laver and Shepsle (1994: 136).
58 The parliamentary bias of France's political institutions was clearly illustrated during the 1986 to 1988 period of cohabitation. Two conservative parties, the Gaullists and the UDF, gained a narrow legislative victory in 1986. Consequently, Socialist President François Mitterrand was forced to name a Gaullist prime minister, Jacques Chirac. Except for some issues concerning foreign relations and defense (on which Mitterrand and the conservatives largely agreed), Mitterrand stood on the legislative sidelines while Chirac functioned as France's political executive. The conservative coalition implemented important policy reforms opposed by Mitterrand, such as the denationalization of many French industries, the reinstitution of a two-round, single-member district electoral law, and changes in labor law (Huber, 1996: 28).
59 Hervieu (1993: 43).
60 Hervieu (1992: 401).
61 Secondo Tarditi *et al.* (1989: 4–5).
62 Keeler (1996).
63 As of 1989, 28.5 percent of mayors were active farmers, and more than one-third were either active or retired farmers.
64 As of 1989, 14.3 percent of senators were farmers.
65 As of 1985, 13.2 percent. Only in the national assembly are farmers even slightly under-represented (3 percent).

162   *Notes*

66 Franklin (1969: 103).
67 INSEE, Annuaire des statistiques, 1986.
68 In the 1970s, the Crédit Agricole became one of the largest banks in the world.
69 For information layoffs by Alcan and Mittal Steel's hostile bid for Arcelor, see "France fearful over deal's effects" by Peggy Hollinger, Sarah Laitner and Mark Mulligan, in *The Financial Times*, London Edition, January 30, 2006, p. 25. For the reaction to PepsiCo's rumored bid for Danone, see "Protectionist sentiments in France worry U.S. execs" by Shelley Emling, in The Atlanta *Journal-Constitution*, November 8, 2005, p. 1D. On encouraging French companies to use poison pills, see "France reveals tools to fight hostile bids" by Martin Arnold and Raphael Minder, in *The Financial Times*, Asia Edition, March 2, 2006, p. 3.
70 "Powerless patriots," in *The Economist*, February 4, 2006.
71 "Sarkozy underlines resolve to block foreign takeovers," in *The Financial Times*, London Edition, March 30, 2007, p. 8.
72 "Powerless patriots," ibid.
73 "France reveals tools to fight hostile bids," ibid.
74 "Yogurt and champagne," in *International Herald Tribune*, July 28, 2005.
75 The Xth and XIth Plans of 1992 and 1995.
76 Three agencies linked to the Ministry of Industry in Paris have been especially active in the promotion of small business in the provinces: the Agence de Développement de la Productique Appliquée (ADEPA), the Agence Nationale de la Valorisation de la Recherche (ANVAR), and the Délégation Régionale de l'Industrie, de la Recherche, et de l'Environnement (DRIRE) (Levy, 1999: 213).

5 Social contract

1 See Adams (1964: 128–159), and Hoshi and Kashyap (2001).
2 With the 1937 Temporary Funds Adjustment Act, stock issues were subject to government control, and corporate bond markets were suppressed. For industrial firms, Adams (1964: 143) shows that new stock issues fell from 60 percent to 75 percent of net funding in 1935 and 1936 to below 20 percent in 1944 to 1945. Corporate bond financing for industrial firms never rose above 15 percent between 1937 and 1945. Additional restrictions occurred with the Corporate Profits, Dividend and Fund Raising Ordinance of April 1939, which forbade firms with capital above ¥200,000 to raise their dividends above the level of November 30, 1938. The Control of Corporate Finance and Accounting Ordinance of October 1940 imposed further restrictions by requiring government approval for dividends above 8 percent (Adams, 1964: 128–159; Hoshi and Kashyap, 2001: 57). The ordinance also permitted the government to determine how internal funds could be used – for example, by requiring the purchase of government bonds. Consequently, shareholders now resembled debt holders since their income was fixed in nominal terms and they had no effective residual claim on earnings.
3 Dore (1984: 131–132), Morris-Suzuki and Seiyama (1989: 88–89).
4 Fukutake (1967: 181).
5 SCAP, Natural Resources Section (1952: 37); Junnosuke (1985: 258–259).
6 Mulgan (2000: 50). For a detailed description of each of the businesses of the agricultural cooperatives, see Zenkoku Nogyo Kyodo Kumiai Chuokai, *Shinpan: Nogyo Kyodo Kumiaiho*, pp. 66–113.
7 SCAP (1952: 114–116).
8 Calder (1988: 262).
9 Dore (1984: 282–287).
10 Masumi (1985: 259), Dore (1984: 415).
11 This legal floor remained in effect until early 1987.

12 In early 1957 there were about 1,150; by 1958 there were around 3,000 special post-master offices.
13 Gourevitch and Shinn (2005: 167–177).
14 Many of these Dietmen come from districts with only a small number of full-time farmers, but Japan has an extraordinarily high number of part-time farmers.
15 See Sakakibara (1993: 29–66) and Okimoto (1989).
16 Seventy-two percent of all rural loans were made through Nokyo in 1980.
17 In 1985, for example, the 15 largely rural prefecture of Hokkaidō, Shikoku, and the Japan sea coast accounted for 23 percent of Japan's public works spending but only 17.4 percent of the population. The four prefectures of the Tokyo metropolitan area by contrast accounted for 24.8 percent of the population but received only 20.7 percent of the public works. See Calder (1989: 240).
18 See Hoshi and Kashyap (2001) and Johnson (1982).
19 For more on the relationship of banks with industry during the century, see Ogura (2002). For more on specific goals of government industrial policy during the postwar period, see Komiya *et al.* (1988).
20 "Shaking up Corporate Japan," in *The Economist*, March 23, 2005.
21 "Defences rest on shaky foundations in Japan, poison pills could act to entrench existing management," by Mariko Sanchanta in *The Financial Times*, London Edition, April 19, 2006, p. 23.
22 "It's Sayonara Koizumi, welcome back Japan Inc.," by William Pesek in *The Financial Times*, London Edition, September 18, 2006.
23 "Land of the rising sum," in *The Economist*, July 12, 2007.
24 "Japan turns to weapons systems for defence from foreign bidders," by Michiyo Nakamoto and Mariko Sanchanta in *The Financial Times*, September 6, 2007.

6 Rural vs. urban conflict

1 This regulation took on the form of a number of emergency decrees, including: (1) constraints on the destructive price competition that had characterized the 1920s; (2) authorizing banking associations to determine binding interest rates on deposits and fees for standardized services; (3) the creation of a bank regulatory agency which, together with the central bank and in consultation with bank associations, was empowered to develop and enforce minimum capital and liquidity requirements and prudential regulations (insider credits, large credit limits, maturity matching requirements); and (4) stricter entry regulations, particularly in the case of credit cooperatives which had to received approval from the appropriate regional cooperative association (Vitols, 2001: 185).
2 When stock exchanges were reopened in early 1932, trading in futures on stocks and bonds, which was considered the most speculative part of securities markets, was completely prohibited. New stock issues were subject to strict control, minimum information content for prospectuses for new securities issues was defined, and the statute of limitations for prospectus fraud was extended. Public (municipal and national) securities were given general priority over industrial securities in access to capital markets. The 1937 Shareholder Law further eroded confidence in the securities markets by weakening the position of the minority shareholders, since votes could no longer be cast by mail. The law provided two ways for shareholders to cast their votes by proxy. First, a shareholder could give his bank authority to cast the votes in the shareholder's name but also forcing shareholders to reveal their identity. Second, and more important in practice, the shareholder's voting right could be ceded to the bank (allowing banks to do proxy voting), enhancing the banks' position with respect to the governance of large corporations.
3 The tax system, for example, favored public bonds (particularly for housing and infra-structure) over industrial bonds. Double taxation of equities (corporation tax plus

individual income tax) stunted the development of equities markets. In addition to these measures, a committee of leading securities issuers (joint-stock banks and the national banks for the credit cooperative and municipal savings-bank sector) was formed to control access to bond markets with priority for public and bank bonds (Vitols, 2001).

4 Revolutionary councils were often loyal to their firms. Their demands often included the end of authoritarian management styles, co-determination in wages and personnel issues, rights to company information, and profit-sharing.

5 As a result of the Works Constitution Act of 1952, enterprises with more than 500 employees were obligated to reserve only one-third of the supervisory board seats for employee representatives. And it was not until the Codetermination Act of 1976 that employee representation on supervisory boards extended to all companies with more than 2,000 employees (O'Sullivan, 1998: 7).

6 See also Höpner (2003a, 2003b).

7 "Hostile Germans BASF can bid for Engelhard, but no one can bid for BASF," in *The Financial Times*, London Edition, January 5, 2006, p. 14.

8 "Germany to act on hostile takeover," by Patrick Jenkins and Hugh Williamson in *The Financial Times*, London Edition, May 4, 2006, p. 27.

7 Voice vs. property

1 After the war, capital, through the support of the Western Allies (particularly the United States), was sufficiently part of the bargain over Austria's economic structure to make it a capitalist economy (prices and production levels decided freely by economic actors).

2 This was accomplished with the nationalization acts of July 26, 1946 and March 26, 1947.

3 The enterprises and plants included the most important lignite mines, the largest iron and steel works, the nonferrous metals mining and smelting works, the most important petroleum extraction and processing installations; a number of firms involved in steel construction and in mechanical engineering, a major chemical concern, and a major shipping company. Outside the manufacturing sector, the three largest credit institutions and the most important electrical energy installations were also nationalized.

4 As early as 1949, the conservative ÖVP (People's Party) sought to limit nationalized industry and its position within the Austrian economy in order to enlarge and privatize and free market. For example, when the Ministry of Property Protection and Economic Planning was dissolved in 1949, its planning responsibility was not transferred to the subsequent ministry. In fact, no more plans were drawn up (Mathis, 1995).

5 In 1966 and again in 1970 the nationalized industries were organized into a state holding company, ÖeIAG (Öesterreichische Industrieverwaltungs-Aktiengesellschaft).

6 For elaboration on these points, see Gugler *et al.* (1997, 2001).

7 In 1948, this program was replaced by the European Recovery Program (commonly known as the Marshall Plan).

8 They downplayed the legacy of Austro-Marxism associated with Otto Bauer, the party's leader, after World War I.

9 Working conditions in the public sector are generally determined by negotiations between unions and state authorities (Traxler, 1993: 292).

10 "Party and union links are sustained by a broad array of twenty-eight satellite organizations that provide the followers of Austria's Left with an integrated system of social and cultural services from cradle to grave" (Katzenstein, 1984: 38).

11 "Pulling the plug," in *The Financial Times*, Europe Edition, August 20, 2004, p. 12.

12 "Austria makes U-turn over Siemes bid VA TECHNOLOGIE," by Eric Frey and Bettina Wassener in *The Financial Times*, London edition, November 9, 2004, p. 28.

13 "Bohler rescued from hostile bidder" by Eric Frey in *The Financial Times*, London Edition, March 30, 2007, p. 22.

14 "Not so welcome in Vienna," in *The Economist*, March 29, 2007.

15 Specifically, Green writes,

> A great deal of trouble may be remedied by certain changes in our banking system. (a) Our banking system should be unified. At present we have 50 different banking systems, all with different regulations. (b) Most of the banks which have failed in the last three years have been small country banks. This difficulty could be avoided if small country banks were branches of strong city banks and could draw on larger resources in time of need. In order to establish branch banking in the United States, Federal laws and some state laws would have to be changed to permit banks to set up branches and to assure control."

16 The Sherman Act of 1890 did not prohibit banks from organizing such groups since it was aimed primarily at large railroads and industrial enterprises. Small business and farmers combined against railroads because these charged lower rates to large customers or important city routes. The Act passed with overwhelming Congressional support; the Senate and House votes were 52–1 and 242–0, respectively. It was specifically designed to prevent the artificial raising of prices by restriction of trade or supply.

17 Federal Power Commission, Holding Company Control of Licenses, Washington, 1933, p. ix.

18 Roy G. Blakey and Gladys C. Blakey, "The Revenue Act of 1935," *American Economic Review*, December, 1935.

8 Key lessons

1 The ideas are in the vein of other scholars who consider the institutional origins of economic systems, such as Weber (1958), Gerschenkron (1962), Olson (1963), Diamond (1997), Haber (1999), Acemoglu and Robinson (2000), Acemoglu *et al.* (2001, 2002), Stulz and Williamson (2003), and Morck *et al.* (2004). They also resonate with those who examine institutional change, such as North and Weingast (1989), North (1990), Stasavage (2002), Thelen (2004), and Pierson (2004), and with those who examine the intersection of politics and the structure of financial institutions such as Zysman (1983), Rosenbluth (1989), and Deeg (1999).

References

Acemoglu, Daron, and James A. Robinson. (2000). "Political Losers as a Barrier to economic development." *American Economic Review* 90 (2): 126–130.

—— (2006). *Economic Origins of Dictatorship and Democracy*. New York: Cambridge University Press.

Acemoglu, Daron, Simon Johnson, and James Robinson. (2001). "The Colonial Origins of Comparative Development: An Empirical Investigation." American Economic Review 91 (5): 1369–1422.

—— (2002). "Reversal of Fortune: Geography and Institutions in the Making of the Modern World Income Distribution." *Quarterly Journal of Economics* 117 (4): 1231.

—— (2004). "Institutions as a Fundamental Cause of Long Run Growth." In Philippe Aghion and Steve Durlauf, eds., *Handbook of Economic Growth*. Amsterdam: North-Holland.

Adams, Thomas Francis Morton. (1964). *A Financial History of Modern Japan*. Tokyo: Research.

Aiginger, K., and G. Tichy. (1982). *Entwicklungschancen der Klein- und Mittelbetriebe in den achtziger Jahren*. Munchen: Olzog.

Albert, Michel. (1993). *Capitalism against Capitalism*. London: Whurr.

Alhadeff, David. (1968). *Competition and Controls in Banking*. Berkeley: University of California Press.

Allen, Franklin, and Douglas Gale. (2000). *Comparing Financial Systems*. Cambridge, MA: MIT Press.

Allen, G. C. (1981). *A Short Economic History of Modern Japan, 1867–1937*. New York: The Macmillan Company.

Alvarez, R. Michael, Geoffrey Garrett, and Peter Lange. (1991). "Government Partisanship, Labor Organization, and Macroeconomic Performance." *American Political Science Review* 85 (June): 539–556.

Amable, Bruno. (2003). *The Diversity of Modern Capitalism*. New York: Oxford University Press.

Anderson, Jonathan. (2005). "How to Think About China? Part 2: The Ageing of China," Asian Economic Perspectives. UBS Investment Research, February 7, 28.

Andrlik, Erik. (1981). "The Farmers and the State: Agricultural Interests in West German Politics." *West European Politics* 4 (1): 104–119.

Aoki, Masahiko. (1994). *The Japanese Main Bank System: An Introductory Overview*. Washington, DC: World Bank.

Arnault, Louis. (1884). *Rapport de la Commission extra-parlementaire du 14 février*

1882 â l'appui d'un project de loi sur les sociétés, suivi de projet de loi soumis au Sénat le 6 décembre 1883. Paris.

Averyt, William F. (1977). *Agropolitics in the European Community: Interest Groups and the Common Agricultural Policy*. New York: Praeger.

Aymé-Martin, Albert. (1931). *Nos Grands Financiers contre la nation*. Paris: Redier.

Baldwin, Peter. (1990). *The Politics of Social Solidarity: Class Bases of the European Welfare State: 1875–1975*. New York: Cambridge University Press.

Bank of Japan. (1935). *Honpō keizai tōkei* [Economic Statistics of Japan]. Tokyo: Bank of Japan.

—— (various years). *Statistical Annual*. Tokyo.

Banno, Junji. (1992). *The Establishment of the Japanese Constitutional System*. London: Routledge.

—— (2001). *Democracy in Pre-War Japan: Concepts of Government, 1871–1937: Collected Essays*. London: Routledge.

Bayliss, Brian, and Alan Butt Philip. (1980). *Capital Markets and Industrial Investment in Germany and France: Lessons for the UK*. Hampshire, England: Saxon House.

Becht, Marco, and J. Bradford DeLong. (2005). "Why Has There Been So Little Block Holding in America?," in Randall K. Morck (ed.), *A History of Corporate Governance Around the World*. Chicago, ILL: University of Chicago Press.

Beck, Thorsten, Asli Demirguc-Kunt, and Ross Levine. (2001). *A New Database on Financial Development and Structure*. Washington, DC: World Bank, Development Research Group, Finance.

—— (2003). "Law and Finance: Why Does Legal Origin Matter?" *Journal of Comparative Economics* 31: 653–675.

Berger, Suzanne, ed. (1981). *Organizing Interests in Western Europe: Pluralism, Corporatism, and the Transformation of Politics*. Cambridge: Cambridge University Press.

Berle, Adolph, and Gardiner Means. (1932). *The Modern Corporation and Private Property*. New York: Transaction Publishers.

Blair, Antonio. (1984). "The Emerging Spanish Party System: Is There a Model?" *West European Politics* 7 (4): 120–155.

Born, Karl Erich. (1983). *International Banking in the 19th and 20th Centuries*. New York: St. Martin's Press.

Boussard, Isabel. (1990). *Les Agriculteurs de la République*. Paris: Economica.

Bouvier, Jean. (1973). *Un Siècle de banque française*. Paris: Hachette.

Boyer, Robert. (1990). *The Regulation School: A Critical Introduction*. New York: Columbia University Press.

Broadbridge, Seymour. (1966). *Industrial Dualism in Japan; A Problem of Economic Growth and Structural Change*. Chicago, IL: Aldine Publishing.

Bronte, Stephen. (1982). *Japanese Finance: Markets and Institutions*. London: Euromoney Publications.

Browne, E. C., and J. Dreijmanis. (1982). *Government Coalitions in Western Denocracies*. New York: Longman.

Bruneau, Thomas, and Alex MacCleod. (1986). *Politics in Contemporary Portugal: Parties and the Consolidation of Democracy*. Boulder, CO: L. Rienner Publishers.

Buck, T., and Tull, M. (2000). "Anglo-American contributions to Japanese and German Corporate Governance after World War Two." *Business History* 42 (2): 119–140.

Calder, Kent. (1988). *Crisis and Compensation: Public Policy and Political Stability in Japan, 1949–1986*. Princeton, NJ: Princeton University Press.

—— (1990). "Linking Welfare and the Developmental State: Postal Savings in Japan." *Journal of Japanese Studies* 16 (1): 31–59.

—— (1993). *Strategic Capitalism: Private Business and Public Purpose in Japanese Industrial Finance*. Princeton, NJ: Princeton University Press.

Calmfors, Lars, and John Driffill. (1988). "Centralisation of Wage Bargaining and Macroeconomic Performance." *Economic Policy* 6 (April): 13–61.

Calomiris, Charles. (2000). *U.S. Bank Deregulation in Historical Perspective*. New York: Cambridge University Press.

Cameron, David R. (1984). "Social Democracy, Corporatism, Labor Quiescence, and the Representation of Economic Interest in Advanced Capitalist Society," In John H. Goldthorpe (ed.), *Order and Conflict in Contemporary Capitalism: Studies in the Political Economy of Western European Nations*, New York: Oxford University Press, pp. 143–178.

Campbell, John L., Rogers Hollingsworth, and Leon Lindberg. (1991). *Governance of the American Economy*. New York: Cambridge University Press.

Cargill, Thomas F., and Naoyuki Yoshino. (2003). *Postal Savings and Fiscal Investment in Japan: The PSS and the FILP*. New York: Oxford University Press.

Carney, Richard. (2004). "National Security and National Finance: A Reassessment of Gerschenkron." EUI Working Paper series, RSCAS No. 2004/21.

—— (2006). "Varieties of Capitalism in France: Interests, Institutions, and Finance." *French Politics* 4: 1–30.

Carré, J. J., P. Dubois, and E. Malinvaud. (1975). *French Economic Growth*. Stanford, CA: Stanford University Press.

Castles, Francis and Peter Mair. (1984). "Left–Right Political Scales: Some "Expert Judgments," *European Journal of Political Research* 12: 73–88.

Chandler, Alfred D. (1977). *The Visible Hand: The Managerial Revolution in American Business*. Cambridge, MA: The Belknap Press of Harvard University Press.

Cleary, M. C. (1989). *Peasants, Politicians, and Producers: The Organization of Agriculture in France since 1918*. New York: Cambridge University Press.

Cohen, Stephen. (1977). *Modern Capitalist Planning*. Berkeley and Los Angeles: University of California Press.

Colbert, Evelyn. (1952). *The Left Wing in Japanese Politics*. New York: International Secretariat, Institute of Pacific Relations.

Cole, Allan B., George O. Totten, and Cecil H. Uyehara. (1966). *Socialist Parties in Postwar Japan*. New Haven, CT: Yale University Press.

Colegrove, Kenneth. (1929). "Labor Parties in Japan." *American Political Science Review* 23 (2): 329–363.

Collick, Martin. (1988). "Social Policy: Pressures and Responses," in J. A. A. Stockwin (ed.), *Dynamic and. Immobilist Politics in Japan*. Honolulu: University of Hawaii Press, pp. 205–236.

Commissariat à l'Intérieur. (1944). "Critique de rapport sur la politique économique d'après guerre présenté par le Comité National d'Etudes de la résistance." June, AN F[la] 3791. *Congressional Record* 1927–1934. Washington, DC.

Corbett, Jenny, and Tim Jenkinson. (1996). "The Financing of Industry, 1970–89: An International Comparison." *Journal of the Japanese and International Economies* 10 (1): 71–96.

—— (1997). "How is Investment Financed? A Study of Germany, Japan, UK and US." *The Manchester School* 65 (1): 69–93.

Courtin, René. (1944). *Rapport sur la politique économique d'après guerre*. Algiers.

Cowhey, Peter F., and Mathew McCubbins. (1995). *Structure and Policy in Japan and the United States*. New York: Cambridge University Press.

Cox, Andrew. (1986). *The State, Finance, and Industry*. Brighton: Wheatsheaf.

Cox, Gary. (1997). *Making Votes Count: Strategic Coordination in the World's Electoral Systems*. New York: Cambridge University Press.

Cox, Gary, and Michael Thies. (1998). "The Cost of Intraparty Competition." *Comparative Political Studies* 31 (3): 267–291.

—— (2001). "How Much Does Money Matter?" *Comparative Political Studies* 33 (1): 37–57.

Crouch, Colin. (2005). *Capitalist Diversity and Change: Recombinant Governance and Institutional Entrepreneurs*. New York: Oxford University Press.

Crouch, Colin, Wolfgang Streeck, Robert Boyer, Bruno Amable, Peter A. Hall and Gregory Jackson. (2005). "Dialogue on 'Institutional Complementarity and Political Economy.'" *Socio-Economic Review* 3: 359–382.

Culpepper, Pepper D. (2003). *Creating Cooperation: How States Develop Human Capital in Europe*. Ithaca, NY: Cornell University Press.

—— (2005). "Institutional Change in Contemporary Capitalism: Coordinated Financial Systems since 1990." *World Politics* 57 (2): 173–199.

Culpepper, D., Peter A. Hall, and Bruno Palier. (2006). *Changing France: The Politics that Markets Make*. New York: Palgrave Macmillan.

Cusack, Thomas R., David Soskice, and Torben Iversen. (2007). "Economic Interests and the Origins of Electoral Systems." *American Political Science Review* 10 (3): 373–391.

Dauphin-Meunier, Achille. (1936). *La Banque de France*. Paris: Gallimard.

Davis, E. P. (1995). *Pension Funds: Retirement Income Security and Capital Markets: An International Perspective*. New York: Oxford University Press.

—— (2001). *Portfolio Regulation of Life Insurance Companies and Pension Funds*. London: Pensions Institute, Birkbeck College.

Deeg, Richard. (1999). *Finance Capitalism Unveiled: Banks and the German Political Economy*. Ann Arbor: University of Michigan Press.

Deeg, Richard, and Gregory Jackson. (2005). "Towards a More Dynamic Theory of Capitalist Variety." *King's College Department of Management Research Papers* 40.

Delaisi, Francis. (1936). *La Banque de France aux mains des 200 familles*. Paris: Comité de vigilance des intellectuels anti-fascistes.

de Man, Hendrik. (1927). *Au delà du Marxisme*. Brussels: l'Eglantine.

—— (1933). *Le Socialisme constructif*. Paris: F. Alcan.

De Swaan, Abram. (1973). *Coalition Theories and Cabinet Formations*. San Francisco, CA: Jossey-Bass.

Deutsche Bundesbank. Various Monthly Reports.

Diamond, Douglas. (1991). "Monitoring and Reputation: The Choice between Bank Loans and Directly Placed Debt." *Journal of Political Economy* 99 (August): 689–721.

Diamond, Jared. (1997). *Guns, Germs, and Steel: The Fates of Human Societies*. New York: W. W. Norton.

Dodd, Lawrence. (1976). *Coalitions in Parliamentary Government*. Princeton, NJ: Princeton University Press.

Dodge, Peter. (1966). *Beyond Marxism: The Faith and Works of Hendrik de Man*. The Hague: Martinus Nijhoff.

Dore, Ronald. (1984). *Land Reform in Japan*. New York: Continuum International Publishing Group.

—— (1986). *Flexible Rigidities*. Stanford, CA: Stanford University Press.

—— (2000). *Stock Market Capitalism: Welfare Capitalism: Japan and Germany versus the Anglo-Saxons*. New York: Oxford University Press.

Dosi, Giovanni, C. Freeman, R. Nelson, G. Silverberg, and L. Soete. (1988). *Technical Change and Economic Theory*. London: Pinter.

Dromer, Lucille. (1978). "Les Limites de la réforme de la Banque de France, juillet 1936." *Recherches et travaux, Institut d'Histoire Economique et Sociale de l'Université de Paris-1* 7 (December): 52–70.

Duchemin, René. (1940). *Organisation Syndicale Patronale en France*. Paris: Librairie Plon.

Dupeux, Georges. (1959). *Le Front Populaire et Les Elections de 1936*. Paris: Librairie Armand Colin.

Dupont, P. C. (1952). *Le Contrôle des Banques et la Direction du Crédit en France*. Paris: Dunod.

Duus, Peter. (1968). *Party Rivalry and Political Change in Taisho Japan*. Cambridge, MA: Harvard University Press.

Dyk, Irene. (1988). "The Austrian People's Party," in Jim Sweeney and Josef Weidenholzer (eds), *Austria: A Study in Modern Achievement*. Aldershot: Avebury, pp. 67–81.

Ebbinghaus, Bernhard, and Philip Manow, eds. (2001). *Comparing Welfare Capitalism. Social Policy and Political Economy in Europe, the USA and Japan*. London: Routledge.

Edquist, Charles. (1997). *Systems of Innovation*. London: Pinter.

Edwards, Jeremy, and Klaus Fischer. (1994). *Banks, Finance and Investment in Germany*. New York: Cambridge University Press.

Emery, H. (1898). "The Results of the German Exchange Act of 1896." *Political Science Quarterly* 13: 286–320.

Ernst, Ekkehard. (2003). "Financial Systems, Industrial Relations, and Industry Specialization: An Econometric Analysis of Institutional Complementarities." *Proceedings of the Öesterreichische Nationalbank Workshops*, 1.

Estevez-Abe, Margarita. (2001). "Welfare Finance Nexus: A Forgotten Link?", in B. Ebbinghaus and Philip Manow, eds., *Comparing Welfare Capitalism: Social Politicy and Political Economy in Europe, the USA and Japan*. London: Routledge, pp. 190–216.

Estrin, Saul, and Peter Holmes. (1983). *French Planning in Theory and Practice*. London: Allen & Unwin.

Examen critique du project de loi sure les sociétés par actions. (1886). Paris.

Fiorina, M. P. (1977). *Congress: Keystone of the Washington Establishment*. New Haven, CT: Yale University Press.

Flora, P. (1983). *State, Economy, and Society in Western Europe, 1815–1975*. Vol. I. London: Macmillan.

—— (1987). *Growth to Limits: Western European Welfare States Since World War II*. London: Walter de Gruyter.

Fohlin, Caroline. (2005). "The History of Corporate Ownership and Control in Germany," in R. Morck (ed.), *A History of Corporate Governance around the World: Family Business Groups to Professional Managers*, NBER series. Chicago, IL: University of Chicago Press, pp. 223–277.

Franklin, S. H. (1969). *The European Peasantry, the Final Phase*. London: Methuen.

Franks, Julian, and Mayer, Colin. (1998). "Bank Control, Takeovers and Corporate Governance in Germany." *Journal of Banking & Finance*, Elsevier, 22(10–11): 1385–1403.

Franks, Julian, Colin Mayer, and Hannes Wagner. (2006). "The Origins of the German Corporation – Finance, Ownership and Control." *Review of Finance*, Springer, 10 (4): 537–585.

Franzese, Robert. (2002). *Macroeconomic Policies of Developed Democracies*. New York: Cambridge University Press.

Freedeman, Charles E. (1993). *The Triumph of Corporate Capitalism in France, 1867–1914*. Rochester, NY: University of Rochester Press.

Freeman, John R. (1989). *Democracy and Markets: The Politics of Mixed Economies*. Ithaca, NY: Cornell University Press.

Frieden, Jeffrey. (1991). "Invested Interests: The Politics of National Economic Policies in a World of Global Finance." *International Organization* 45 (4): 425–451.

Fukui, Haruhiro, and Shigeko N. Fukai. (1996). "Pork Barrel Politics, Networks, and Local Economic Development in Contemporary Japan." *Asian Survey* 36 (3): 268–286.

Fukutake, Tadashi. (1967). *Japanese Rural Society*. New York: Oxford University Press.

Furushima, Toshio. (1951). *Gaisetsu Nihon nōgyō gijutsushi*. Tōkyō: Yōkendō.

Garon, Sheldon. (1987). *The State and Labor in Modern Japan*. Berkeley: University of California Press.

Garvy, George. (1977). *Money, Financial Flows, and Credit in the Soviet Union*. Cambridge, MA: Harvard University Press.

Gaudibert, Jean Claude. (1977). *Le dernier empire français*. Paris: Seghers.

Gerlich, Peter. (1981). "Government Structure: The Principles of Government," in Kurt Steiner (ed.), *Modern Austria*. Palo Alto, CA: Society for the Promotion of Science and Scholarship, pp. 209–222.

Germain-Martin, Henry. (1954). "France," in Bekchart (ed.), *Banking Systems*. New York: Columbia University Press.

Gerschenkron, Alexander. (1962). *Economic Backwardness in Historical Perspective, a Book of Essays*. Cambridge, MA: Belknap Press of Harvard University Press.

Gilson, R. J., and Mark Roe. (1999). "Lifetime Employment: Labor Peace and the Evolution of Japanese Corporate Governance." *Columbia Law Review* 99 (2): 508–540.

Glaeser, Edward, and Andrei Shleifer. (2003). "The Rise of the Regulatory State." *Journal of Economic Literature* 41 (2): 401–425.

Golden, Miriam. (1993). "The Dynamics of Trade Unionism and National Economic Performance." *American Political Science Review* 87 (June): 439–454.

Goldthorpe, John H., ed. (1984). *Order and Conflict in Contemporary Capitalism*. New York: Oxford University Press.

Gourevitch, Peter, and James Shinn. (2005). *Political Power and Corporate Control: The New Global Politics of Corporate Governance*. Princeton, NJ: Princeton University Press.

Gueslin, André. (1978). *Les Origines du Crédit Agricole (1840–1914)*. Université de Nancy II.

—— (1984). *Histoires des Crédits Agricoles*. Paris: Economica.

—— (1992). "Banks and State in France from the 1880s to the 1930s: The Impossible Advance of the Banks," in Youseff Cassis (ed.), *Finance and Financiers in European History, 1880–1960*. Cambridge: Cambridge University Press, pp. 63–92.

Gugler, Klaus, Alex Stomper, Josef Zechner, and Susanne Kalss. (1997). "The Separation of Ownership and Control: An Austrian Perspective," in European Corporate Governance Network *et al.* (eds), *The Separation of Ownership and Control: A Survey of 7 European Countries: A Preliminary Report*. Brussels: European Corporate Governance Network.

—— (2001). "The Separation of Ownership and Control in Austria," in Frabrizio Barca and Marco Becht (eds), *The Control of Corporate Europe*. New York: Oxford University Press.

Guillen, Mauro. (2000). "Corporate Governance and Globalization: Is There a Convergence across Countries?" *Advances in International Comparative Management* 13: 175–204.

Guinnane, Timothy W. (2001). "Delegated Monitors, Large and Small: The Development of Germany's Banking System, 1800–1914." Working Papers 835, Economic Growth Center, Yale University.

Haber, Stephen. (1999). *Industry and Underdevelopment: The Industrialization of Mexico, 1890–1940*. Stanford, CA: Stanford University Press.

Haber, Stephen, Douglass North, and Barry Weingast, eds. (2007). *Political Institutions and Financial Development*. Stanford, CA: Stanford University Press.

Hall, Peter. (1986). *Governing the Economy: The Politics of State Intervention in Britain and France*. New York: Oxford University Press.

Hall, Peter, and David Soskice, eds. (2001). *Varieties of Capitalism: The Institutional Foundations of Comparative Advantage*. New York: Oxford University Press.

Hall, Peter, and Daniel W. Gingerich. (2004). "Varieties of Capitalism and Institutional Complementarities in the Macroeconomy: An Empirical Analysis." *MPIfG Discussion Paper 04/5*.

Hall, Peter, and Kathleen Thelen. (2009). "Institutional Change in Varieties of Capitalism." *Socio-Economic Review* (7) 1: 7–34.

Halliday, Jon. (1978). *A Political History of Japanese Capitalism*. New York: Monthly Review Press.

Hamon, Augustin. (1938). *Les Maîtres de la France*. Paris: Sociales Internationales.

Hanami, T., ed. (1989). *Industrial Conflict Resolution in Market Economies: A Study of Australia, the Federal Republic of Germany, Italy, Japan, and the USA*. Boston, MA: Kluwer Law and Taxation Publishers.

Hancké, Bob, Martin Rhodes, and Mark Thatcher, eds. (2007). *Beyond Varieties of Capitalism: Conflict, Contradictions, and Complementarities*. New York: Oxford University Press.

Hankel, Wilhelm. (1981). *Prosperity Amidst Crisis: Austria's Economic Policy and the Energy Crunch*. Boulder, CO: Westview Press.

Hardach, Karl. (1980). *The Political Economy of Germany in the Twentieth Century*. Berkeley: University of California Press.

Hazama, Hiroshi. (1997). *The History of Labor Management in Japan*. New York: St. Martin's Press.

Henry, José-Pierre, and Marcel Régulier. (1986). *Le Crédit Agricole*. Paris: Presses Universitaires de France.

Herrigel, Gary. (1993). "Large Firms, Small Firms, and the Governance of Flexible Specialization: The Case of Baden Württenberg and Socialized Risk," in Bruce Kogut (ed.), *Country Competitiveness*. New York: Oxford University Press, pp. 15–35.

Hervieu, Bertrand, ed. (1992a). *Les Agriculteurs français aux urnes*. Paris: L'Harmattan.

—— (199b). "Dix Remarques sur le vote des agriculteurs," in Bertrand Hervieu, ed., *Les Agriculteurs français aux urnes*. Paris: L'Hartmann.

—— (1993). *Les Champs du Futur*. Paris: François Bourin.

Hiscox, Michael. (2001). *International Trade and Political Conflict: Commerce, Coalitions, and Mobility*. Princeton, NJ: Princeton University Press.

Hoffmann, Susan. (2001). *Politics and Banking: Ideas, Public Policy, and the Creation of Financial Institutions*. Baltimore, MD: Johns Hopkins University Press.

Hollingsworth, J. Rogers, and Robert Boyer, eds. (1997). *Contemporary Capitalism: The Embeddedness of Institutions*. Cambridge: Cambridge University Press.

Hollingsworth, J. Rogers, Philippe C. Schmitter, and Wolfgang Streeck, eds. (1994). *Governing Capitalist Economies*. New York: Oxford University Press.

Höpner, Martin. (2003a). "European Corporate Governance Reform and the German Party Paradox." Max-Planck-Institute for the Study of Societies Program for the Study of Germany and Europe Working Paper No. 03.1.

—— (2003b). "What Connects Industrial Relations and Corporate Governance? Explaining Institutional Complementarity." Max-Planck-Institute for the Study of Societies Working Paper.

Hoshi, Takeo, and Anil Kashyap. (2001). *Corporate Financing and Governance in Japan*. Cambridge, MA: MIT Press.

Hoston, Germaine. (1986). *Marxism and the Crisis of Development in Prewar Japan*. Princeton, NJ: Princeton University Press.

Huber, John D. (1996). *Rationalizing Parliament: Legislative Institutions and Party Politics in France*. New York: Cambridge University Press.

Hurst, James. (1973). *A Legal History of Money in the United States*. Lincoln: University of Nebraska Press.

Inglehart, R., and H. D. Klingemann. (1976). "Party Identification, Ideological Preference and the Left–Right Dimensions among Western Pass Publics," in I. Budge, I. Crewe, and D. Farlie (eds.), *Party, Identification and Beyond: Representations of Voting and Party Competition*. London: Wiley.

International Labour Office (ILO). (1950). *Labour–Management Co-operation in France*. Geneva: ILO.

Institut National de la Statistique et des Études Économiques (INSEE). (Various years).

Iwasaki, Uichi. (1921). *The Working Forces in Japanese Politics*. New York: Columbia University.

Jackson, Gregory. (2001). "The Origins of Nonliberal Corporate Governance in Germany and Japan." in W. Streeck and K. Yamamura (eds.), *The Origins of Nonliberal Capitalism: Germany and Japan*. Ithaca, NY: Cornell University Press, pp. 121–170.

Jackson, Gregory, and Sigurt Vitols. (2001). "Pension Regimes and Financial Systems: Between Financial Commitment, Market Liquidity and Corporate Governance," in Bernhard Ebbinghaus and Philip Manow (eds.), *The Varieties of Welfare Capitalism: Social Policy and Political Economy in Europe, Japan and the USA*. London: Routledge.

Johnson, Chalmers. (1982). *MITI and the Japanese Miracle: The Growth of Industrial Policy, 1925–1975*. Stanford, CA: Stanford University Press.

Journal Officiel. (Various years). Documents Parlementaires, Chambre des Deputés.

Junnosuke, Masumi. (1985). *Postwar Politics in Japan, 1945–1955*. Berkeley: University of California Press.

Katzenstein, Peter. (1978). *Between Power and Plenty*. Madison: University of Wisconsin Press.

—— (1985). *Small States in World Markets: Industrial Policy in Europe*. Ithaca, NY: Cornell University Press.

—— (1987). *Policy and Politics in West Germany: The Growth of a Semisovereign State*. Philadelphia, PA: Temple University Press.

Keeler, John. 1987. *The Politics of Neocorporatism in France: Farmers, the State, and Agricultural Policymaking in the Fifth Republic*. New York: Oxford University Press.

—— (1996). "Agricultural Power in the European Community: Explaining the Fate of CAP and GATT Negotiations." *Comparative Politics* 28 (2): 127–149.

Kerr, H. H. (1987). "The Swiss Party Systems: Steadfast and Changing," in H. Daalder (ed.), *Party Systems in Denmark, Austria, Switzerland, The Netherlands and Belgium.* London: Pinter.

Kilbourne, Richard H. (1995). *Debt, Investment, Slaves: Credit Relations in East Feliciana Parish, Louisiana, 1825–1885.* Tuscaloosa: University of Alabama Press.

King, Desmond, and Stewart Wood. (1999). "The Political Economy of Neoliberalism: Britain and the United States in the 1980s," in Herbert Kitschelt, Peter Lange, Gary Marks, and John D. Stephens (eds), *Continuity and Change in Contemporary Capitalism..* Cambridge: Cambridge University Press: pp. 371–397.

King, Robert G., and Ross Levine. (1993a). "Finance and Growth: Schumpeter Might Be Right." *Quarterly Journal of Economics* 108: 717–738.

—— (1993b). "Finance, Entrepreneurship, and Growth: Theory and Evidence." *Journal of Monetary Economics* 32: 513–542.

Kishimoto, Koichi. (1988). *Politics in Modern Japan.* Tokyo: Japan Echo.

Kobayashi, Masaaki. 1985. "Japan's Early Industrialization and the Transfer of Government Enterprises: Government and Business." *Japanese Yearbook of Business History* 2: 54–79.

Komiya, Ryutaro, Masahiro Okuno, and Kotaro Suzumura. (1988). *Industrial Policy of Japan.* San Diego: Academic Press.

Kornai, Janos. (1979). "Resource-Constrained vs. Demand-Constrained Systems." *Econometrica* 47: 801–819.

Koshiro, Kazutoshi. (2000). "Formal and Informal Aspects of Labor Dispute Resolution in Japan." *Law and Policy* 22 (3–4): 353–367.

Kroszner, Randall S., and Philip E. Strahan. (1999). "What Drives Deregulation? Economics and Politics of the Relaxation of Bank Branching Restrictions." *Quarterly Journal of Economics* 114 (4): 1437–1467.

Kuisel, Richard F. (1981). *Capitalism and the State in Modern France: Renovation and Economic Management in the Twentieth Century.* New York: Cambridge University Press.

Kume, Ikuo. (1998). *Disparaged Success: Labor Politics in Postwar Japan.* Ithaca, NY: Cornell University Press.

La Porta, Rafael, Florencio Lopez-de-Silanes, and Andrei Shleifer. (2002). "Government Ownership of Banks." *Journal of Finance* 57 (1): 265–301.

—— (2008). "The Economic Consequences of Legal Origins." *Journal of Economic Literature* June.

La Porta, Rafael, Florencio Lopez-de-Silanes, Andrei Shleifer, and Robert W. Vishny. (1998). "Law and Finance." *Journal of Political Economy* 106 (6): 1113–1155.

Lamoreaux, Naomi. (1991). "Bank Mergers in Late Nineteenth-century New England: The Contingent Nature of Structural Change." *Journal of Economic History* 3: 537–557.

—— (1994). *Insider Lending: Banks, Personal Connections, and Economic Development in Industrial New England, 1784–1912.* Cambridge: Cambridge University Press.

Lamoreaux, Naomi, and Jean-Laurent Rosenthal. (2005). "Legal Regime and Contractual Flexibility: A Comparison of France and the United States during the Era of Industrialization." *American Law and Economic Review* 7: 28–61.

Lardy, Nicholas. (1998). *China's Unfinished Economic Revolution.* Washington, DC: Brookings Institution.

Laver, Michael, and Ian Budge, eds. (1992). *Party Policy and Government Coalitions.* New York: St. Martin's Press.

Laver, Michael, and W. Ben Hunt. (1992). *Policy and Party Competition.* New York: Routledge.

Laver, Michael, and Norman Schofield. (1990). *Multiparty Government: The Politics of Coalition in Europe*. New York: Oxford University Press.

Lazonick, William. (1991). *Business Organization and the Myth of the Market Economy*. Cambridge: Cambridge University Press.

LeFranc, E. and J. Itard. (1935). "La classe ouvrière a un plan," in *Le Populaire*, March 13.

Levine, Ross. (1997). "Financial Development and Economic Growth: Views and Agenda." *Journal of Economic Literature* 35: 688–726.

—— (1998). "The Legal Environment, Banks, and Long Run Economic Growth." *Journal of Money, Credit, and Banking* 30: 596–620.

—— (2005). "Law, Endowments, and Property Rights." *Journal of Economic Perspectives* 19 (3): 61–88.

Levine, Ross, and Sara Zervos. (1998). "Stock Markets, Banks, and Economic Growth." *American Economic Review* 88: 537–558.

Levine, Ross, Norma Loayza, and Thorsten Beck. (2000). "Financial Intermediation and Growth: Causality and Causes." *Journal of Monetary Economics* 46: 31–77.

Levy, Jonah. (1999). *Tocqueville's Revenge: State, Society, and Economy in Contemporary France*. Cambridge, MA: Harvard University Press.

Lewis, W. Arthur. (1950). *The Principles of Economic Planning*. London: G. Allen & Unwin.

Lijphart, Arend. (1999). *Patterns of Democracy: Government Forms and Performance in Thirty-six Countries*. New Haven, CT: Yale University Press.

Lockwood, William M. (1954). *The Economic Development of Japan: Growth and Structural Change, 1868–1938*. Princeton, NJ: Princeton University Press.

Lorwin, Val R. (1954). *The French Labor Movement*. Cambridge, MA: Harvard University Press.

Mackie, T.T. and R. Rose. (1990). *International Almanac of Electoral History*. London: Macmillan.

Makuch, N., J. Peyne, and P. Prunet. (1978). *Le Crédit Agricole*. Paris: Berger, Levrault.

Manow, Philip. (2001a). "Welfare State Building and Coordinated Capitalism: Germany and Japan Compared." in Wolfgang Streeck and Kozo Yamamura (eds.), *The Origins of Non-Liberal Capitalism*. Ithaca, NJ: Cornell University Press.

—— (2001b). "Comparative Institutional Advantages of Welfare Regimes and New Coalitions in Welfare Reforms," in Paul Pierson (ed.), *The New Politics of the Welfare State*. New York: Oxford University Press, pp. 146–164.

Margairaz, Michel. (1972). *Les Propositions de Politique Economique Financiere et Monétaire de la SFIO, de 1934 à 1936: La Reflation*. Paris: Université de Paris.

Martin, Cathie Jo, and Duane Swank. (2008). "The Political Origins of Coordinated Capitalism: Business Organizations, Party Systems, and State Structure in the Age of Innocence." *American Political Science Review* 102: 181–198.

Massumi, Junnosuke. (1985). *Postwar Politics in Japan, 1945–55*. Berkeley, CA: Institute of East Asian Studies, University of California, Berkeley, Center for Japanese Studies.

Mathis, Franz. (1995). "Between Regulation and Laissez Faire: Austrian State Industries after World War II," in Günter Bschoff, Anton Pelinka, and Rolf Steininger (eds), *Austria in the Nineteen Fifties*. New Brunswick, NJ: Transaction Publishers, pp. 79–90.

Matsunami, N. (1979). *The Japanese Constitution and Politics*. Washington, DC: University Publications of America.

Mavgordatos, George. (1984). "The Greek Party System: A Case of Limited but Polarised Pluralism." *West European Politics* 7 (4): 156–169.

McCubbins, Mathew, and Frances Rosenbluth. (1995). "Party Provision for Personal Politics: Dividing the Vote in Japan," in Mathew McCubbins and Peter Cowhey (eds), *Structure and Policy in Japan and the United States*. New York: Cambridge University Press.

Milgrom, Paul and John Roberts. (1990). "The Economics of Modern Manufacturing: Technology, Strategy, and Organization." *American Economic Review* 80: 511–528.

—— (1995). "Complementarities, Industrial Strategy, Structure and Change in Manufacturing." *Journal of Accounting and Economics* 19: 179–208.

Ministere de l'Agriculture. (1981). *Cent ans de ministere de l'agriculture*. Paris.

Miyashita, T. (1957). "Reconstruction of Zaibatsu," Nippon Shihon Shugi Taikei [The System of Japanese Capitalism]. Tokyo.

Morck, Randall, and Masao Nakamura. (2005). "A Frog in a Well Knows Nothing of the Ocean: A History of Corporate Ownership in Japan," in Randall Morck (ed.), *A History of Corporate Governance Around the World*. Chicago, IL: University of Chicago Press.

Morck, Randall, Daniel Wolfenzon, and Bernard Yeung. (2004). "Corporate Governance, Economic Entrenchment and Growth." *NBER Working Paper No. 10692*. Cambridge, MA: National Bureau of Economic Research.

Morin, Francois. (2000). "A Transformation in the French Model of Shareholding and Management." *Economy and Society* 29 (1).

Morris-Suzuki, Tessa, and Takuro Seiyama. (1989). *Japanese Capitalism since 1945: Critical Perspectives*. Armonk, NY: M.E. Sharpe.

Mulgan, Aurelia. (2000). *The Politics of Agriculture in Japan*. New York: Routledge.

—— (2001). *"Japan Inc." In the Agricultural Sector: Reform or Regression?* Canberra, ACT: Australia-Japan Research Centre.

Myers, Stewart C. (1984). "Capital Structure Puzzle." *Journal of Finance* 39 (3): 575–592.

Myers, Stewart C., and Nicholas Majluf. (1984). "Corporate Financing and Investment Decisions When Firms have Information That Investors Do Not Have." *Journal of Financial Economics* 13: 187–221.

Myrdal, Gunnar. (1968). *Asian Drama*. New York: Pantheon.

Nelson, Richard R., ed. (1993). *National Innovation Systems*. New York: Oxford University Press.

Neville-Rolfe, Edmund. (1984). *The Politics of Agriculture in the European Community*. London: Policy Studies Institute.

Nicoletti, G., S. Scarpetta, and O. Boylaud. (1999). "Summary Indicators of Product Market Regulation and Employment Protection Legislation for the Purpose of International Comparisons." *OECD Economics Department Working Paper* No. 226. Paris.

Nordlinger, Eric. (1981). *On the Autonomy of the Democratic State*. Cambridge, MA: Harvard University Press.

North, Douglass C. (1990). *Institutions, Institutional Change and Economic Performance*. New York: Cambridge University Press.

North, Douglass C., and Barry Weingast. (1989). "Credible Commitment in Early Modern Europe: The Evolution of Institutions Governing Public Choice in Seventeenth-century England." *Journal of Economic History* 4: 803–832.

Odaka, Konosuke. (1993). "'Japanese-Style' Labour Relations," in Tetsuji, Okazaki and Okuno-Fujiwara (eds.), *The Japanese Economic System and its Historical Origins*, New York: Oxford University Press.

Ogura, Shinji. (2002). *Banking, the State, and Industrial Promotion in Developing Japan, 1900–1973*. New York: Palgrave.

Okimoto, Daniel. (1989). *Between MITI and the Market: Japanese Industrial Policy for High Technology.* Stanford, CA: Stanford University Press.

Olson, Mancur. (1963). "Rapid Growth as a Destabilizing Force." *Journal of Economic History* 23 (4): 529–552.

—— (1965). *The Logic of Collective Action: Public Goods and The Theory of Groups.* Cambridge, MA: Harvard University Press.

O'Sullivan, Mary A. (1998). "The Political Economy of Corporate Governance in Germany." *Jerome Levy Institute Working Paper* No. 226.

Pagano, Marco, and Paolo Volpin. (2001). "The Political Economy of Corporate Governance." *Centre for Economic Policy Research* Discussion Paper No. 2682.

—— (2005). "Shareholder Protection, Stock Market Development, and Politics," *CSEF Working Papers 149,* Centre for Studies in Economics and Finance (CSEF). University of Naples, Italy.

Park, Gene. (2004). "The Political-Economic Dimension of Pensions: The Case of Japan." *Governance* 17 (4): 549–572.

Pelinka, Anton. (1988)."The Peculiarities of Politics in Austria: The Constitution, Federalism, Parliamentary and Social Democracy," in Jim Sweeney and Josef Weidenholzer (eds), *Austria: A Study in Modern Achievement.* Aldershot: Avebury, pp. 47–54.

Perotti, Enrico, and Ernst-Ludwif von Thadden. (2005). "The Political Economy of Corporate Control." *Tinbergen Institute Discussion Papers 05–102/2.* Tinbergen Institute.

Perotti, Enrico, and Armin Schwienbacher. (2007). "The Political Origins of Pension Funding." *CEPR Discussion Paper No. DP 6100.*

Petry, Francois. (1994). "The Role of Cabinet Ministers in the French Fourth Republic," in Michael Laver and Shepsle (eds.), *Cabinet Ministers and Parliamentary Government.* New York: Cambridge University Press.

Phelps, Edmund. (2006). "Dynamic Capitalism." *Wall Street Journal,* October 10.

Philip, André. (1944). "Les Reformes de Structure," in *Pour la Rénovation de la République.* Paris: Parti Socialiste.

Pickles, Dorothy M. (1953). *French Politics: The First Years of the Fourth Republic.* London: Royal Institute of International Affairs.

Pierce, Roy. (1983). *French Politics and Political Institutions.* Washington, DC: University Press of America.

Pierson, Paul. (2004). *Politics in Time: History, Institutions, and Social Analysis.* Princeton, NJ: Princeton University Press.

Piore, Michael, and Charles Sabel. (1984). *The Second Industrial Divide.* New York: Basic Books.

Pizzorno, Alessandro. (1978). "Political Exchange and Collective Identity in Industrial Conflict," in Colin Crouch and Alessandro Pizzorno (eds.), *The Resurgence of Class Conflict in Western Europe,* Vol 1, London: Macmillan, pp. 277–298.

Price, John. (1997). *Japan Works: Power and Paradox in Postwar Industrial Relations.* Ithaca, NY: ILR Press.

Przeworski, Adam, and Michael Wallerstein. (1982). "The Structure of Class Conflict in Democratic Capitalist Societies." *American Political Science Review* 76 (2): 215–238.

Rajan, Raghuram, and Rodney Ramcharan. (2008). "Landed Interests and Financial Underdevelopment in the United States." *NBER Working Papers* No. 14347.

Rajan, Raghuram, and Luigi Zingales. (1998). "Financial Dependence and Growth." *American Economic Review* 88: 559–586.

—— (2003). "The Great Reversals: The Politics of Financial Development in the 20th Century." *Journal of Financial Economics* 69: 5–50.

Ramseyer, J. Mark, and Frances Rosenbluth. (1995). *The Politics of Oligarchy: Institutional Choice in Imperial Japan.* New York: Cambridge University Press.

Regini, Marino. (1984). "The Conditions for Political Exchange: How Concertation Emerged and Collapsed in Britain and Italy," in J. H. Goldthorpe (ed.), *Order and Conflict in Contemporary Capitalism: Studies in the Political Economy of Western European Nations.* New York: Oxford University Press, pp. 124–142.

Revue des Sociétés, V (1887), p. 410; C5426.

Rioux, Jean-Pierre. (1987). *The Fourth Republic, 1944–1958.* New York: Cambridge University Press.

Roe, Mark. (1994). *Strong Managers, Weak Owners.* New York: Princeton University Press.

—— (2003). *Political Determinants of Corporate Governance.* New York: Oxford University Press.

Rogowski, Ronald. (1989). *Commerce and Coalitions: How Trade Affects Domestic Political Alignments.* Princeton, NJ: Princeton University Press.

Rosenbluth, Frances. (1989). *Financial Politics in Contemporary Japan.* Ithaca, NY: New York: Cornell University Press.

Sacks, Paul M. (1980). "State Structure and the Asymmetrical Society." *Comparative Politics* April: 349–376.

Sakakibara, Eisuke. (1993). *Beyond Capitalism: The Japanese Model of Market Economics.* New York: University Press of America.

Saloutos, Theodore. (1974). "New Deal Agricultural Policy: An Evaluation." *The Journal of American History* 61 (2): 394–416.

Sani, G., and G. Sartori. (1983). "Polarization, Fragmentation and Competition in Western Democracies," in H. Daalder and P. Mair (eds.), *Western European Party Systems.* Beverly Hills, CA: Sage, pp. 307–340.

Scalapino, Robert. (1967). *Democracy and the Party Movement in Prewar Japan.* Los Angeles: University of California Press.

SCAP, Natural Resources Section. (1945–1951, 1952). *Agricultural Programs in Japan.*

Scharpf, Fritz W. (1987). "Game-Theoretical Interpretations of Inflation and Unemployment in Western Europe." *Journal of Public Policy* 7 (3): 227–257.

—— (1991). *Crisis and Choice in European Social Democracy.* Ithaca, NY: Cornell University Press.

Schmidt, Helmut. (1985). *A Grand Strategy for the West: The Anachronsim of National Strategies in an Interdependent World.* New Haven, CT: Yale University Press.

Schmitter, Philippe, and Gerard Lehmbruch, eds. (1979). *Trends Toward Corporatist Intermediation.* Beverly Hills, CA: Sage.

Schweikart, Larry. (1988). "Jacksonian Ideology, Currency Control, and 'Central Banking': A Reappraisal." *The Historian* LI (November): 781–802.

Sheingate, Adam. (2001). *The Rise of the Agricultural Welfare State: Institutions and Interest Group Power in the United States, France, and Japan.* Princeton, NJ: Princeton University Press.

Shin'ichi Gotō. (1973). Honpō ginkō gōdōshi [History of Bank Mergers in Japan]. Tokyo: Kin'yu zaisei jijō kenkyūkai.

Shirk, Susan L. (2007). *China: Fragile Superpower.* New York: Oxford University Press.

Shleifer, Andrei. (1998). "State vs. Private Ownership." *Journal of Economic Perspectives,* 12: 133–150.

Shleifer, Andrei, and Robert Vishny. (1994). "Politicians and Firms." *Quarterly Journal of Economics* 109: 995–1025.

Shonfield, Andrew. (1965). *Modern Capitalism: The Changing Balance of Public and Private Power*. New York: Oxford University Press.

Shugart, Matthew S., and John M. Carey. (1992). *President and Assemblies: Constitutional Design and Electoral Dynamics*. New York: Cambridge University Press.

Simon, Miguel Cantillo. (1998). "The Rise and Fall of Bank Control in the United States: 1890–1939." *American Economic Review* 88 (5): 1077–1093.

Skocpol, Theda. (1992). *Protecting Soldiers and Mothers: The Political Origins of Social Policy in the United States*. Cambridge, MA: Belknap Press of Harvard University Press.

Skocpol, Theda, and Edwin Amenta. (1985). "Did Capitalists Shape Social Security?" *American Sociological Review* 50 (4): 572–575.

Social Expenditure Database, 1980–1996. CD-ROM. Paris: OECD.

Soma, Masao. (1986). *A History of Japan's Electoral System*. Kyushu: Kyushu University Press.

Stasavage, David. (2002). "Credible Commitment in Early Modern Europe: North and Weingast Revisited." *Journal of Law, Economics, and Organization* 18 (1): 155–186.

Streeck, Wolfgang. (1989). "Successful Adjustment to Turbulent Markets: The Automobile Industry," in Peter J. Katzenstein, (ed.), *Industry and Politics in West Germany: Toward the Third Republic*. Ithaca, NY, and London: Cornell University Press, pp. 113–156.

Streeck, Wolfgang, and Philip Schmitter, eds. (1986). *Private Interest Government: Beyond Market and State*. Beverly Hills, CA: Sage.

Streeck, Wolfgang, and Kozo Yamamura, eds. (2001). *The Origins of Nonliberal Capitalism: Germany and Japan in Comparison*. Ithaca, NY: Cornell University Press.

Stulz, René, and Rohan Williamson. (2003). "Culture, Openness, and Finance." *Journal of Financial Economics* 70 (3): 313–349.

Tarditi, Secondo, Kemmeth Thomason, Pierpaolo Pierani, and Elisabetta Croci-Angelini, eds. (1989). *Agricultural Trade Liberalization and the European Community*. Oxford: Oxford University Press.

Taylor, M. and M. Laver. (1973). "Government Coalitions in Western Europe." *European Journal of Political Research* I: 205–248.

Thelen, Kathleen. (2004). *How Institutions Evolve: The Political Economy of Skills in Germany, Britain, the United States and Japan*. New York: Cambridge University Press.

Traxler, Franz. (1993). "Austria." *De Gruyter Studies in Organization* 45.

Tsebelis, George. (1995). "Decision Making in Political Systems: Veto Players in Presidentialism, Parliamentarianism, Multicameralism and Multipartism." *British Journal of Political Science* 25 (3).

Ueda, Kazuo. (1999). "The Financial System and Its Regulations," in T. Okazaki and M. Okuno-Fujiwara (eds.), *The Japanese Economic System and its Historical Origins*. New York: Oxford University Press.

Umegaki, Michio. (1988). *After the Restoration: The Beginning of Japan's Modern State*. New York: New York University Press.

United Nations Population Division. (2005). *World Population Prospects: The 2004 Revision*. New York.

U.S. Congress. (various years). *Congressional Record*. Washington, DC: U.S. Government Printing Office.

U.S. Department of Agriculture. (1931). *Yearbook of Agriculture*. Washington, DC: U.S. Government Printing Office.

180   *References*

U.S. Department of Commerce, Bureau of the Census. (1976). *Historical Statistics of the United States: Colonial Time to 1970*. Washington, DC: U.S. Government Printing Office.

U.S. Department of Commerce, Bureau of the Census. (1989). *State Personal Income: 1929–87*. Washington, DC: U.S. Government Printing Office.

U.S. Department of Commerce, Bureau of the Census. (various years). *Statistical Abstract of the United States*. Washington, DC: U.S. Government Printing Office.

U.S. Department of Labor, Bureau of Labor Statistics. (various years). *Employment and Earnings*. Washington, DC: Government Printing Office.

Varshney, Ashutosh. (1995). *Democracy, Development, and the Countryside: Urban-Rural Struggles in India*. New York: Cambridge University Press.

Vavasseur, A. A. (1894). *Commentaire de la loi du 1er août 1893 sur les sociétés par actions*. Paris.

Verdier, Daniel. (2003). *Moving Money*. New York: Cambridge University Press.

Vinen, Richard. (1991). *The Politics of French Business, 1936–1945*. New York: Cambridge University Press.

Vitols, Sigurt. (2001). "The Origins of Bank-Based and Market-Based Financial Systems: Germany, Japan, and the United States," in Wolfgang Streeck and Kozo Yamamura (eds.), *The Origins of Nonliberal Capitalism: Germany and Japan*. Ithaca, NY: Cornell University Press, pp. 171–199.

—— (2005). "Changes in Germany's Bank-Based Financial System: Implications for Corporate Governance." *Corporate Governance: An International Review* 13 (3): 386–396.

Vittas, Dimtri (ed.). (1978). *Banking Systems Abroad: The Role of Large Deposit Banks in the Financial Systems of Germany, France, Italy, the Netherlands, Switzerland, Sweden, Japan and the United States*. London: Inter-Bank Research Organization.

Wada, Junichiro. (1996). *The Japanese Election System: Three Analytical Perspectives*. New York: Routledge.

Weber, Max. (1958). *The Protestant Ethic and the Spirit of Capitalism*. New York: Scribner's.

Whitley, Richard. (1999). *Divergent Capitalisms: The Social Structuring and Change of Business Systems*. Oxford: Oxford University Press.

Will, Michael R. (1969). "Recent Modifications in the French Law of Commercial Companies." *International and Comparative Law Quarterly* 18 (4): 980–997.

Williamson, Oliver. (1975). *Markets and Hierarchies: Analysis and Antitrust Implications*. New York: Free Press.

Willmore, Larry. (1999). *Public versus Private Provision of Pensions*. United Nations Department of Social and Economic Affairs Discussion Paper No. 1.

Wilson, G. A., and Olivia J. Wilson. (2001). *German Agriculture in Transition: Society, Policies, and Environment in a Changing Europe*. New York: Palgrave.

Wilson, John. (1957). *French Banking Structure and Credit Policy*. Cambridge, MA: Harvard University Press.

Wright, Gordon. (1948). *The Reshaping of French Democracy*. New York: Reynal and Hitchcock.

—— (1964). *Rural Revolution in France: The French Peasantry in the Twentieth Century*. Stanford, CA: Stanford University Press.

Wu, Friedrich. (2006). "What Could Brake China's Rapid Ascent in the World Economy?" *World Economics* 7 (3).

Yamamura, Kozo. (1967). *Economic Policy in Postwar Japan: Growth Versus Economic Democracy*. Berkeley: University of California Press.

—— ed. (1997). *The Economic Emergence of Modern Japan*. Cambridge: Cambridge University Press.

Zenkoku, Ginkō Kyōkai Rengōkai. (1989). *The Banking System in Japan*. Tokyo: Federation of Bankers Association of Japan.

Zysman, John. (1983). *Governments, Markets, and Growth: Financial Systems and the Politics of Industrial Change*. Ithaca, NY: Cornell University Press.

Index